Family and Succession Law in Denmark

Family and Succession Law in Denmark

Second Edition

Hans Viggo Godsk Pedersen &
Ingrid Lund-Andersen

This book was originally published as a monograph in the International Encyclopaedia of Laws/Family and Succession Law.

General Editors: Roger Blanpain, Frank Hendrickx
Volume Editor: Walter Pintens

DJØF Publishing

Wolters Kluwer

Published by:
Kluwer Law International B.V.
PO Box 316
2400 AH Alphen aan den Rijn
The Netherlands
Website: www.wklawbusiness.com

Sold and distributed in North, Central and South America by:
Wolters Kluwer Legal & Regulatory U.S.
7201 McKinney Circle
Frederick, MD 21704
United States of America
Email: customer.service@wolterskluwer.com

Sold and distributed in Denmark by:
DJØF Publishing
Gothersgade 137
DK 1123 Copenhagen
Denmark
Website: www.djoef-forlag.dk

Sold and distributed in all other countries by:
Turpin Distribution Services Ltd.
Stratton Business Park
Pegasus Drive, Biggleswade
Bedfordshire SG18 8TQ
United Kingdom
Email: kluwerlaw@turpin-distribution.com

ISBN 978-90-411-8259-3 (Kluwer)
ISBN 978-87-574-3737-9 (DJØF Publishing)

This title is available on www.kluwerlawonline.com

The Authors

Hans Viggo Godsk Pedersen (born 1947) is Professor at the Department of Law, University of Southern Denmark. He obtained his cand. jur. in 1975 and his PhD in Law in 1985. From 1975 to 1982, he worked at the Århus School of Economics; and as an Associate Professor since 1979. From 1982 to 1997, he worked at the Law Department of the Copenhagen Business School as an Associate Professor. He did research within the field of credit security law. Among the books he has published are *Kaution (Guarantee),* 10th edn (2013); *Om ejerpantebreve & skadeløsbreve (On Mortgage Deeds & Letters of Indemnity)* (1990); *Bankgarantier (Bank Guarantees),* 2nd edn (2003); and on subjects as domestic relations and right of inheritance, amongst others is *Familie- og arveret (Law of Domestic Relations and Inheritance),* 8th edn (2013) in cooperation with Anitta Godsk Pedersen.

Ingrid Lund-Andersen (born 1949) is Professor at Faculty of Law, the University of Copenhagen. She obtained her Law Degree from the University of Copenhagen in 1976 and her doctoral dissertation, *Familieøkonomien* (*Financial Relations in the Family*) in 2011. From 1976 to 1978, she was employed at the Counsel for Prosecution. From 1978 to 2010, she worked at the University of Aarhus, School of Law. She is the co-author of several books, among others, *Familieret (Family Law),* 2st edn (2012), *Arveretten* (*Succession Law*), 5th edn (2014) and *Nordisk Samboerrett* (*Nordic Cohabitation Law*) (2014). Her research fields are Family Law, the Rights of the Child and the Legal Position of Cohabitants and she has published numerous articles on these subjects in national and international journals. She is a national expert at the Commission on European Family Law (CEFL).

The Authors

Table of Contents

The Authors 3

List of Abbreviations 13

Preface 15

General Introduction 17

Chapter 1. General Background of the Country 17

Chapter 2. Historical Background of Family and Succession Law 18

Chapter 3. Sources of Family and Succession Law 19

§1. CONSTITUTION 19

§2. LEGISLATION 19

§3. TREATIES 19

§4. JURISPRUDENCE 20

Chapter 4. The Courts Administering Family and Succession Law 21

Part I. Persons 23

Chapter 1. The Status of a Person 23

§1. DEFINITION OF A PERSON 23
I. Natural Persons 23
II. Legal Persons 24

§2. CAPACITY 24
I. Introduction 24
II. The Conditions under Which a Person Is Made Incapable of Acting Legally 25
A. Minors 26
B. Adults Who Are Put Under and Declared Incapable of Acting in Legal Matters 26
1. Guardianship 27
2. Legal Incapacity 30
III. Legal Incapacity and Valid Contracts 31
IV. Legal Incapacity and Invalid Contracts 32
V. The Liability for Torts 34
A. Minors 34
B. Adults of Unsound Mind 35

§3. ABSENTEES 35
I. Missing Persons 35
II. Presumption of Death and Return of the Absentee 36
A. Presumption of Death by Court Judgment 37
B. The Absentee Turns Up Unexpectedly 37
III. Division of an Absentee's Assets without Court Decision 38
IV. The Division of the Missing Person's Property after Twenty Years 38
V. The Disappearance of an Heir 39

Chapter 2. Registration of Civil Status 40

§1. THE RIGHT OF REGISTERED PERSONS TO HAVE THEIR REGISTERED INFORMATION PROTECTED 41

§2. THE RIGHT TO OBTAIN INFORMATION ABOUT REGISTERED PERSONS 42

Chapter 3. Personality Rights 43

§1. THE RIGHT TO LOOK AFTER ONESELF AND ONE'S OWN INTERESTS 43
I. Physical Integrity 43
A. A Woman's Right to Abortion 43
B. Suicide and Euthanasia 44
C. Organ Donations 45
D. Circumcision of Women 46
II. Psychological Integrity 46

§2. THE DUTY TO TAKE CARE OF OTHER PEOPLE 47
I. The Legal Rights of Children 48
A. Parents' Chastisement of Their Children 48
B. Child Pornography 49
II. The Protection of Drug Addicts, Alcoholics and Vagabonds 49

Chapter 4. Names 51

§1. Composition of a Name 51

§2. Last Name 51
I. Acquisition of the Last Name 51

§3. First Name 52

§4. Middle Name 53

§5. Change of Name 53

Chapter 5. Nationality 54

§1. Definitions 54

§2. Acquisition of Danish Nationality 54

§3. Loss of Danish Nationality 57

§4. The Nordic Countries 58

Chapter 6. Domicile and Residence 59

Chapter 7. Mentally Handicapped Persons 60

§1. The Elderly Demented and Persons with a Mental Disability 60

§2. Persons With a Mental Illness 61

Part II. Family Law 63

Chapter 1. Marriage 63

§1. The Nature of Marriage 63

§2. The Capacity to Marry 63

§3. The Formalities of Marriage 65

§4. The Effects of Marriage 66

§5. Void and Voidable Marriages 67

§6. Registered Partnership 69

Chapter 2. Divorce 70

§1. Grounds 70
I. Separation 70
II. Divorce 71

§2. Procedure 73

§3. Effects 75

Chapter 3. Cohabitation without Marriage 76

§1. General Aspects 76

§2. Family Law Aspects 76

Chapter 4. Filiation 79

§1. Paternity 79

§2. New Problems 85

Chapter 5. Adoption 87

§1. Background 87

§2. The Adoption Requirements 88

§3. The Legal Effects of Adoption 90

§4. The Annulment of Permissions to Adopt 90

Chapter 6. Parental Authority 92

§1. Contact 94

§2. Contracts for Personal Work 95

§3. Financial Maintenance 95

Chapter 7. Guardianship 97

§1. Disposal on Behalf of Minors and of Adults Who Are Incapable to Act in Legal Matters 97

§2. Placement of the Assets 99

Chapter 8. Kinship and Relationships of Affinity 100

Part III. Matrimonial Property Law 103

Chapter 1. Rights and Obligations of Spouses 103

§1. General Principles 103

§2. The Household Expenses 103

§3. The Matrimonial Home 105
- I. Real Property 106
- II. Furniture and Household Effects, Etc. 107
- III. Tenancy 108

§4. Transactions between Spouses 108
- I. Ordinary Bilateral Contracts 108
- II. Gifts 109
- III. Invalid Gifts and Annulled Transfers 111

Chapter 2. The Marriage Settlement 114

§1. Separate Property Contracts 114

§2. Other Ways of Making Contracts for Separate Property 116

Chapter 3. The Legal Matrimonial Regime 118

§1. General Principles 118

§2. Personal Possessions and Rights 119

§3. Ways of Holding Separate Property 123

§4. The Control of the Property 124

§5. The Relationship with the Creditors 125

§6. Division of Matrimonial Property 127
- I. Grounds for Division During Marriage 128
- II. Assets and Liabilities of the Estate 130
- III. Rules for Unequal Division of Community Assets 132

IV. Claims for Compensation 134
V. The Qualitative Division 135
A. General Principles 135
B. Joint Right of Spouses to Select Assets Prior to Division 136
VI. Agreement Modifying a Contract 137

§7. Claims Raised against Separate Property on Division 139

Part IV. Succession Law 141

Chapter 1. Intestate Succession 141

§1. The Opening of the Succession 141
I. Death 141
II. Missing Persons and Absentees 141

§2. The Heir 142
I. Capacity to Succeed 142
II. Commorientes 142
III. Unworthiness to Succeed 143

§3. The System of Descent 143
I. The Classes of Heirs 143
A. Surviving Spouse 143
1. The Surviving Spouse's Position When the Deceased Has Living Beneficiaries 144
2. The Spouse as the Sole Beneficiary 146
B. Descendants 146
C. Ascendants 147
D. Collaterals 147
II. Representation 148
III. The Anomalous Succession 148
IV. Adoption 148
V. Undivided Possession of the Estate 149
A. Conditions Applying to the Undivided Estate 150
B. The Effect – Control 151
C. The Division 152
D. Compensation Right: Annulment of Presents 154
E. Execution of Division of the Undivided Estate 155

§4. The Rights of the State on the *Bona Vacantia* 156

Chapter 2. Testamentary Succession 158

§1. Capacity to Make a Will 159

§2. Different Types of Wills 160
I. Normal Wills 160
II. Emergency Wills (Nuncupative Wills) 161
III. Non-compliance of the Recognized Procedures Concerning Format 161

§3. The Joint Will 162

§4. Revocation of a Will 163

§5. Provisions in a Will 164

§6. Restrictions 165
I. The Legitim 165
A. The Quantitative Competence 166
B. The Qualitative Competence 167
II. Maintenance Provisions 168

§7. Interpretation of a Will 169

Chapter 3. Acts *Inter Vivos* Related to the Estate 170

§1. Estate Planning 170

§2. Donations 171
I. Death Bed Donations 171
II. Death-Risk Donations 172
III. Death Donations 172
A. Presents Given During Life versus Death Donations 173
B. Death Donations versus Mutually Burdening Agreements 174

§3. Trusts 175

§4. Insurance Contracts 175

§5. Others 177

Chapter 4. Acquisition and Administration of the Estate 179

§1. The System of Acquisition 179

§2. The Administration of the Estate 179
I. The Distribution of the Estate 179
II. The Distribution to the Surviving Spouse 180
III. Private Distribution of the Estate 180

IV. Distribution of the Estate by an Authorized Manager 181
V. Advertisement for Creditors 183

Selected Bibliography 185

Index 187

List of Abbreviations

CEFL	Commission on European Family Law
CISG	Convention on International Sale of Goods
CPR	Central Persons' Register
DKK	Danish Krone
EC	European Community
EU	European Union
EEA	European Economic Area
GP	General Practitioner
IHT	Estate and Gift Tax Act
NATO	North Atlantic Treaty Organization
UN	United Nations

List of Abbreviations

Preface

This monograph is intended for the use of foreign lawyers desiring information about the Danish family and succession law. Hans Viggo Godsk Pedersen is the author of the General Introduction, Part 3, Matrimonial Property Law, and Part 4, Succession Law. Ingrid Lund-Andersen has written Part I, Persons, and Part 2, Family Law.

The law is stated as at 1 September 2015.

Hans Viggo Godsk Pedersen
Ingrid Lund-Andersen

General Introduction

Chapter 1. General Background of the Country

1. Denmark has a population of about 5.6 million; of which about 2.3 million are men and approximately 2.4 million are women of individuals aged 15 years old and above. A little more than 1 million couples are married, although some of them are separated. Due to the fact that a man often marries a woman who is somewhat younger than him, and that men often die at an earlier age than women, there are many more widows than widowers – about 227,000 compared to 70,000 respectively.

It is remarkable that approximately 187,000 men are divorced without having remarried while the same applies to approximately 244,000 women. As the figures show, men are more likely to remarry than women. That the rate of divorces is high in Denmark is proved by the fact that at present, the number of divorces is about 18,800 a year while the number of marriages is about 27,500 a year.

Furthermore, it is remarkable that not all unmarried adults are living alone. Approximately 632,000 persons or 316,000 couples are in a steady relationship – that means as husband and wife. As the figures show one out of four couples chooses not to marry. As far as persons of the same sex are concerned, about 3,600 partnerships are registered and about 800 persons of the same sex are married.

Chapter 2. Historical Background of Family and Succession Law

2. Since the fifteenth century, the husband has been considered the head of the family in Denmark. The property rights of the spouses were a kind of community property settlement. However, as the spouses were not equal, it was not a settlement like the community property settlement that is in force now. Only the husband had the right to dispose of the community property. The important changes in this system were made by legislation in the last part of the nineteenth century and especially in 1925 by the Act of Parliament governing the legal effects of marriage; an Act which – with few amendments – is still regulating matrimonial property law. The changes in the system were made in order to make the spouses equal as far as economic and personal matters were concerned. As it appears in Part 3, the legislation operates with a kind of community property settlement which allows each spouse to deal independently with the property he/she has acquired before or during the marriage so that each spouse is personally liable for this property to his/her own creditors.

Also as regards inheritance, women traditionally held a weaker position than men in the sense that women would only inherit half as much as men. However, in 1857, this was changed so that men and women would inherit equally. Of course, this was part of the development taking place to make rights equal for men and women. Furthermore, there has been a development in this century to the effect that a spouse should hold a stronger position in relation to the other spouse's children and other relatives. For instance, since 1954 the surviving spouse has had the opportunity to remain in undivided possession of the entire joint estate, so that the children would not inherit before the longest living of the spouses died. To this should be added that the size of the estate inherited by the surviving spouse was increased from one-fourth to a third in 1964 and to half in 2008. In addition, the surviving spouse in 1964 was given a right to take out assets up to a certain amount from the estate even if this would mean that the children would get no inheritance.

Chapter 3. Sources of Family and Succession Law

§1. Constitution

3. In Denmark the Constitution does not contain articles that have a link with family law. This means that the Parliament is not bound by Constitutional constraints when regulating this field.

§2. Legislation

4. As already mentioned, the primary sources in Danish family and succession law are Acts of Parliament. Although there are some court decisions, it is to be noticed that these decisions must be seen only as an interpretation of the legislation.

Regarding marriage, the most important Acts are the Act of Parliament No. 148 of 8 May 1991 (Consolidated Act No. 1096 of 07 October 2014), the Marriage and Matrimonial Causes Act, as subsequently amended, and Act No. 56 of 18 March 1925 (Consolidated Act No. 1053 of 12 November 2012) as subsequently amended. Division of the family assets is governed by Act No. 594 of 14 June 2011, the Division of Family Assets Act, as subsequently amended.

Concerning children, the most important Acts are Act No. 460 of 7 June 2001 (Consolidated Act No. 1097 of 7 October 2014), the Children Act, as subsequently amended, Act No. 499 of 6 June 2007 (Consolidated Act No. 1085 of 7 October 2014), the Parental Responsibility Act, as subsequently amended and Act No. 388 of 14 June 1995 (Consolidated Act No. 647 of 12 June 2013), the Guardianship Act, as subsequently amended. The last one also contains regulation of guardianship for adults who are incapable of dealing with legal matters.

Succession is primarily regulated by Act No. 515 of 6 June 2007 (Consolidated Act. No. 652 of 12 June 2013), the Inheritance Act, as subsequently amended and Act No. 383 of 22 May 1996 (Consolidated Act No. 737 of 25 June 2014), the Administration of Estates Act, as subsequently amended.

§3. Treaties

5. Denmark has ratified some Nordic Conventions on Marriage, Guardianship, Inheritance and Administration of the Estate. The Nordic cooperation has a relatively long tradition.

Besides the Nordic Conventions, Denmark has ratified the UN Convention of 20 June 1956 on the recovery abroad of maintenance and the Hague Convention of 5 October 1961 on the conflicts of laws relating to the form of testamentary dispositions; of 1 June 1970 on the recognition of divorces and legal separations; of 2 October 1973 (before this the 1958 Convention) on the recognition and enforcement of decisions relating to maintenance obligations and of 25 October 1980 on the Civil Aspects of International Child Abduction. Also, the European Council

Convention of 20 May 1980 on recognition and enforcement of decisions concerning custody of children and restoration of custody of children has been ratified by Denmark.

Due to the fact that Denmark has ratified the above-mentioned conventions, it is of less importance that the EU Convention on Jurisdiction & Judgments has also been ratified by Denmark.

§4. JURISPRUDENCE

6. The field of family and succession law is regulated in relatively great detail by Parliamentary Acts. The courts interpret the Acts in cases brought before them, but due to the fact that it is interpretation of the Acts, case law is not a main source of law. According to Danish tradition, a number of books on the subject have been published. Although these are to some extent textbooks, they are very often used when interpreting the legislation. In fact, when a case is brought before the court it is almost unthinkable that the lawyer would not have searched in the published jurisprudence for an interpretation of the Act which would be in conformity with his/her client's wishes.

Chapter 4. The Courts Administering Family and Succession Law

7. In Denmark there are no Family Courts. Therefore, cases have to be brought before the ordinary courts. Cases concerning division of the estate have to be settled by the Probate Court. However, in fact few cases are settled by the courts for two reasons.

Many cases are settled under an administrative procedure by the regional state administration. For instance, if the spouses agree, legal separation and divorce can be settled by the regional state administration. If one of the spouses does not agree, the case must be settled by the courts.

Cases concerning division of the estate are to be settled by the Probate Court. Probably due to the fact that in most cases it seems obvious how the Probate Court would settle the case if it was heard, almost all spouses divide the estate by private agreement – sometimes assisted by lawyers.

This does not mean that all disputes are settled in exactly the way the Probate Court was supposed to settle them. Some spouses may have special reasons for another division of the estate.

Part I. Persons

Chapter 1. The Status of a Person

§1. Definition of a Person

8. When defining the concept of a *person* from a legal point of view, this concept is itself based on another concept, namely that of *legal status*,[1] which involves the ability to have legal rights and obligations, but which does not cover a third concept, namely that of *legal capacity*, which is dealt with in §2 and which must be distinguished from legal status. A person, from the legal point of view, is a person with legal status, namely a person in possession of legal rights and legal duties. The concept of legal status covers the legal right to the protection of liberty, privacy and integrity. A person is still a person in this sense even though he/she is put under guardianship and may be legally incapable of acting as described below in §2.

I. Natural Persons

9. A person in the legal sense is first a *natural person*. All normal adults have the ability to enjoy legal rights and to be made subject to legal duties. A person also has political and social rights collectively with other persons in the community. The ability covers everybody, including children, the mentally ill and all handicapped persons so that in fact everybody is a person in this legal sense. Thus, a child can own a farm and be a legal person in those contracts which the running of the farm involves, even though the child himself/herself cannot enter into these contracts, his/her guardian must do that. The child will also be made liable for compensation if he/she himself/herself or a person employed by him/her on the farm causes damage to a third person or to his/her estate. Persons under guardianship due to mental illness or mental handicap may also own farms, run factories or inherit large sums of money. Legal status, accordingly, is an inherent right belonging to all individuals from the moment of their birth until the moment of their death. Even before birth, the unborn child is a person, able to inherit and entitled to compensation, if he/she loses a breadwinner.

1. By way of comparison, in English law legal personality is defined as follows: a person in law means any entity accepted by the law as having certain defined rights and obligations. Such persons may be natural (human beings) or artificial (corporations). See P.W.D. Redmond & Peter Shears, *General Principles of English Law*, 4 (7th edn, M&E Law 1993).

Even though the concept of legal status implies the protection of liberty, privacy and integrity, this is a somewhat modified truth in modern society since the private life and private interests of the individual must often yield to other interests on which society sets a higher value. Children, the elderly, the mentally ill, handicapped persons, prisoners and foreigners are among those groups that must suffer limitations to their rights. For example, the right to have a family is limited through the provisions which entitle public authorities to expel aliens, imprison criminals and to refuse permission to adoption. A child conceived through artificial insemination may not know his/her donor father.

II. Legal Persons

10. Second, a corporation can be defined as a *legal person* and has, as such, legal rights and legal duties. In other words, a corporation is an artificial person composed of one or several natural persons. The corporation is recognized by the law as having a separate personality from its human members. A 'corporation sole' is one that consists of one human member only at any one time or of the successive holders of certain offices, for example, bishops, the Queen, the Public Trustee, etc. A 'corporation aggregate' consists of many members simultaneously (e.g., limited companies). Corporations are – e.g., cooperatives – companies with limited liability or with limited partnership, associations, societies and unions as well as public authorities, whether central government or local authorities.[2]

§2. Capacity

11. After a brief introduction follow the conditions for the establishment of guardianship for minors and adults. In the case of minors, guardianship and legal incapacity go together. For adults, however, the establishment of guardianship and the divestment of legal capacity do not necessarily go together but involve separate decision-making. Accordingly, the establishment of guardianship is considered separately from legal incapacity.

The provisions concerning those areas, where the ward, despite his/her legal incapacity, can still act and enter into *valid* contracts, will be described next. The legal effects of his/her entering into *invalid* contracts will also be dealt with. The rules governing the liability for torts of a minor and a person of unsound mind unable to act rationally in the Liability for Torts Act are described at the end of this chapter.

I. Introduction

12. Legal capacity can be defined as a person's ability to: (1) dispose of his/her property, (2) enter into contracts, and (3) be made liable for torts. A person who

2. Inger Dübeck, *Personers Rettigheder (The Rights of Persons)*, 7–33 (1st edn, DJØF 1996).

lacks one or more of these abilities is considered legally incapable to act. His guardian must act on his/her behalf in order to dispose of his/her property or in order to enter into contracts. There are special provisions for liability for torts which will be described in greater detail below.

The question about appointment of guardians, their powers and duties and the ward's access to influence decisions made on his/her behalf, are dealt with in Part II, Chapter 7 (Guardianship).

A young person has no legal capacity, he/she is a minor. Normally his/her parents will have the parental responsibility, and will act on his/her behalf. Otherwise his/her guardian will do this.

An adult may also be made legally incapable of acting, but this presupposes first of all that he/she is put under guardianship, and furthermore that he/she is declared legally incapable of acting. Thus the decision about legal incapacity is a separate decision made according to special considerations. Legal incapacity presupposes the establishment of guardianship, whereas guardianship can be established without declaring the person in question legally incapable.

In the case of an adult, the guardian is usually found among his/her closest relatives and his/her desires in this respect are normally complied with. The attitude of his/her family members to this question is also consulted, and if the family cannot agree about the appointment, a third person, perhaps a professional, may be selected.

13. The law dealing with legal incapacity was amended by the 1995 Guardianship Act (Today Act No. 1015 of 20 August 2007) to cover most aspects of legal incapacity, such as the conditions for appointing guardians, the causes of legal incapacity, the scope of guardianship and the duties of guardians, the administration of the property of the legally incapable person, the ability of the legally incapable person to dispose of what he/she has earned by his/her own work and the nullity of contracts into which a legally incapable person has entered. Only the rules governing the liability for torts of minors and persons of unsound mind unable to act rationally are found elsewhere, namely in the Liability for Torts Act.[3]

II. The Conditions under Which a Person Is Made Incapable of Acting Legally

14. A person is incapable to act for two reasons: (1) if he/she is a child or young person, that is, a minor; and (2) if he/she is an adult put under guardianship and also declared incapable of acting.

3. The former provisions for the liability for torts, which were contained in the 1992 Legal Capacity Act, were transferred to the Liability for Torts Act No. 599 of 8 Sep. 1996 with later amendments, most recently by Act No. 266 of 21 Mar. 2014.

A. Minors

15. Minority is regulated in the Guardianship Act Chapter 1, sections 1–4. A person does not have legal capacity from birth. In fact he/she does not acquire legal capacity until he/she reaches the age of 18, according to section 1(1)(1). He/She acquires legal capacity on his/her 18th birthday at midnight. Until he/she comes of age, the possessor of the parental authority is his/her guardian (described below in Chapter 3). If both parents possess the parental authority, they are both guardians. They act jointly on behalf of the minor, but one guardian may authorize the other to act on his/her behalf (sections 2 and 3).

According to section 1(2), minors, i.e., young persons under 18, have no legal capacity in the sense that they cannot: (1) dispose of their property; or (2) enter into contracts. The provisions for liability for torts are found in the Liability for Torts Act section 24(a).

An exception to the age limit of 18 is made in the Guardianship Act section 1(1)(1), in respect of young persons under 18 who enter into marriage before they reach that age. Young persons under 18 cannot marry, unless they have the permission of the state administration according to the Marriage and Matrimonial Causes Act, section 1(1)(2). When they have this permission to marry, they automatically acquire legal capacity, unless the state administration, when granting the permission to marry, makes it a condition that the young person under 18 remains a minor and a ward (Guardianship Act section 1(1)(2)).[4]

In cases where the young person under age who applies for permission to marry is wealthy, permission is made conditional that legal capacity is not conferred, if on the one hand neither he/she nor his/her partner is capable of administering his/her capital and assets, but on the other hand they need the permission to marry, for example, because the couple have a child or are expecting one.

If a minor has married and is divorced both before he/she reaches the age of 18, he/she retains the legal capacity to act regardless of the fact that the marriage no longer exists.

B. Adults Who Are Put Under and Declared Incapable of Acting in Legal Matters

16. In the following, the conditions for establishing permanent or temporary guardianship will be described. Below, the conditions for declaring an adult incapable of acting are dealt with.

4. The term 'ward' will be used from now on referring to persons who are either (1) under 18; or (2) under 18 with permission to marry but without legal capacity according to the decision of the regional state administration; or (3) adults divested of their capacity to act.

1. Guardianship

17. Chapter 2, sections 5–7, of the Act deals with the situation where the need for appointment of a guardian is permanent. There are special provisions for the establishment of temporary guardianship in specific situations in Chapter 8 of the Act.

The *duties of the guardian* are laid down in Chapter 4 of the Act, the main provisions being sections 24 and 25 and the additional provisions sections 26–31. According to section 24, it is the duty of the guardian to look after the interests of his/her ward depending on how wide the scope of his/her guardianship is. The guardian must see to it that any capital which his/her ward may possess is preserved and also gives a reasonable interest. The guardian must furthermore see to it that any income which comes to his/her ward is used for the benefit of his/her ward. This involves that the guardian may spend his/her ward's income not only to cover his/her ward's most basic needs but for such purposes which he/she considers useful for his/her ward. The parents of minors may – in their capacity of guardians – use the child's income for his/her maintenance within reason and taking the position of the child into consideration. This provision is connected with the duty imposed on each of the parents to maintain their child according to the Children's Maintenance Act section 13, which will be described below in Chapter 6 §3. Both in the case of children and adult wards, the guardian may, if the ward's income proves insufficient, spend his/her capital within reasonable bounds, but he/she needs the approval of the state administration in order to do so.[5] If a guardian considers it justified that the ward looks after his/her own needs, he/she may provide him/her with cash which the ward may decide how to spend. The guardian should do this in case his/her ward is a young person coming up to the age of 18 or if he/she is a mentally handicapped person living in a community home and functioning well.

The ward is entitled to have some say in important decisions about his/her affairs. The guardian must consult him/her, unless he/she is under 15 years of age or incapable of understanding the importance of the decision. If the ward is married, the guardian must also consult the spouse. There is a prohibition against the ward's standing surety on the ward's behalf for the debt of a third person. The state administration supervises the way guardians, appointed in the administration, administer the capital of their wards, and the guardians must present an account of their administration. If a guardian neglects his/her duties, he/she is liable to pay compensation to his/her ward for any damage caused deliberately or by negligence (sections 26–31).

According to Chapter 2 of the Act, there are three situations in which a *permanent* guardian can be appointed for an adult: (1) if a person is unable to look after his/her own affairs for reasons of mental illness, senility or retarded mental

5. This provision, which covers both children and adult wards, is intended to be used primarily for the benefit of adult wards. The older the ward, the less is the need to preserve the capital intact, and in case of an older ward, the guardian is expected to use the capital, when the need arises.

development or any other form of enfeebled health, and if there is a need for it (section 5(1)); (2) if a person is unable to take care of his/her own financial affairs due to illness or seriously enfeebled health, if he/she himself/herself applies for it (section 5(2));[6] (3) joint guardianship (section 7).

According to Chapter 8 of the Act, *temporary guardianship* for special purposes can be established according to sections 48–50.

a. Permanent Guardianship in Case of a Serious Health Condition (Section 5(1))

18. The implementation of guardianship according to section 5(1) presupposes that three tests are passed: (1) A legal test according to which the person must be unable to look after his/her own affairs. This need not mean that he/she is totally incapable of looking after himself/herself. All that is required is a significant deviance from what is considered normal conduct. This may vary according to the size of his/ her capital and assets or the complication of the functions he/she has to perform. (2) A medical test which requires the presence of some kind of mental illness or disability. The medical test also covers the demented person whose frailty condition is due to age or any other reason, even the serious abuse of alcohol and narcotics. (3) A need's test which involves the appointment of a guardian for a person who has a very important problem to solve and no family or close relatives to support him/her.

b. Permanent Guardianship at the Request of the Person Himself/Herself (Section 5(2))

19. The conditions for appointing a guardian according to section 5(2) are not as strict as those under section 5(1). Thus, the health of the person in question need not be as bad, and the requirement of proof of bad health is relaxed. A medical certificate is required in all cases. It is for the state administration to estimate whether or not the conditions for guardianship are fulfilled both under section 5(1) and (2). Thus, the person's own application for guardianship is not decisive in itself, and the state administration will need to meet the applicant in order to assess if his/her desire for guardianship is maintained and has been considered by the applicant in all its aspects.

c. Limited Permanent Guardianship (Section 5(3))

20. The provisions in section 5(1) and (2) date back to the former Legal Capacity Act. But a new provision was introduced in the 1995 Act in section 5(3) according to which guardianship can be limited to certain economic affairs – e.g., certain assets – just as it can be limited to certain personal matters excluding economic

6. Guardianship according to s. 5(2) is an alternative to joint guardianship under s. 7, which will be described later.

affairs.[7] This provision affords the possibility of devising individualized guardianship arrangements adjusted to individual circumstances, for example, a person in an old people's home may have need of a guardian to act on his/her behalf for special purposes. Thus the guardianship can be limited to financial circumstances exclusively, if the need for a guardian is only in this area. It may be further limited to concern only part of the capital and assets, for example, to a holding of securities, real estate, certain income or to specified tasks. It may also be limited to certain personal circumstances, for example, to seeing to it that the person under guardianship is put in an institution.

d. Joint Permanent Guardianship (Section 7)

21. If a person requests it, and there is a need for help to administer his/her capital and assets or other financial affairs, and the person himself/herself is inexperienced or suffers from bad health, a guardian can be appointed to act together with the applicant (section 7(1) and (3)). As this kind of guardianship is dependent on an application from the person involved, there is no special medical criterion in the provision, it is sufficient that the need for guardianship is due to inexperience, weak health generally or other similar conditions. It is a task for the state administration to decide on the base of a meeting with the applicant, whether or not he/she is sufficiently able to cooperate with the guardian. If it turns out that they do not cooperate well, another joint guardian can always be appointed later on. It is possible to limit the joint guardianship to certain assets or affairs (section 7(2)).

e. Temporary Guardianship (Chapter 8)

22. Section 47 of the Act covers situations where there is a conflict between the ward and the guardian. In such situations, the ward may be either a minor or an adult under guardianship. For example, if the guardian himself/herself must enter into a contract with the ward, the guardian cannot both look after his/her own interests in this matter and those of his/her ward. Therefore, a special guardian must be appointed for the purpose of making this particular contract only. Similarly, if the ward and the guardian have conflicting interests in other legal matters, or a conflict of interests arising out of some personal problem, for example, disagreement over a choice of career or a marriage partner, a guardian for special purposes can be appointed. The practical situation will often be a conflict between parent and child. It may also arise, if the ward is to inherit money from a deceased person in connection with the administration of the deceased person's estate. Section 47 of the Act covers all these situations.

If the permanent guardian is away for a period of time or otherwise temporarily prevented from looking after the interests of his/her ward, a provisional guardian can also be appointed. This becomes necessary, if the guardian falls ill, for example,

7. An example of a personal matter for the management of which such limited guardianship is established is where a person is so weak that he/she cannot himself/herself cope with the decision about leaving his/her home and moving to an institution but needs a guardian to make that decision for him/her.

and the provisional guardian is appointed to look after all the affairs generally of the ward in the intermediate period. These situations are dealt with in section 48 of the Act.

According to section 49, it is possible to appoint a special guardian in case of need for an adult who is otherwise functioning normally, but who is temporarily prevented from looking after his/her own affairs. Guardianship in these situations may only last for as long as the adult himself/herself is prevented and the obstruction lasts. The tasks of the guardian are specified, he/she is not given a general appointment.

f. The Scope of Guardianship

23. Sections 8–10 of the Act deal with the permanently appointed guardian. According to section 8(1) of the Act, a decision made under sections 5 and 7 should be adjusted to the needs of the person for whom the guardian is appointed and may not go further than strictly necessary. If his/her condition is temporary, the period of guardianship can be limited (section 8(2)). A decision about guardianship can be amended after some time has elapsed to something less radical, if the circumstances of the person have changed (section 9). This is the case if the health of the person under guardianship improves, in which case the section 5 decision can be substituted by joint guardianship under section 7.

On the other hand, the decision can also be to extend guardianship. Thus, a guardianship-decision which was limited to certain assets according to section 5(3) can be extended later on to cover all his/her assets. Similarly, a person under section 5 – guardianship who has retained his/her capacity to act, but who proves unable to act appropriately or comes under a bad influence from a third person, may later on be deprived of his/her legal capacity according to section 6.

Decisions about guardianship (section 5) divestment of legal capacity (section 6), and joint guardianship (section 7) must be rescinded according to section 10 if the conditions for guardianship or divestment of legal capacity are no longer present.

The scope of guardianship for the temporarily appointed guardian according to Chapter 8 of the Act is always limited to special tasks, and the appointment is for a temporary period only.

2. Legal Incapacity

24. A young person does not acquire legal capacity until he/she reaches the age of 18 (or marries before that) as mentioned above. The person under 18 is thus legally incapable of acting, and the guardian must act on his/her behalf. An adult who is put under guardianship does not necessarily lose his/her legal capacity. But in cases where guardianship is established according to section 5, the guardianship comprising his/her financial circumstances, his/her legal capacity to act can be taken away under section 6. Section 6(1)(1) is worded as follows:

> *In connection with the establishment of guardianship under Section 5 covering financial matters, a person can at the same time be divested of his ability to*

act, on condition that this is necessary in order to prevent that the person in question exposes his capital and assets, income or other financial interests to risks of considerable diminishment or to prevent financial exploitation of him.

This type of guardianship is used for persons who are not only infirm but are also active. This is the case of persons who are manic-depressive or schizophrenic. They are often intrepid and involve themselves in all sorts of transactions. Legal incapacity is imposed in order to protect them from their *own* bad or harmful actions and also to protect them against persuasion, exploitation and abuse from *third persons.* It was mentioned above that guardianship under section 5 may be limited to certain assets or affairs. But in the case of divestment of legal capacity according to section 6(1)(2), the decision must always cover all assets and affairs of the ward, there is no possibility of limiting the decision. It is a question of all or nothing.

The person who has been divested of his/her capacity to act is in Danish called *umyndig,* that is, he/she has become a 'ward'.[8] Technically, this means two things according to section 6(2), namely that he/she is unable to: (1) dispose of his/her property, and (2) enter into contracts.

III. Legal Incapacity and Valid Contracts

25. In this context, unless otherwise stated, the provisions now to be described cover all persons termed wards,[9] that is, young persons according to section 1(2) or adults deprived of legal capacity section 6(2). The provisions about this are to be found in the Guardianship Act, Chapter 6, sections 42 and 43. Section 42(1) is concerned with the ward's ability to dispose of: (1) income derived from his/her personal work; (2) a gift, a legacy or a bequest by will intended for his/her independent disposal; (3) pocket money which his/her guardian has given him/her for his/her free disposal. As concerns income derived from personal work, only young persons over the age of 15 can dispose of this. Under that age his/her parents must act on his/her behalf in this respect also. The ward can spend the earnings, the gift, the legacy or the pocket money freely, also by entering into contract with a third party, for example, by selling it, by cancellation or by notification and other similar actions. As a counterpart, he/she is liable with his/her whole capital and assets not just with his/her earnings or the gift, etc. for his/her proper performance under the contract. This also covers liability for compensation in case of a faulty performance. In the case of earnings, his/her free disposal extends to substitute income in the form of sickness and unemployment benefit, but not to a pension or to compensation for damage to persons or things.

In regard of the ward's undertaking of personal work or service, if he/she is an adult ward, he/she needs the permission of his/her guardian to enter into contracts for such work. In the case of young persons, special and rather complicated provisions for such contracts are found in the Parental Authority Act, the main rule of

8. The term 'ward' will be used from now on referring to the person who has been divested of the legal capacity to act.
9. See *supra* para. 24, n. 8.

which is that the young person needs the permission of his/her parents to undertake such work.[10]

If the ward buys something, thus spending his/her earnings, the gift or pocket money, he/she may also dispose freely of what he/she has bought and over what substitutes for it. Thus, if he/she buys a television which is later stolen, he/she is entitled to the insurance money just as he/she is entitled to compensation in the case of liability (section 42(2)(1)). However, his/her powers to dispose do not permit him/her to enter into debts, for example, under a hire/purchase contract (section 42(2)(2)).

In all cases, the guardian can with the approval of the state administration deprive the ward of his/her powers to dispose under section 42 if this is necessary out of the consideration for the welfare for the ward (section 42(2)(3)). This does not cover situations where the guardian merely disagrees with the dispositions of the ward but must be done out of consideration for the ward only.

An adult ward and a young person over the age 15 may with the permission of the guardian and the approval of the state administration undertake a trade or other business on their own. This means that he/she can also enter into any contracts and even incur debts by way of the exercise of his/her trade, but the permission will normally fix the extent to which he/she can act on his/her own. The permission can be revoked by the guardian with the approval of the regional state administration. A third party must know or ought to know about the revocation otherwise the ward will be bound by the contract (section 43(1)–(3)).[11]

IV. Legal Incapacity and Invalid Contracts

26. In the case of invalid contracts, the provisions in the Guardianship Act, Chapter 7, sections 44–46 cover all persons termed 'wards', that is, persons who fall within the scope of sections 1 and 6. The provisions do not regulate the ward's access to rescind the contract because he/she has that right in any case, whatever the circumstances. The provisions are concerned only with the other party to the contract and regulate his/her access to rescind the contract. The provision in section 44 deals with the cancellation of the invalid contract, section 45 with the restoration of whatever goods have been exchanged, and compensation. Section 46 has a rule about invalid contracts made by a person who is not a ward but is of unsound mind and unable to act rationally.

Section 44(1) covers the situation where a ward has entered into a contract on his/her own without being capable of doing so because of lack of legal capacity. In this case, the other party to the contract may rescind the contract, unless the guardian approves the contract as made or the contract is discharged completely and exactly according to its terms by the ward. The first example of such an exception is a case where the ward buys a moped by hire purchase, the contract may be approved subsequently by the guardian or because the ward comes of age and approves or fulfils the contract himself/herself. A second example of a contract made by a ward that is

10. See Ch. 6, §2.

11. Svend Danielsen, *Værgemålsloven med kommentarer*, 593–608 (DJØF 2006),

strictly invalid, but that is valid in the circumstances, is when the ward is given a certain amount of cash for which he/she buys something foolish, for example, a 7 year old who buys sweets for GBP 10. In this case the other party to the contract is protected by law, because it is in the interest of society that he/she should be able to rely on the reception of cash even though the minor was not supposed to buy sweets, but shop for his/her mother.[12]

It is a special situation where the other party to the contract is aware not only of dealing with a person who lacks legal capacity, but, furthermore, of the fact that he/she has no special permission to enter into this particular contract. In this case, according to section 44(2), the other party may only rescind the contract after the lapse of the period fixed by the two parties when they made the contract or – if no such time limit has been fixed – after the lapse of a reasonable period of time within which the ward was to obtain the approval of the guardian.

According to section 44(3) in contracts where the ward has entered into a contract for personal work, and the employer knows that he/she is a ward, the employer cannot rescind the contract as long as the ward fulfils his/her part of the contract. This rule does not apply in those cases where the employer is unaware of the fact that the employee is a ward or has good reasons to believe that the ward is allowed to enter into the contract. In these cases the employer may rescind the contract freely.

If a contract is annulled according to the provisions of section 44 because of a person's legal incapacity, section 45(1) provides that both parties must restore to the other party whatever payment has been made under the contract whether in kind or cash, and if this is impossible, pay compensation for its value. The ward, however, is only obliged to pay compensation to the extent that he/she has actually benefited from the contract. The compensation is usually fixed at the amount for which the thing was bought. These rules also apply, when both parties, not only one, are wards or if the guardian exceeds his/her capacity to act on behalf of his/her ward. The other party to the contract must restore all payments regardless of the fact that he/she made the contract in good faith.

Section 45(2) extends the ward's liability to pay compensation in those cases where the ward has misled the other party to the contract by stating that he/she was authorized even though he/she was not, and regardless of whether payment has been made or not. In these cases the ward must pay a suitable compensation for the losses the other party has suffered. Such losses are posting, freight, storage and other ordinary commercial costs but not the loss of profit. In other words, the direct loss, which the other party suffers from having relied on the contract, is compensated, but not his/her loss for non-fulfilment of the contract. The lowest amount at which this compensation can be fixed is the value of the goods (section 45(1)).

If the ward is guilty of offence, for example, fraud or forgery, the ordinary rule for compensation applies (section 45(3)).

Section 46(1) contains a provision which covers persons with a multitude of mental conditions who because of the mental condition enter into contracts of whatever nature. Such contracts are made invalid, if two tests are passed: (1) a medical test

12. This provision has been established by the practice of the courts and is popularly termed 'The Cash Rule'. It would not apply if the minor were in possession of a GBP 100 note.

which requires that the person suffers from mental illness or disability, is seriously demented or temporarily deranged, or suffers from a similar condition; (2) a legal test which requires that he/she was unable to act rationally for these reasons. Persons, who fall within the scope of sections 5 and 7 of the Act, that is, persons for whom a guardian is appointed for seriously health conditions or if he/she himself/herself requests it, retain their legal capacity and may enter into contracts which are damaging for them. Such contracts will fall within the scope of section 46. The provision in section 45(1) applies to the settlement between the parties, but there is a special provision in section 46(3) which covers the situation where the sensible party to the contract was unable to detect the mental condition of the other party. In this case, he/she is entitled to a reasonable compensation.[13]

V. The Liability for Torts

27. The Liability for Torts Act[14] now contains the two provisions for liability in tort for children (section 24(a)) and adults of unsound mind (section 24(b)).

A. *Minors*

28. According to section 24(a) minors under 15 are fully liable for their torts according to the same rules which apply to persons above this age. Section 24(a) applies only to tortious liability but not to torts arising from a breach of contract, in which case section 44 of the Guardianship Act applies. The provision only applies to the tort of negligence. The legal standard of 'negligence' is here adjusted by the courts to a comparison between the actual action of the child causing the damage and a hypothetical action of a socially well-adjusted child of the same age in a similar situation.

The compensation itself may, however, be reduced or lapse completely for reasons of fairness. Reductions may be made by the courts for reasons of the child's lack of development, the nature of the action[15] and other circumstances. One such example of 'other circumstances' is the relationship between the minor's ability to pay for the damage he/she has caused, and the ability of the person suffering the damage to sustain it. When considering reduction, it is also an element whether or not the person sustaining the damage was insured or not. Compensation is never reduced if the person causing the damage has a 'third party liability insurance'.[16]

The holder of custody of a child living at home is liable for damages which the child is liable for under the law of torts up to Danish Krone (DKK) 7,500 for each damage. If the parents have joint custody, they have joint and several liability.[17]

13. Svend Danielsen, *Værgemålsloven med kommentarer*, 609–647 (DJØF 2006).
14. See *supra* para. 17, n. 5.
15. For example, the court will estimate whether the child performed the damaging action with intent, or whether it was merely done negligently.
16. Bo von Eyben og Helle Isager, *Lærebog i erstatningsret*, 131–142 (8th edn, DJØF 2015).
17. Section 1 in Act No. 363 of 13 May 2009 on Liability for Children's Damages.

B. Adults of Unsound Mind

29. Section 24(b) covers persons suffering from various mental conditions, and because of that cause damage to other persons for which they are liable. As in the case of invalid contracts two tests must be passed: (1) a medical test which requires that the person suffers from mental illness or disability, is temporarily deranged, or suffers from a similar condition; (2) a legal test which requires that he/she was unable to act rationally for these reasons. A person in one of these conditions who causes damage is liable for the damage under the same rules as persons of sound mind. This means that a person who is of unsound mind is not exempted from liability. To the extent that the liability is caused by negligence, the courts will estimate whether or not the person causing the damage has acted differently from how a normal person would have acted.

The amount of the compensation may be reduced or lapse entirely if the courts so decide when considering the mental condition of the person causing the damage for reasons of fairness. Reductions may be made by the courts because of the person's state of mind, the nature of the action and other circumstances. One such example of 'other circumstances' is the relationship between the ability of the person causing the damage to pay for it, and the ability of the person suffering the damage to sustain it. When considering reduction, it is also an element whether or not the person sustaining the damage was insured or not. Compensation is never reduced if the person causing the damage has a third-party liability insurance (section 24(b)(1)).

According to section 24(b)(2), there will be no reduction of damage if the person causing the damage has abused alcohol or narcotics, and this abuse has put him/her in a state of mind covered by section 24(b)(1). Section 24(b)(2) does not apply in cases of chronic alcoholism, pathological intoxication or forced intoxication.[18]

§3. Absentees

30. The provisions now in force in this area date back to 1946 and were in 1995 due to the introduction of the Guardianship Act. The Act, which is called the Missing Person's Act (Act No. 766 of 4 August 2005) deals with missing persons in Chapter 1; presumption of death by court judgment in Chapter 2, and lapse of the judgment, if the absentee turns up unexpectedly, which is provided for in the Act's Chapter 4; division of an absentee's assets without court decision, Chapter 3 of the Act. A special Chapter 5 of the Act provides for the division of the missing person's possessions after twenty years; and finally in Chapter 6, the Act regulates the case where an heir has either disappeared or his/her existence is unknown.

I. Missing Persons

31. The legal status of missing persons is regulated in the Act's sections 1–4. A person is considered an absentee when he/she has either disappeared from his/her

18. Bo von Eyben og Helle Isager, *Lærebog i erstatningsret*, 125–128 (8th edn, DJØF 2015).

usual surroundings, or a long time has elapsed, since his/her closest of kin have had any news of him/her, so that he/she is in all likelihood dead. He/She may also have disappeared in circumstances that make it seem likely that he/she is no longer alive. This was the case for a person who was last seen alive in Riga in 1941, when he went out, despite his wife's warnings, into the town in which there were riots. A guardian was appointed for him in 1949.

According to section 1 of the Act, a guardian is appointed when this is found to be necessary. The appointment may be made at the request of the interested parties and the provisions in the Guardianship Act about temporary guardianship apply to the appointment.

The assets of the missing person are governed by the same rules which apply to the administration of the capital and assets of wards. This involves that the missing person's capital and assets are kept for him/her in the same form in which they were taken over by the guardian.[19] There are two instances where the assets of the missing person are not just kept for him/her but are converted in some way. In the first instance, the Probate Court decides, if the possessions of the missing person should be sold rather than be kept for him/her, and the profit of the sale administered by an approved bank. In the second instance, the Minister of Justice decides, if the income and assets of the missing person may be used for his wife's or children's maintenance and education. For special reasons, the income may also be used to maintain and educate other persons who were formerly wholly or partly maintained by the now missing person (section 2).

In those cases where the missing person was married and his/her spouse is of age, that part of their joint estate which belongs to the missing person is administered by his/her spouse and his/her guardian jointly under the supervision of the Minister of Justice. Any inheritance or any gift which comes to the spouse is kept out of the joint estate in case of division of assets, taking place at a later stage between the missing person and his/her heirs (sections 3 and 4).

II. Presumption of Death and Return of the Absentee

32. In Chapter 1 of the Act the situation was considered when a person has been missing for a longer period of time but no decision with regard to his/her possible destiny is made. In this section two closely connected situations will be discussed. One of these is the situation where a court judgment is made according to which the missing person is considered deceased. In the second situation the presumed deceased person turns up unexpectedly.

19. According the Ch. 5 of the Guardianship Act, the capital and assets of a ward must be preserved unchanged. Cash, shares and bonds, mortgage deed and other securities are put into an approved bank but the guardian administer real estate, movables and amounts of cash below the sum of DKK 75,000.

A. Presumption of Death by Court Judgment

33. In those cases where a person has disappeared and it is unknown what has happened to him/her,[20] the court decides that he/she must be considered dead. Proceedings in the court can start after public summons when five years have elapsed since the missing person was last known to be alive (section 6(1)). If the missing person, at that time, was known to be in peril of his/her life or there are other reasons which indicate a probability amounting to certainty that he/she is dead, for example, if the ship or aircraft, on which he/she was known to be on board, has disappeared, the time limit is shortened to six months (section 6(2)). The spouse of the missing person, his/her heirs and other persons with due interest according to the law may start proceedings.[21]

The proceedings start at a court in Denmark, if the domicile of the missing person was known to be here or he/she was at least known to be staying here. The court appoints a lawyer to look after the interests of the missing person (section 9). At the first court hearing the person who started the proceedings, the missing person's spouse, his/her closest relatives and all other persons who are supposed to have some knowledge about the circumstances of the missing person are summoned. At the court hearing, the person who started the proceedings puts his/her explanation or proof to the court about the fate of the missing person. On the basis of the proof or the explanation, the court decides, if the disappearance has lasted for the period required, and whether the proof of his/her death is sufficient or not. If the proof of death is considered insufficient, the court may summon the missing person to a meeting in court and furthermore ask any other party in possession of possible further information to pass this information on to the court.

The person who started the proceedings must publish the summons in the *Danish State Journal.* The court may decide to publish the summons in other newspapers or in the other media in this country or abroad. Another court meeting is held after the lapse of at least one month. After the lapse of this period and if nothing turns up to weaken the proof at this meeting, the court makes a judgment of presumption of death and at the same time indicates from which date this judgment takes effect (section 13).

B. The Absentee Turns Up Unexpectedly

34. Once judgment has been made according to which a person is presumed dead, there is a second ten-year time limit which starts running from the date the judgment was made. Within this period the missing person may turn up and demand his/her possessions back from those persons to whom they were distributed as

20. It is a different situation if a person has disappeared but it is certain that he/she is dead. In these cases the probate court can make a decision according to which the missing person is declared dead even though no death certificate can be issued. This was the case at the shipwreck of the ship Hans Hedtoft off the coast of Greenland in 1959, when twenty-five persons on board the ship at its wreck were declared dead.
21. Registered partnership between persons of the same sex gives access for one of the partners to start the proceedings if the other partner goes missing.

bequests once he/she was presumed dead (section 17(1)). Information may also turn up to prove that the missing person died at a different time from the one fixed in the judgment. In this case, a person who would be entitled to inherit in these altered circumstances has the same time limit within which he/she may demand his/her inheritance (section 17(2)).

No heir is obliged to give back more than he/she has received. The creditors of the heir are also obliged to return whatever assets they have had attached by legal proceeding. If an heir has sold or spent a legacy he/she must pay a compensation corresponding to the value of the assets at the time of sale or consumption. The compensation cannot exceed an amount which corresponds to the value of the assets at the moment when they are to be repaid. His/her obligation to pay back can be reduced in certain circumstances if the spending was considered reasonable, for example, towards his/her own or his/her family's maintenance. He/she cannot be made to pay back, if the assets are lost without his/her fault, nor is he/she responsible for the interest of the assets which was due before the day of the missing person's return (section 18).

An insurance Company which has paid a life insurance to the heirs may demand the sum paid back. The demand may be reduced, if it was spent towards the maintenance of the heir and his/her family. A widow's pension and a similar pension which has been paid out on the basis of a presumption of death cannot be demanded back. If an heir has acquired any of the missing person's assets by fraud he/she is liable in all circumstances without a time limit. If the missing person's spouse has married again after the judgment was made, the former marriage remains dissolved whether or not the judgment is proved to be wrong because the missing person is alive (sections 20–23).

III. Division of an Absentee's Assets without Court Decision

35. The proceedings described above are of course cumbersome. In case the missing person owns very little – the upper limit of the total value is fixed at an amount of DKK 2,000 in the Act – the proceedings can be dispensed with (section 16). According to this provision, the missing person's assets can be distributed between his/her heirs after a period of one year from the last day he/she was known to be alive without a formal judgment. The Probate Court makes a decision about the time of death, and his/her goods are distributed as if his/her death took place at that time.

IV. The Division of the Missing Person's Property after Twenty Years

36. Another way of distributing a missing person's assets without a formal judgment is the case when he/she has gone missing, and his/her goods have been administered as provided by section 2 according to the decision of the Probate Court for a period of twenty years. If no proceedings for a court judgment have been started, the Probate Court summons the missing person and his/her heirs according to the proceeding in the Act's Chapter 2, as described above. The Probate Court is invited to do so by the Minister of Justice or any interested party. In this case there is no limit to the value of his/her assets, and they may exceed DKK 2,000. If the missing person does not turn up, but he/she has heirs who do, his/her assets are divided as if he/she had died after the expiry of the twenty-year limit. If nobody turns up, the assets are made over to the State (the Act's Chapter 5, section 24).

V. The Disappearance of an Heir

37. In the case of the distribution of assets after a deceased person, where certainty cannot be obtained whether or not an heir has survived the testator, special provisions have been laid down in Chapter 6 of the Act. Thus, no inheritance is put aside for him/her, but he/she has a right to demand his/her inheritance from those who have inherited within a period of ten years after the testator's death. If it turns out that the heir died within this period of time himself/herself leaving an heir, the new heir becomes entitled to the inheritance by the same rights which the deceased heir would have had, had he/she lived. If an heir is proved to have survived the testator, he/she inherits even though his/her whereabouts are unknown (Chapter 6, sections 25–27).

Chapter 2. Registration of Civil Status

38. The original legislation dealing with personal registration of all persons living in Denmark dates back to the first National Registration Act of 1924. The Act was amended in 1965 to facilitate the introduction of electronic data processing in personal registration and to create a legislative warrant for the introduction of the Central Persons' Register (CPR). In 1978, private persons were given access to information from the CPR register.

Denmark used to have two registers: (1) one at the national level, introduced in 1965, the CPR register; (2) one – the original register – at the local level called the Local Authority Register. The two registers have been amalgamated and now consist of only one electronic CPR register. The Act which now regulates this one register is Consolidation Act No. 5 of 9 January 2013. Its title is: 'Central Persons Register Act'. Overall responsibility for the CPR register rests with the Danish Ministry of Social Affairs and the Interior jointly with the local authorities. The Minister lays down the rules for the tasks of the local authorities in this area. The purpose of the legislation is to ensure that all persons living in Denmark have a CPR number and that the register contains fundamental information about all persons with a CPR number. Its purpose is, furthermore, to ensure that persons with a CPR number are registered as living where they do in fact live or stay. The system is operated as follows: everybody who is registered as living in Denmark on the basis of having been born here or having moved here is given a CPR number. The Ministry for Social Affairs and the Interior must inform each person of his/her CPR number when registration takes place at the person's birth or for the first time after having moved to Denmark or if the number is changed The Local Authority must see to it that all persons living within its area are registered on their address in the local authority. A person is considered to live in the local area where he/she has his/her home on a permanent basis. The Act defines this as the place where a person sleeps regularly when he/she is not temporarily absent on holiday, business, due to illness or to other similar causes, and where he/she has his/her belongings. If a person is without fixed abode he/she must be registered as living where his/her usual place of abode is regardless of its character. If a person has several places of abode or several homes, the local authority must decide to which of these the person is most closely attached, and register him/her as living there. If a child's parents do not live together and the child lives with each parent at different times, the local authority must register the child as living with the parent where he/she stays the greater part of the time. If a person lives onboard a boat or in a mobile home, he/she must be registered as living where the boat or the mobile home stays most of the time. The local authority is entitled to collect information from the person himself/herself, from his/her landlord, the post office, his/her unemployment benefit fund, bank or other institutions in order to find out where the persons actually lives.

The provisions of the Act are divided according to whether a person moves within Denmark from one local authority to another or moves to Denmark from abroad. If a person moves from one local authority to another, it is the duty of that person to register with his/her new local authority within a period of five days. The person must provide information about his/her CPR number, his/her full name, his/her former address and local authority, his/her future address and local authority and the date when he/she moved. The information must be given in writing and on a special form, if the local authority requires this. The registration must cover all persons who move with him/her. Exceptions to this duty are military service or imprisonment.

39. If a person moves to Denmark from abroad he/she can only register in the CPR register if his/her stay in Denmark exceeds three months. If the person is an EU or EEA citizen or comes from one of the Nordic countries (including the Faeroe Islands) that person must only register if his/her stay in Denmark exceeds six months. Shorter visits abroad do not cause these time limits to lapse. Registration of all citizens from abroad – except those from the Nordic countries – can only take place if the person has a residence permit or can prove that he/she is not required to have one. Diplomats or persons covered by conventions concerning military affairs, such as North Atlantic Treaty Organization (NATO), or their families, are not required to register. Persons moving to Denmark from abroad must provide information about their full name, a possible Danish CPR number, date and place of birth, last address where the person used to live abroad, the date when he/she moved to Denmark, his/her future address in Denmark, his/her civil status, date of marriage if he/she is married and by whom, possible membership of the Danish state church or an evangelical-Lutheran community abroad, any children, spouse and parents not covered by the registration and nationality. The local authority can require proof of this information and require the person who applies for registration to attend in person at the local authority office.

40. Persons who leave Denmark must be registered as no longer living in Denmark. Stays abroad for longer periods than six months must always be registered in this way. The person is considered as having left Denmark, if he/she stays away for a longer period than six months. However, shorter stays abroad do not have this effect. Persons who work abroad for the Danish state do not have to register as having left Denmark. Persons who for reasons of work stay overnight abroad for a period longer than six months but who spend their weekends, days off and holidays in Denmark have a right to remain registered in Denmark.

§1. The Right of Registered Persons to Have Their Registered Information Protected

41. All persons who have been registered as described above have a right to apply to their local authority to obtain name and address protection so that their name, address and CPR number are not passed on to other private persons. This protection is granted for a year, but lapses unless the person in question wishes it to lapse sooner or the local authority decides that there are special circumstances which entitle the person to a longer period of protection. All persons registered in the local authority are furthermore entitled to demand that they be not included in directories, or not made contact with for the purpose of collecting statistical or scientific information. As mentioned below, the Ministry for Social Affairs and the Interior can otherwise pass on information for such purposes. All registered persons can demand that they are not made contact with by businesses for marketing purposes.

§2. The Right to Obtain Information About Registered Persons

42. Information contained in the CPR register and older registers can be passed on according to the Act on Processing of Personal Data, Act No. 429 of 31 May 2000, to other public authorities. But the public authority may only pass on such information which it has itself received from the CPR register if this is allowed by provision in an Act of Parliament or if the Ministry for Interior and Health gives its permission to do so. The CPR Registers Act contains provisions which allow the Ministry for Social Affairs and the Interior to pass on information for use in scientific research or for statistical purposes. But as mentioned above, individual persons can demand that information for such purposes be not handed on in their case. The Ministry for Social Affairs and the Interior may also pass on information from the CPR register to companies and individual businesses about persons who are identified individually. The information which the Ministry may pass on covers the person's present name and address, unless the name and address have been protected, the person's profession, a request that the person does not want to be communicated with for marketing purposes, if the person has died or disappeared, has left the country and information about a new address, if the person is a ward and the name and address of the guardian as well as any changes in this information.

43. The local authorities may pass on information to anybody who requests information (i.e., private persons) about a registered person's present name and address – unless protected – profession, etc., in fact the same kind of information which the Ministry for Social Affairs and the Interior can pass on to public authorities except civil status. Information about civil status can be passed on to banks, however, except for information about separation from a spouse. Credit enquiry agencies are entitled to be provided with information about a person's name, address and CPR number regardless of the fact that they are protected. The local authority may also pass on information which is protected to persons who have a legal interest in obtaining the information. The Act contains provisions for how public authorities must use the CPR numbers of their clients. The Ministry for Social Affairs and the Interior must also lay down rules for the destruction of CPR registers in case of outbreak of war or if similar conditions obtain.

Chapter 3. Personality Rights

44. Danish Personality Law deals with the individual's legal rights to respect of liberty, privacy and integrity.[22] A central question is concerned with the legal protection of the individual's autonomy and integrity.

In this section, two main principles will be dealt with: (§1) the right to look after oneself and one's own interests; (§2) the duty to take care of other people's affairs from a public or private interest's point of view.

§1. The Right to Look after Oneself and One's Own Interests

45. The right to look after one's own interest is exercised by self-determination in regard to one's own life and circumstances. This problem has two aspects: (section I) a person's physical integrity, for example, the right to dispose of one's own life; (section II) a person's psychological integrity, which is concerned with his/her right to a religious, philosophical or political conviction as well as his/her right to privacy.

I. Physical Integrity

46. A person's physical integrity is traditionally viewed under the following headings: (section A) free access to abortion for a woman; (section B) can a person take his/her own life or refuse medical treatment; (section C) organ donation and organ transplants. A new issue in this area concerns the circumcision of women, which is practiced in some immigrant families (section D).

A. A Woman's Right to Abortion

47. In Denmark, the ethical dilemma between a woman's free access to abortion on one hand and the embryo's and later foetus' right to live is decided so that the woman's desire takes precedence over the embryo's right, at least as long as it is very young. According to the Danish Health Act (Consolidation Act No. 1202 of 14 November 2014), a woman has a right to make decisions about her own life and body, just as she has the right to refuse to start a family and to be a parent. In Denmark, there are provisions in the Health Law according to which the access to abortion is free until the expiry of the twelfth week of the pregnancy (section 92). The woman decides if she wants a termination of the pregnancy and it is free of charge if she lives in Denmark. Women who come to Denmark from abroad must pay to have the abortion. The consultant surgeon decides if the twelve-week period has expired. However, he/she may refuse to carry out the abortion for medical reasons, which speak against the abortion. After the twelfth week, all decisions about

22. This chapter is based on Inger Dübeck, Personers Rettigheder ('The Rights of Persons'), (1st edn, DJØF, 1996).

abortion must be made by the region board on abortion to which the woman must apply (section 97). If she is under 18 and has not married, she needs the consent of her parents unless the region board dispenses with this consent. Permission to abortion is given based on medical, eugenic, ethical or social indications. The social indication is based on the consideration to the woman's retarded development, youth, immaturity and if she functions badly in her social context.

An unexpected result of the in vitro-fertilization method was that it augmented a woman's chances of pregnancy when more eggs than one from her were fertilized. A woman may thus risk having twins, even quadruplets in which case she may desire to have an 'embryo reduction'. In 2003, the Act was amended so as to permit reduction of embryos or foetuses, that is, in those cases where the woman is expecting twins, triplets or quadruplets. No permission is required if the reduction is carried out before the twelfth week of pregnancy. After the twelfth week the reduction is allowed only if there are special circumstances, for example, a risk of damage to the mother's health if she were to give birth to all the children she is expecting. In this case the county board must give its permission to the reduction.

The woman who chooses to interrupt her pregnancy outside the authorized medical system can no longer be punished for doing so, but the doctor who performs the operation is liable to punishment with imprisonment up to two years, and persons who perform such an operation without a medical degree with imprisonment up to four years.

B. Suicide and Euthanasia

48. According to the Health Act, the dignity and integrity of patients must be respected as well as their right to decide about receiving medical treatment. The main rule of the Act is contained in section 15 according to which no medical treatment may be started or continued without the informed consent of the patient unless special rules provide otherwise. 'Informed consent' refers to a requirement in the Act according to which he/she must be given sufficient information – indeed he/she has a right to it – about his/her condition by the medical staff, where he/she is being treated. A consent to treatment can be given in writing but it may also be implied. Patients over 15 are entitled to give informed consent under the guidance of the person with parental authority. Patients not yet 15 cannot give informed consent to medical treatment, the person with parental authority must do so on behalf of the young person/child. If a patient lacks the ability to give informed consent, his/her guardian or a close relative may give the consent in his/her place. Immediate treatment necessary to ensure that the patient survives or that his/her chance of survival is improved can be given without consent. The Act contains rules about consent in special cases. For example, the situation where a patient has started a hunger strike. If the patient has been informed about the consequences of the hunger strike, the medical staff may not interrupt it. If a patient refuses blood transfusion this refusal must be respected. A dying patient may refuse treatment which will prolong his/her life. If a dying patient is unable to exercise his/her right of decision, the medical staff is allowed not to start treatment and to stop a treatment already begun. A dying patient is entitled to receive painkillers, sedatives and similar medication even though this may hasten the advent of death.

There are rules about the so-called life-testament. In such a document anybody over 18 who is not a ward can express his/her wishes concerning medical treatment in the situation where he/she is no longer able to give his/her consent to medical treatment. The life-testament may provide that the person writing the testament does not wish to be given life-prolonging treatment if he/she is dying or if he/she has become severely disabled due to illness, an accident, old age, heart failure or from another similar cause, if the disability will cause the patient to be unable to take care of himself/herself physically or mentally. If the medical staff is considering starting life-prolonging treatment of a dying patient and the patient is unable to give his/her consent, the medical staff must get in touch with the central register, where copies of such life-testaments are kept. The patient's wish must be respected if he/she is dying. If he/she is going to be severely disabled, his/her wish in the life-testament is only a guideline for the medical staff.

In present Danish law, there are no rules which either permit or prohibit suicide. A person who helps somebody else to die is liable to punishment though the punishment may be reduced if done out of compassion for a hopelessly sick person. In other words, even though suicide and attempts to commit suicide are not punishable, assistance from a third person in carrying out a decision to take one's own life, is punishable. The Psychiatry Act (Consolidation Act No. 1729 of 2 December 2010) permits forced commitment of a person to a hospital in order to prevent him/her from committing suicide, but it is generally assumed that the police, doctors, family and other persons who have special care for a suicide candidate have an extended duty to help him/her.

C. Organ Donations

49. Denmark introduced the concept of 'brain death' as a supplement to the concept of the 'heart death' by law in 1990. A person may be declared dead, either because he/she has stopped breathing and his/her heart no longer beats irrevocably or because his/her brain has stopped functioning also irrevocably. The choice between the two options is free, and in case a doctor is able to ascertain that his/her patient's brain has ceased functioning, he/she must declare that person dead. The time of death is put down in the death certificate as the time when the patient's brain or heart stopped functioning. In relation to other legislation, for example, the law of inheritance, insurance and social benefits, the time of death is the point in time at which the doctor found that the patient had died either according to the heart death criterion or the brain death criterion. A patient who is found to have died according to the brain death criterion may have his/her heart and breathing kept going artificially in a respirator with a view either to organ transplantation from the patient's living tissue, or to save the unborn child of a pregnant woman, if the birth is imminent, or out of consideration for the family of the patient. In practice it is possible to keep the respirator going for twenty-four or even forty-eight hours. In case of organ transplantation of organs such as kidneys, the pancreas, heart and liver, the organs must be transplanted immediately after their having been removed from the body of the patient whose brain is no longer functioning, even though his/her breathing and his/her heart function are kept going by the respirator. However, this is only permitted if there is a patient actually ready and waiting for the transplantation. The introduction of the 'death of the brain'– criterion by legislation has thus established the possibility of transplantation of vital organs, with the result that these organs can be removed before the patient's heart stops functioning but after irrevocable cessation of his/her brain function. Transplantation from deceased persons requires a previous permission from the deceased donor. This permission must be in writing, and the permission given after the donor's 18th year. A person may also have given his/her permission orally, which presupposes that the deceased donor's close relatives give information about this. Close relatives cannot object to organ donation from the deceased person, if the permission was given in writing. A donor may have registered his/her permission at the National Hospital's Donor Register.

In the case of donors who are alive, the person from whom the organs are taken must consent in writing to the organ donation, and the person must be over 18. A person under 18 may consent to organs being donated from him/her while he/she is alive if the person with parental authority consents.

Medical autopsy (as opposed to forensic autopsy) can be carried out on persons who have died in hospital or were brought dead to hospital, Autopsy may be carried out, if the deceased has given his/her previous consent after his 18th year. If there is no previous consent, an autopsy may not be performed if the deceased person or his/her closest relatives have expressed their opposition to it or if an autopsy can be assumed to be contrary to the deceased person's or his/her relatives' convictions. Neither can it be carried out if other special circumstances speak against it.

D. Circumcision of Women

50. Some African immigrant families in Denmark caused great scandal when it became known recently that they practiced circumcision of their daughters. In 2003, the scandal caused the Danish Parliament to amend the Penal Code so that a new section 245(a) was introduced, according to which the persons who cause bodily harm by cutting away or otherwise removing the female external sexual organs either partially or completely can be punished with imprisonment up to six years. If the bodily harm was grievous, the sentence can rise to ten years. As parents started sending their daughters back to Africa to have the operation performed, section 7 of the Act was amended so that this was punishable too in Denmark even though the offence took place abroad.

II. Psychological Integrity

51. Denmark has acceded to the European Convention on Human Rights and incorporated its provisions into Danish law in 1992. The provisions are now found in Act No. 750 of 19 October 1998 on the European Convention of Human Rights as Denmark is a member of the EU, the provisions of the EU and EC Treaties on fundamental and human rights are also binding on Denmark. The Danish Constitution contains a catalogue of human rights.

In May 2000, the former Private and Public Registers Acts were abolished and an Act on the Processing of Personal Data (Act No. 429 of 31 May 2000) took their place. The Act deals with electronic data processing as well as with non-electronic processing of personal data in a register. According to section 7 of the Act, no data processing may take place which involves information about an individual's race or ethnic background, political, religious or philosophical convictions, trade union membership, his/her health or sexual conduct unless the registered person gives his/her consent or the registration is necessary to protect either the registered person's or other persons' vital interests. The prohibition is extended to cover the handing on of such information. Public authorities are also covered by section 7, but they have an additional duty not to register or pass on information about a person's criminal offences, serious social problems or purely private matters (section 8). Examples of such private matters are a person's membership of other associations than trade unions, a serious accident with consequences for the person's personal and social life, suicide attempts, family disputes, separation and divorce applications as well as adoptions. Such information may be passed on if the registered person has given his/her consent, a serious private or public interest is at stake which takes precedence over the private interest which underlies the requirement to keep the information secret or it is necessary for the information to be passed on for the functioning of the public authority in question. Information about a person's debt to a public authority may be passed on to credit enquiry agencies.

In the Public Administration Act (Consolidation Act No. 433 of 22 April 2014) it is laid down that certain circumstances impose a duty of confidentiality on public authorities and limit the public authorities' access to pass on such information to other public authorities. According to section 28 of the Act, such information concerns a person's race, religion, skin colour, political convictions, membership of societies, sexual conduct and criminal offences as well as information about health or social problems, the abuse of drugs and other stimulants unless the person in question gives his/her consent, or such information can be passed on according to other Acts or vital interests indicate that the information should be passed on with a greater weight than the consideration for keeping them secret, such information cannot be passed on from one public authority to another. In the Act on Right of Access to Documents (Act No. 606 of 12 June 2013) all information which concerns a person's private and financial circumstances, that is, information which belongs to the person's sphere of privacy are excepted from the right of access to information.

§2. The Duty to Take Care of Other People

52. Above, the rules concerning a person's physical and psychological integrity were dealt with. Here, a person's social integrity will be described. The duty to look after other people's affairs from a private or public point of view means that the right to self-determination (personal integrity) is limited in order to protect a weak or incapacitated person either from doing damage to himself/herself or from damage caused by his/her surroundings. Under Danish law, no infringement of an individual's self-determination may be made unless it is warranted by law, that is, in an Act of Parliament, by administrative or judicial practice, or if the individual himself/herself has consented, or if it is a case of self-defence. If an infringement of a person's integrity is made legal, there is a need to give access for the person whose integrity is infringed to a complaints system as a safeguard against unlawful infringements. It must also be possible to impose a legal sanction if the legal infringement exceeds its bounds. This topic will be dealt with below in relation to the legal rights of children; and in relation to the protection of drug addicts. The legal rights of the mentally handicapped, the demented elderly persons and the mentally ill will be dealt with below in Chapter 7.

I. The Legal Rights of Children

53. The concept of the legal rights of children involves that children should be entitled to have their own point of view and to express it freely in accordance with their age and maturity. Questions about the legal rights of children have surfaced in relation to parents' chastisement of their children and child pornography.

Danish law about the legal rights of children is centred round a concept of the holder(s) of the custody's duty to take care of their child. This principle is embodied in the Parental Responsibility Act (Consolidation Act No. 1085 of 7 October 2014), section 2. The principle is based on ethical considerations and strengthened by many centuries of legal case law. The duty of the holder of the custody authority involves a duty to take care of their children's physical, personal and psychological needs. The Parental Responsibility Act enabled divorced parents to share custody.

The rules concerning the holder of the custody's function as a guardian of their child are laid down in the Guardianship Act. The duty of the parents to maintain their children, is regulated in the Children's Maintenance Act (Consolidation Act No. 1100 of 7 October 2014), sections 13 and 14, which will be described in Part 2, Chapter 6. The duty of the parents to maintain their children is so fundamental that the duty is transferred to the State, if the parents neglect it. According to the Social Services Act (Consolidation Act No. 150 of 16 February 2015) section 58, the local authority can decide to forcibly remove a child from its home and place it in an institution or in family care if there is a risk of causing damage to the child's health or development because the child is not taken care of, is treated violently or the child has problems with abuse/addiction, has become criminal or suffers from other behavioural problems.

A. *Parents' Chastisement of Their Children*

54. The 1995 Parental Responsibility Act was amended in 1997 and parents' chastisement of their children was forbidden (Act No. 416 of 6 October 1997). According to section 2(2) of the Act, the child has a right to be cared for and to be secure. It must be treated with respect for its person and may not be subjected to corporal punishment or other humiliating treatment.

B. Child Pornography

55. In 2003 the Penal Code, section 235 was amended so as to bring the Act in accordance with the additional protocol to the United Nation's Children's Convention. In the new section 235(1) a person who spreads pornographic photos and films or other similar material which show persons under the age of 18 in sexual contexts can be punished by a fine or be imprisoned for a period of up to two years. If the offence is grave the punishment is imprisonment up to six years. The new provision made the so-called fictitious child pornography an offence and extended the age limit of children from 15 to 18 years of age. The six-year upper limit was also introduced at this time.

According to section 235(2) any person, who possesses or for payment becomes acquainted with obscene photographs or films, other obscene visual reproductions or similar of persons under the age of 18, shall be liable to a fine or to imprisonment for any term not exceeding one year. This provision does not include possession of obscene pictures of a person who has reached the age of 15, if the person has consented to the possession (section 235(3)).

II. The Protection of Drug Addicts, Alcoholics and Vagabonds

56. In ordinary circumstances medical treatment cannot be initiated or continued, unless the patient consents as described above. The patient is required to give his/ her 'informed consent' according to section 15 of the Health Act. This also applies to the drug addict, the alcoholic and the vagabond. There is no possibility of using force in ordinary medical treatment of this group of persons or any other group of persons for that matter, unless forced treatment is necessary under the Epidemics Act or the Psychiatry Act.

57. The Epidemics Act (Act No. 814 of 27 August 2009) makes it possible to admit patients to hospital under compulsion, if there is danger of an epidemic, and treat them against their will.

58. The Psychiatry Act (Consolidation Act No. 1729 of 2 December 2010) defines what is to be understood by force or compulsion, namely that it takes place against the desires of the patient whether it is admission to hospital, retention in hospital or treatment. The Act also provides for forced fixation of patients and for their being locked up. Certain conditions must be present for the provisions of the Act to apply which concern both the mental state of the patient and the medical estimates of the necessity of the use of force.

Act on Retention of Drug Addicts in Treatment (Consolidation Act No. 1128 of 20 October 2014) provides for the retention of drug addicts but only in connection with a contract which the drug addict makes with the staff of the institution where he/she is to receive treatment (i.e., to break his/her addiction). The drug addict decides for himself/herself whether or not he/she wants the treatment, but once he/she has entered into a contract for treatment, he/she can be detained against his/her will in the institution where treatment takes place. The drug addict may terminate the contract at any time, however, though he/she can still be detained if he/she has become a danger either to himself/herself or to other people. Forced retention must only take place within a total of six months from the day the contract was made, and the total period of compulsory retention may only last for two months. A compulsory retention may only last for a maximum of fourteen days. The Act makes it voluntary for the County Councils whether or not to implement the provisions of the Act.

Chapter 4. Names

§1. Composition of a Name

59. The Danish Names Act dates back to 1904. It was revised in 1961, 1981 and again in 2005 (Act No. 524 of 24 June 2005. See also consolidation Act No. 1098 of 7 October 2014). The reform of 1961 represented an attempt to create equality of treatment as to name-giving between men and women and between children born within or out of wedlock. According to the Act, a name consists of last name (Chapter 1 of the Act), which will be described below under §2; first name (Chapter 3 of the Act) and middle names (Chapter 2 of the Act), described below under §3.

The Government may enter into an agreement with other countries regarding the relationship between Danish and foreign legislation on personal names, including the protection of names and the naming legislation to be applied to foreign nationals living in Denmark, and to Danish nationals living abroad (section 25(1)).

§2. Last Name

60. In former times, the last name was usually called the family name. The last name is now acquired by christening, by adoption or by application to the civil registrar.

The person(s) with custody must choose a last name for the child. If this giving of a name does not take place within six months after the birth of the child, the child will be given its mother's name automatically (section 1(2)). This provision applies to a child born within or out of wedlock.

The holder(s) of the custody will normally choose that the child is to carry the name which the father and/or the mother had when the child was born. If one of the parents carries the last name of a former spouse, the parents may instead choose the last name this parent had before he/she married.

I. Acquisition of the Last Name

61. Last names borne by more than 2,000 individuals are not protected and may be adopted by any individual (section 2). A name may be adopted as a last name provided one of the following conditions is met (section 4):

- The name has previously been the applicant's last name.
- The name is, or has been, borne as a last name by one of the applicant's parents, grandparents, great-grandparents or great-great-parents.
- The name is, or has been, the applicant's middle name.
- The name is the last name of the applicant's mother's or father's current or former spouse, provided the consent of the stepfather or stepmother concerned is obtained. A cohabitant shall be considered a legal spouse provided the cohabitants declare that they live together as a married couple, and who either lived

together for a minimum of two years or have children under the age of 18 together or will bear the name concerned as their last name.
- The name is the last name of the applicant's current or former foster mother or foster father. Provided the consent of the party concerned is obtained.
- The name is the last name which the applicant is entitled to adopt pursuant to the other provisions, with a modification of the gender-determined ending of the name if the name is rooted in a culture that permits is.
- The applicant knows and has obtained the consent of the individuals in who bear the name as their last name.

If spouses wish to bear the same last name, one spouse may adopt the last name of the other with the latter's consent (section 5(1)). The same applies to individuals who are not married but who declare that they live together as a married couple, and who either lived together for a minimum of two years or have children under the age of 18 together or will bear the name concerned as their last name (section 5(2)).

Two names, both of which may be used individually as a last name, may together be adopted as a single last name if the names are joined by a hyphen (section 8(1)). An individual who bears a last name consisting of several names joined by hyphens may choose to drop one of the names.

An adopted child acquires the last name of the adopting parent, unless the permission for adoption provides that the child is to keep its own name or carry this name together with the name given by adoption (section 9(1)). If the adoption is rescinded, the child shall retain the right to bear the last name which was given by adoption. These provisions also apply if the child was adopted by an adoption under a foreign adoption order (section 9(2)).

A last name will be annulled if another last name is adopted (section 10).[23]

§3. First Name

62. The provisions concerning first and middle names are dealt with in Chapter 2 and 3 of the Act, sections 11–15. According to section 12, a child must, as a minimum, have one first name. The person(s) with parental responsibility for a child must, no later than six months after the birth of the child, choose a first name to which the child is entitled. Apart from naming by christening in the established church or in one of the recognized religious communities or by an adoption order applications pertaining to naming of individuals must be submitted to the civil registrar (section 16). The first name chosen must be a proper first name and may not be such as to cause the child any unpleasantness later on in life. For example, a boy may not be given a girl's name and vice versa. The Minister of Social Affairs and the Interior publishes a list of names for boys and girls which may be adopted.

---

23. Henrik Estrup & Nikolaj Aarø-Hansen, *Navneloven med kommentarer (Act on Names)*, 35–132 (DJØF 2006).

§4. Middle Name

63. A child can be given one or more middle names (section 11). A middle name may, for example, be the middle name of child's father or mother or a name by the child's grandparents. A middle name may be dropped. A middle name will be annulled if it is adopted as a last name. An adoptive child is entitled to adopt a middle name from his/her adoptive parent's or parent's family or from his/her original family. The child shall retain the right to bear a middle name acquired on the basis of adoption following the nullification of adoption.[24]

§5. Change of Name

64. A given name may be changed by application to the civil registrar (section 16). The registrar will make a decision in every case and will forward the application to the stats administration if a case is to be decided by the state administration.

The child must consent to his/her name being changed if he/she is over the age of 12 (section 22(1)). If the child is under the age of 12, his/her attitude to the change in name must be ascertained to the extent that this is possible given the child's maturity or level of understanding and the nature of the case. The child's attitude to the suggested change must, insofar it is possible, be taken into account when a decision is made. In exceptional cases, the change of name may be agreed by the state administration even though consent from a child over the age of 12 has not been obtained.

If a child bears the same middle name or last name as a non-custodial parent, a declaration from the said non-custodial parent must be obtained to a decision to change the name in question (section 23). This applies if the child bears the first name of the parent concerned as a middle name or last name. The duty of consultation shall not apply if the act of obtaining the declaration may be deemed to cause significant damage to the child or unduly delay the case. An application to change a child's middle name or last name may be refused if it goes against the best interest of the child or the parent that has submitted a declaration.

A foreign national may, upon application, be permitted to change his or her name in accordance with the adoption of a name of change of name effectuated pursuant to legislation in the individual's country of citizenship (section 24(1)). However, a name may not be adopted, if it is inappropriate or may cause offence, or if it is unsuitable for use as a name in this country.[25]

24. Henrik Estrup & Nikolaj Aarø-Hansen, *Navneloven med kommentarer (Act on Names)*, 135–192 (DJØF 2006).
25. Henrik Estrup & Nikolaj Aarø-Hansen, *Navneloven med kommentarer (Act on Names)*, 193–243 (DJØF 2006).

Chapter 5. Nationality

§1. Definitions

65. In present Danish law, the concepts of 'Danish citizenship', 'Danish nationality' and 'Danish subject' are synonymous. This means that only persons in possession of Danish citizenship are Danish nationals and on the other hand, all persons who are Danish citizens are also Danish nationals.

The original legislation in this area dates back to a regulation from 15 January 1776. The two most important reforms in this century were carried out in 1925 and 1950. The revision in 1950 was a result of a Nordic cooperation. The present Danish Act on Danish Nationality is Consolidation Act No. 422 of 7 June 2004.

Danish nationality is the condition for enjoying certain legal rights. Possession of Danish nationality also imposes certain legal duties. The most important legal rights are the following: (1) the right to stay and work in Denmark; (2) the right to seek protection in Danish Embassies abroad; (3) franchise and eligibility according to the Danish Constitution, sections 29, 30, 42, 88 and the Act concerning Danish parliamentary elections, elections to the European Parliament and to the Danish local authorities;[26] (4) the right to a position as a civil servant in central government, the Danish Constitution, section 27; (5) the right to receive social assistance on a permanent basis and a social pension – with certain exceptions; (6) the right to carry on an independent trade or business; (7) the right to be appointed as a juror or lay judge; (8) the right to government grants for the purposes of higher or university education. Several of these rights can also be claimed by EU citizens as nationals of other Member States according to the EC Treaty. Certain exceptions are allowed, for example, a Member State can restrict certain posts in its public administration so that only nationals of that Member State can hold such posts (the EC Treaty, Article 39(4)). The most important legal duty is conscription or compulsory military service.

The acquisition of Danish nationality according to the Danish Nationality Act, sections 1–6, will be dealt with under II. The loss of Danish nationality (sections 7–9 of the Act), will be described under III.

§2. Acquisition of Danish Nationality

66. The acquisition of Danish nationality is connected with birth (section 1), the marriage of a young person's parents (section 2), adoption (section 2(a)), declaration (sections 3–5) and naturalization (section 6).

According to section 1 of the Act, Danish nationality is acquired by birth, if either the child's father or mother is Danish. If the parents of the child are not married,

26. Anybody over the age of 18 who has lived in Denmark on a permanent basis for three years immediately before the election has franchise and is eligible to local authority elections regardless of citizenship. The EC Treaty Art. 19 grants the right both to stand for and to vote in local authority elections and in elections to the European Parliament to all EU citizens but not the right to vote in elections or to stand for the national Parliaments.

and if only the child's father is Danish, the child acquires Danish nationality only if it was born in Denmark. Foundlings who are found in Denmark acquire Danish nationality, until other information becomes available.[27]

If a child born of a Danish man and a foreign woman has not acquired Danish nationality at birth, the child acquires Danish nationality at the marriage of its parents on condition that the child is under 18 and unmarried (section 2). The 1925 Act had a provision according to which a foreign woman acquired Danish nationality by marriage with a Danish man. This provision was abolished in the 1950 Act, and from then on, only the couple's children acquire nationality. The foreign woman who marries a Danish man must acquire Danish nationality by naturalization according to section 6.

A foreign child under 12 who is adopted by Danish adoption license becomes a Danish national, if the adopting parents are married and at least one of the spouses is a Danish national. A child adopted by an unmarried Danish national also acquires Danish nationality (section 2(a)). According to this provision, Danish *nationality* is acquired on the day that the adoption takes legal effect. In case of adoption of children from abroad, this means from the date the child arrives in Denmark. The provisions of section 2(a) apply equally to adoptions by foreign adoption licenses, if these are recognized by the Danish Adoption Act.

According to section 2(b), a marriage has no legal effects as regards the acquisition of Danish nationality under the Act, if is entered into by a person who is already married, as long as both marriages are in force. This provision was introduced in 2002 and it means that a marriage cannot be the foundation for automatic acquisition of nationality as long as both marriages exist.

A national of Finland, Iceland, Norway or Sweden can acquire Danish nationality by making a declaration to a County Governor, the Prefect of Copenhagen, the High Commissioner of the Faroe Islands or the High Commissioner of Greenland (section 3(1)). A declaration can be made by persons who: (i) have attained the age of 18, but not yet 23; (ii) reside in Denmark at the date of the declaration; (iii) have resided in Denmark for an aggregate period of not less than ten years, of which an aggregate period of not less than five years must be within the last six years; (iv) are unpunished and have not been sentenced to measures pursuant to Part 9 of the Criminal Code; (v) are not charged with a criminal offence (section 3(2)). According to section 3(3), a declaration can also be made by persons who: (i) have acquired nationality in Finland, Iceland, Norway or Sweden in another manner than by naturalization; (ii) have attained the age of 18; (iii) have resided in Denmark during the last seven years and (iv) have not, during that period, been sentenced to imprisonment or any measure which can be considered equivalent to imprisonment. For purposes of subsection 2(iii) hereof, residence in another Nordic country is equivalent to residence in Denmark, but only insofar as residence in the other Nordic country precedes, by not less than five years, the making of the declaration and the declarant's 16th birthday.

---

27. Section 1 was amended in 1998. The amendment abolished the former provision which treated chil dren born in a marriage differently from children born outside a marriage. The present provision follows the European Convention of 6 Nov. 1997 on Nationality.

According to section 4, a person – after having acquired nationality by birth and after having lived in Denmark until his/her 18th birthday but having later lost the Danish nationality – can recover nationality by submitting a declaration to the state administration. It is a condition that the person in question has lived in Denmark for two years immediately before submitting the declaration. Residence in another Nordic country until the declarant's 12th birthday is equivalent to residence in Denmark (section 4(3)). If the person in question is a citizen in another country, a declaration under section 4 can only be submitted, if the person can prove that he/she by acquiring Danish nationality loses his/her nationality of other countries (section 4A).

If a person has acquired nationality by declaration under section 3 or 4, nationality is also acquired under section 5 by that person's children – including adopted children – unless it is expressly stated that a child is not to be included in the acquisition of nationality. It is a condition for a child's acquisition of nationality that the person submitting the declaration has custody of the child or has joint custody that the child is unmarried, is under the age of 18 and lives in Denmark. For an adopted child it is a condition, that the adoption license is valid under Danish law. Moreover it is a condition that it is proved that such acquisition will cause the child to lose its nationality of other countries unless the other parent of the child retains his/her nationality thereof and shares custody of the child.

Danish nationality can be acquired by naturalization according to section 44 of the Danish Constitution and section 6 of the Danish Nationality Act. In practice, naturalization is done by an Act of Parliament in which the name of each individual naturalized person is listed explicitly. Whether or not a person is naturalized depends wholly on the discretion of Parliament in each individual case. This means that nobody has a right to Danish nationality under section 6. The grant of nationality is entirely a matter for the discretion of the Danish Parliament. There are certain 'rules of thumb', however, concerning the length of the applicant's legal residence in Denmark. Normally, a stay of nine years without interruption is required, but the period is reduced to two years for citizens of another Nordic country and six years for (non-Nordic) applicants, who have been married to a Danish citizen for at least three years and who are still married to that person. Refugees and stateless persons must have lived in Denmark for a period of eight years from the date when the person in question was first issued with a residence permit. The applicant must be 18 years of age. Furthermore, it is taken into consideration how the conduct of the applicant has been, whether or not paid his/her taxes, paid back social assistance or maintenance payments. If he/she has not done so, this precludes naturalization. In practice, great emphasis is put on whether or not the applicant masters the Danish language and has knowledge of Danish social conditions. Once a person is naturalized, he/she has the same legal rights and duties as a person who acquired nationality from birth. Nationality is acquired on the same date as the day on which the Act of Parliament came into operation. Children of a naturalized person acquire nationality under section 5.[28]

---

28. Birgit Kleis & Niels Beckman, *Indfødsretsloven (Act on Danish Nationality)*, 40–68 (DJØF 2004).

§3. Loss of Danish Nationality

67. Danish nationality will be lost according to section 7 under the following circumstances: (1) when a Danish citizen acquires foreign nationality by application or explicit consent; (2) when a Danish citizen acquires foreign nationality by entering a public service in a foreign country; (3) when an unmarried child under the age of 18 becomes a foreign citizen by the fact that either parent holding or sharing custody of the child acquires a foreign nationality according to (1) or (2) above, unless the other parent retains Danish nationality and shares custody of the child.

According to section 8, a person who was born abroad and who has never lived in Denmark or stayed here under conditions which indicate ties with Denmark loses his/her Danish nationality as from his/her 22nd birthday unless the person in question becomes stateless. However, the Danish Minister of Justice may – on application – grant permission that Danish nationality is retained, if the application is handed in before the applicant's 22nd birthday. Such permission is usually granted, if the applicant can prove some ties with Denmark, such as a certain command of the Danish language, holiday stays in Denmark, exchange of letters with relatives living in Denmark or ties with Danish circles abroad. Residence in a Nordic country for an aggregate period of not less than seven years is equivalent to residence in Denmark. Permission is not normally granted, until the applicant's 21st birthday. A child of a person who loses nationality under section 8, will also lose his/her nationality when it was originally acquired through that person unless the loss will mean that the child becomes stateless.

According to section 8(A), if a person in connection with the acquisition of Danish nationality has committed fraud, for example, by giving false or misleading information, or who has fraudulently omitted to give relevant information, loses citizenship by court judgment if the information was important for the grant of nationality. According to section 8(B(1)), a person convicted of violation of one or more provisions of Part 12 (offences against the State's independence and security) and Part 13 (offences against public authorities) of the Criminal Code may be deprived of his/her Danish nationality by court order unless this will make a person concerned stateless. Where a person is punished abroad for an act which may, under subsection (1) lead to deprivation of his/her nationality, such person can be deprived of his/her nationality pursuant to section 11 of the Criminal Code (section 8(B(2)).

According to section 9, the Minister of Justice may release a Danish citizen from his/her Danish nationality, if that person wishes to acquire or already has acquired foreign nationality. It is normally a condition for granting the release that the applicant becomes a foreign national before the expiry of a certain time limit. Release from Danish nationality is not normally granted to persons who are resident in Denmark and who wish to remain here or to persons having to do Danish military service. In practice, a release is granted on condition that the applicant moves from Denmark within a certain time limit. A release from Danish nationality cannot be refused to persons who are foreign nationals and who live in another country.[29]

29. Birgit Kleis & Niels Beckman, *Indfødsretsloven (Act on Danish Nationality)*, 69–84 (DJØF 2004).

§4. THE NORDIC COUNTRIES

68. Denmark made an agreement with Finland, Norway and Sweden in 1969 and in 1998 all the Nordic countries agreed to Iceland acceding to this agreement – according to which residence in a Nordic country is placed on the same footing as residence in Denmark, see more in detail above §3.

Chapter 6. Domicile and Residence

69. Domicile is where a person has his/her permanent home or, if he/she is living abroad, where he/she intends to return to permanently. Residence is the place where a person happens to be living. A person can be resident in several countries at the same time, but can have only one domicile.

A definition of a person's domicile is found in section 6 of Consolidation Act No. 5 of 94 January 2013 on the Central Persons Register, where a person's domicile is defined as the place where he/she usually sleeps, when he/she is not temporarily absent due to holiday, business travel, illness and the like, and where he/she has all his/her possessions. As described above in Chapter 2, a person must register his/her civil status where he/she has his/her domicile or residence. If he/she has several residences, he/she must register where the most permanent residence is, which is thus considered to be his/her domicile.

As regards Danish nationality, this is normally acquired by birth according to the nationality of the parents, regardless of their domicile. As described above, it is a condition that an applicant for Danish citizenship, who has not acquired Danish citizenship by birth, has lived in Denmark – or synonymously has had his/her domicile in Denmark – for a certain period of time.

The main rule in Denmark is that a person's legal capacity is regulated by the law in the country where he/she has his/her domicile. This rule has been laid down by the practice of the Danish courts and is not found in any Act of Parliament. The alternative to the rule of domicile is the nationality principle which is followed in most European countries, when determining a person's legal capacity. An exception to the Danish principle of domicile is found in the Cheque Act, Consolidation Act No. 558 of 25 August 1986, section 58(1), according to which a foreigner's ability to enter into cheque obligations are deemed to be those of the country of which he/she is a citizen.

The Convention on International Sale of Goods (CISG) (Act No. 733 of 7 December 1988 which implements the United Nations' Convention of 11 April 1980) provides that in the absence of a special agreement between buyer and seller, the legal provisions of the country, where the seller is domiciled, apply.

Chapter 7. Mentally Handicapped Persons

70. Mentally handicapped persons fall into many categories. Here they will be divided into two groups: the first group is the elderly demented persons and persons with a mental disability, described under §1 and the second group the persons suffering from a mental illness (§2). The persons described under §1 all have in common that they do not fall within the scope of the provisions in the Act on Use of Coercion in Psychiatry Act of 1998 (Act No. 1111 of 1 November 2006), whereas the group under §2 does. Thus, in principle, there is no access to use force where the first group of persons is concerned, but there is in the second. Aspects of this problem will be examined under §1 and §2.

§1. The Elderly Demented and Persons with a Mental Disability

71. According to the Danish Constitution, section 71(2) and (6), a person cannot be confined or imprisoned, except where this is authorized by law. If a person has been detained, and the detention has been decided not by the court but by an administrative authority, the question about the legality of the detention must be put to the court, unless it is authorized in the legislation concerning foreigners. Under the Social Services Act (Consolidation Act No. 150 of 16 February 2015), the county councils must provide institutional care, boarding houses or community care for adults with a mental or physical handicap. According to the Social Services Act, sections 124–128, there are a number of legal safeguards for persons with a serious mental or physical handicap in connection with the use of security wards, isolation and fixation. The use of constraint and security wards may only take place in exceptional circumstances, if it is found to be absolutely necessary in the individual situation, for example, if the patient's behaviour represents a danger to himself/herself or to others. If the patient resists and there is no court decision according to which he/she must be put into a security ward, the county council must consider whether or not another measure is more suitable.

These provisions must be seen in connection with the provisions in section 5 of the Guardianship Act, described above in Chapter 1. Section 5(1) and (2) of the Guardianship Act covers the elderly demented person and the mentally handicapped, and makes it possible to appoint a personal guardian for these persons, either because they cannot look after their own affairs (1), or because they themselves request the appointment of a guardian (2). The appointment of a guardian is done in those situations – apart from the situation where there is a financial problem to be solved – where a major life decision must be made and the patient himself/herself is unable to make it and has no close relatives to make it for him/her. Guardianship will never entitle a guardian to decide that the patient must be put under constraint in an institution or in a hospital. In the health legislation there are provisions which require the assent of the patient to medical treatment. The practical situation where it can be useful to appoint a guardian is the situation where a person is becoming increasingly demented due to old age, and it is necessary to make a decision about putting that person in a home for the elderly or an institution, and there are no close relatives to whom the decision can be entrusted, or if the family cannot reach an agreement. The guardian will also have a useful role in cases where an application has been made to put the elderly person in an institution, but the application is refused by the social welfare office and indeed in any case where it is necessary to contact the social welfare authorities, and the guardian can look after this on behalf of the elderly person and see to it that the elderly person is consulted.

A woman may request abortion after the twelfth week of pregnancy, if there is a danger that the child will be born with a serious mental or physical illness. The woman may also request abortion if she herself, because of a mental or physical illness or weak intelligence, is unable to look after her child. This was described above in Chapter 3. According to the Health Act (Act No. 1202 of 14 November 2014), all persons over 18 may apply for sterilization (section 105). The application must be made to a medical doctor or to the county board. Sterilization of women will only be carried out if pregnancy involves danger to her life and health. Her husband may be sterilized instead of her but only by express permission. Sterilization of persons under 18 is not allowed, unless there are exceptional circumstances (section 107(3). In all cases for couples who are not under 18, sterilization is allowed if there is danger that a child will be born with a serious physical or mental disability, and it is considered necessary to prevent her from having children. Similarly, permission will be granted if the applicant or her spouse due to mental illness or a serious mental handicap will be unable to look after a child safely. Permission is given by the county boards. The provisions for castration are different in their aim and scope. Permission is granted by the Danish Health and Medicines Authority, and only if the applicant's sexual urge exposes him to the risk of committing a crime or involves deep mental suffering or social deroute (section 115). Permission is not given, if the applicant is under the age 18.

§2. Persons With a Mental Illness

72. The Psychiatry Act applies to the use of constraint in psychiatric treatment of persons who are committed to a psychiatric ward in hospital (section 1). From this follows, that the provisions for constraint cannot be used towards persons who are not in a psychiatric ward. The Act does not cover persons in social welfare institutions, which was dealt with above under §1. Neither does it cover for persons who are in prison unless they are transferred to a psychiatric ward. Day patients in psychiatric wards do not fall within the scope of the Act, and they cannot be retained or treated by constraint. There are three forms of detention in the Act: (1) commitment by constraint (Chapter 3); (2) retention by constraint (Chapter 3); (3) detention of extraordinarily dangerous persons (Chapter 11). There are four other forms of constraint: (1) forced medical treatment; (2) fixation by constraint; (3) the use of physical force; and (4) fixation to protect the patient (Chapters 4 and 5). The enumeration of the different forms of constraint is not exhaustive. Less serious forms of constraint may be used in order to preserve peace, quiet and order in the wards.

It is a general principle in the Act that the use of constraint should be limited as much as possible, and commitment and treatment in a psychiatric ward requires the acceptance of the patient, insofar this can be obtained. The doctor who commits the patient and treats him/her must advise the patient about the treatment and stay in hospital and the possibility of recovery. The chief physician of the ward must make a plan for the treatment, advise the patient about it and obtain his/her consent. Constraint cannot be used until everything possible to make the patient cooperate voluntarily has been done (sections 2–4).

Commitment by constraint and detention by constraint in a psychiatric ward may only take place, if the patient is mentally ill or in a situation equal to that. On the other hand, the abuse of drugs and alcohol is not put on an equal footing with mental illness and cannot legitimate commitment or treatment by constraint.

Commitment by constraint must always take place for the purposes of treatment, even in those situations where the committed person is very dangerous. It is also a condition that the committed person's chances of recovery would be diminished, or he/she represents a considerable danger to himself/herself or to others, if he/she is not committed (section 5). These conditions apply for every commitment and every detention by constraint. Commitment by *constraint* requires a certificate issued by a doctor. The police must sign the commitment papers and carry out the commitment. Detention by constraint may only take place if the conditions laid down in section 5 are fulfilled (section 10). If the patient demands to be discharged, the chief physician must inform him/her within twenty-four hours whether he/she can be discharged or detention by constraint must take place. The time limit is forty-eight hours, if the patient demands discharge within the first twenty-four hours of his/her stay in hospital. When the conditions in section 5 are no longer present, the detention must be terminated immediately. The patient and his/her adviser must be informed at once (section 11). Treatment by constraint may only be done if the patient fulfils the conditions laid down in section 10. If medication by constraint becomes necessary, only approved medications in ordinary doses and with the fewest possible side effects must be used. The decision about treatment by constraint is made by the chief physician (section 12(4)). According to section 14(2) only belts, hand and foot straps and gloves may be used and only if necessary (1) to prevent a patient from getting himself/herself or others into imminent danger of injury to body or health, (2) to prevent him/her from pursuing or seriously molesting his/her co-patients or (3) to prevent him/her from causing malicious damage to the ward (section 14(2)). This decision is made by the physician in charge but may be made by the nursing staff, if quick action is necessary. A guard must always be present for patients fixated with a belt (section 16). The use of force is permitted for persons committed to a psychiatric ward who must be detained or transferred to another part of the hospital, but only if the conditions in section 14(2) are fulfilled. A special patient appeal tribunal in every county must be established to which patients can appeal, if they are made subject to treatment by constraint, fixation by constraint or the use of force (sections 34–36).

Part II. Family Law

Chapter 1. Marriage

§1. The Nature of Marriage

73. In Denmark, marriage is defined as a legal relationship between a two persons of opposite sex or between two persons of the same sex.

Prior to every marriage, there is an engagement in the sense that the couple has made an agreement to marry later. Danish law attaches no significance to engagement. Thus, the legal effects of engagement are few, whereas the legal effects of marriage are many. Danish law has no provisions concerning the return of gifts on cancellation of an engagement. If the couple has given each other gifts, and these gifts are assumed to be conditional on the marriage taking place, they must be returned, if the marriage is called off. Gifts for purely personal use, for example, Christmas and birthday presents, will not normally have to be returned. This, however, does not, in Danish law, apply to the engagement ring.[30]

§2. The Capacity to Marry

74. The present Danish Marriage and Matrimonial Causes Act dates back to 1969 but has been amended several times, most comprehensibly in 1989 when the conditions for separation, divorce and maintenance contributions were modernized.[31]

To be legally valid, a marriage must be voluntary, between two single persons who are over 18 and capable of marrying and who are not closely related. Each of these conditions will now be looked at, beginning with the age and capability conditions. These conditions are laid down in Chapter 1, sections 1–11(b) of the Marriage and Matrimonial Causes Act (Consolidation Act No. 1096 of 7 October 2014).

A person must normally be over 18 to marry. Young persons under 18 cannot marry, unless they have the permission of the state administration (section 1(1)(2)). When they have this permission, they automatically acquire legal capacity, unless the state administration,[32] when granting the permission, makes it a condition that

30. Ingrid Lund-Andersen & Irene Nørgaard, *Familieret (Family Law)*, 61 (2th edn, DJØF 2012).
31. Ingrid Lund-Andersen & Irene Nørgaard, *Familieret (Family Law)*, 62–63 (2th edn, DJØF. 2012).
32. The state administration and its nine local departments has been established as the state authority that handles tasks in areas where it is considered to be an advantage that administration and related

the young person under 18 remains a minor and a 'ward'. This is described in Part I, Chapter 1, §2.

In the same way, a young person under the age of 18 who has not been married before cannot marry without the consent of the parents. If one of the parents is either deceased, mentally ill, mentally disabled, without share in the parental authority, or if his/her consent cannot be obtained except without considerable difficulty or delay, then the consent of the other parent is sufficient (section 2). The parents' consent must be written down on a special form and applies to the marriage of the minor to one particular person only, it cannot be given for the general purpose of the ward's marriage to any person.

A person who is under guardianship according to section 5 of the Guardianship Act, or who has been deprived of his/her legal capacity to act under the Act's section 6 cannot marry except with the consent of the guardian (section 3).

If either the parents or the guardian refuse to grant this permission, the county office may give it, if it finds that there are no reasonable grounds for refusing the permission (section 4). In any case, if a marriage is contracted in contravention of these provisions, the marriage will still be valid; it cannot be annulled.

Closely related persons cannot marry under Danish law. The Danish Marriage and Matrimonial Causes Act (section 6) defines closely related persons first, as persons in the direct ascending or descending line as well as brothers and sisters. A marriage which infringes the provision can be annulled (section 23). Second, marriage shall not be contracted without permission of the Minister of Social Affairs and the Interior between persons, of whom one has been married to the other person's relative in lineal ascent or decent (section 7). Marriage between an adopted child and one of its adopting parents is also prohibited for as long as the adoption decision stands (section 8). The adoption decision can be revoked, however, if the two – adopted child and adopting parent – wish to marry.

75. A person who has either been married or been living in a registered partnership cannot marry again, while the former marriage or partnership exists. Danish law thus prohibits bigamy (section 9). A marriage which infringes the provision can be annulled (section 23). A person who infringes this provision is liable to punishment, which may involve a sentence in jail, under the Penal Code, section 208. Just as a person cannot marry until a former marriage or partnership has been dissolved, neither can he/she marry again, if the family assets and property of the former marriage or partnership have not yet been divided up (section 10). This rule applies, if the partners of the former marriage or partnership are dividing up their assets and property by private agreement. If the assets have to be divided by court decision, the partners are allowed to marry again as soon as the court procedure has commenced, they need not wait for the final decision of the court. These rules apply also in the case, where the former marriage or partnership is dissolved not by divorce, but by one of the partners having died. These rules do not apply, if either the partner of the former marriage/partnership or the heirs of the deceased spouse give their consent to the new marriage. A special permission to the second marriage can be

---

contact between authorities and citizens are taken care of at local level. The state administration belongs to and refers to the Ministry for Social Affairs and the Interior.

granted, if a whole year has passed since the divorce, or even within the year, if it seems likely that the former spouse/partner or the heirs refuse to consent out of spite, or if the former spouse has disappeared or lives abroad (section 10(2)).

As of 1 July 2002, a new marriage condition has been laid down in section 11(a). According to this rule, a marriage may only be contracted when both parties are Danish citizens or have legal residence in Denmark in pursuance of sections 1–3(a), section 4 b or section 5(2) of the Aliens Act, or in pursuance of residence permission after sections 6–9(f) of the Aliens Act. The state administration may, in pursuance of section 11(a)(2), grant a permission to contract marriage to a foreigner who does not have legal residence if special circumstances, especially the length of a foreigner's stay in Denmark, speak in favour hereof. Regardless of the length of a foreigner's stay, an exemption will be possible if the couple has or is expecting a child together, or in case of a serious disease or a serious handicap. In those cases where only one of the parties is a Danish national, citizen in of one of the other Nordic countries, or has a residence permit in pursuance of sections 6–9(f) of the Aliens Act, marriage may only be contracted if both parties declare that they are familiar with the rules laid down in section 9(1)(i) and (2–14 and 30) of the Aliens Act on family reunion, see section 11(b) of the Marriage and Matrimonial Causes Act. This does not apply if the person living in Denmark is either a EU/EEA national issued with a residence permit under section 6 of the Aliens Act, a Swiss national with a residence permit under section 6 of the Aliens Act.

§3. The Formalities of Marriage

76. The formalities of marriage are laid down in Chapter 2, sections 12–22(a) of the Act. A marriage cannot take place, unless the conditions for entering into marriage are fulfilled. The mayor's office in each of the local authorities in Denmark examines in each case, if the marriage conditions are fulfilled and issues a license. The marriage ceremony must then take place within four months of the date of the license. The prospective spouses must apply for a license to the mayor's office in the local authority, where either partner is living, and they may choose freely between them. If neither partner is domiciled in Denmark, they may apply to the mayor's office, where they are actually staying. It is a condition that their stay in Denmark is legal. A fee of DKK 500 is payable by the foreign spouses for the issue of the license (sections 13(3)). Similarly, they may have to pay for translation of the required documents or for the assistance of an interpreter at the marriage ceremony itself. The application has to be digital, see section 58(d)(1) of the Act, unless special circumstances exist.

The prospective spouses may choose freely between a church wedding and a civil wedding (section 15(1)). The partners may have the banns read in church from the pulpit, but this procedure has no legal significance. The partners may have the banns read in church, even though they have decided on a civil wedding. Spouses who have opted for a civil wedding may have their marriage blessed afterwards by a clergyman in the Danish State Church. A church wedding may be held in the Danish State Church, the denomination of which is Lutheran, or in the authorized religious community of the other denominations. It is an indispensable condition in both cases that one of the partners belongs either to the Danish State Church or to an authorized religious community. The Ministry of Social Affairs and the Interior can give such an authorization. A marriage may also be held within a non-authorized religious community, if one of the partners belongs to it, and the community has a Minister of Religion authorized to perform marriages (section 16).

77. A church wedding in the Danish State Church must be celebrated by one of its clergymen according to rules laid down by the Ministry of Religious Affairs, that is, regulations concerning which clergymen have the right and duty to perform marriages. A church wedding outside the Danish State Church is performed by those clergymen who have a special authorization from the Ministry. Access to a civil wedding is open to everybody, and the wedding is performed by the mayor of the local authority or by the person he/she authorizes to perform the ceremony. The wedding ceremony may take place only on condition that a license no more than four months old is produced to the effect that all the conditions of marriage are fulfilled according to section 13. If – due to illness – one of the partners may not be well enough for the wedding ceremony to be performed, the ceremony may be performed immediately, even though the examination of the conditions of marriage has not yet been completed. A marriage ceremony may never take place, if it is known to the marriage authorities that the conditions of marriage have not been fulfilled (sections 17–19).

The marriage ceremony must always be performed in the presence of at least two witnesses. Both partners must be present at the marriage ceremony simultaneously and must – on being questioned by the person invested with the authority to perform the ceremony – reply that it is their intention to marry one another; whereupon they are declared husband and wife. A marriage is valid only on condition that it is made before the proper wedding authorities in accordance with the proper regulations. But a marriage which does not fulfil these formalities, and therefore becomes invalid, can be approved subsequently by the Ministry of Social Affairs and the Interior and thus become valid (sections 20–21).[33]

§4. The Effects of Marriage

78. Once two persons have been married, this leads to the creation of new rights and new obligations between them. From the legal point of view the effects of marriage can be divided up under four main headings: (1) the spouses have a mutual duty to support and maintain each other. This duty is a civil law duty and applies between the spouses. It is also a public law duty laid down in the Active Social-policy Act (Consolidation Act No. 1193 of 13 November 2014). Thus, if a spouse fails in his/her civil law duty, and the other spouse must apply for social assistance to live, the spouse becomes liable for this towards the social welfare authorities; (2) the legal matrimonial regime is deferred community of property with special provisions for the spouses' ability to dispose and to enter into debt. An exception is

33. Ingrid Lund-Andersen et al., *Familieret (Family Law)*, 177–178 (5th edn, DJØF 2003), and Ingrid Lund-Andersen & Irene Nørgaard, *Familieret (Family Law)*, 64 (2nd edn, DJØF 2012).

made if the spouses agree to have separate estates; (3) the spouses have a mutual right of inheritance after one another; (4) the marriage cannot be dissolved at will. The rights and obligations of the spouses according to Danish law are described below in Part 3 (Matrimonial Property Law), Chapter 1. In this chapter only some of the more personal aspects of the effects of marriage will be referred to briefly.

The new unity of the married couple is regulated in the Legal Effects of Marriage Act (Consolidation Act No. 1193 of 13 November 2014). Its section 1 lays down the one fundamental principle in Danish matrimonial law, namely that 'husband and wife must support each other mutually and jointly take care of the requirements of the family'. This statement of the Act implies not only that the spouses are put on a perfectly equal footing and that none is dependent on the other, but also that they must keep their mutual interests in view in all their actions and that they must discuss and negotiate all matters of common interest between them. Apart from this statement of principle, the Act does not contain any express rules about the personal relationship between the spouses. As described in Part I, Chapter 4, perfect equality as to their surname was introduced in the Names Act. During the existence of the marriage, the spouses have a legal duty to be faithful to each other. This is implied by the fact that the unfaithfulness of one spouse to the marriage, that is, his/her adultery, gives the other spouse the right to a divorce immediately without any previous period of separation (section 33 of the Marriage and Matrimonial Causes Act). However, if the couple have separated, the duty of faithfulness no longer obtains. The Act does not regulate the sexual relationship between the spouses at all. This follows from the abolition of the former provisions according to which one spouse became entitled to separation or divorce, if the other was to blame in their sexual relationship. Thus the former mutual duty for the spouses to have sex with each other no longer exists in the Danish law of matrimony.

§5. Void and Voidable Marriages

79. Generally speaking an annulment is like a divorce in that it ends the marriage. But, whereas a divorce is granted, because the marriage has broken down, an annulment is granted, if the marriage was not valid in the first place, or if it is defective in some way. It is, in one sense, as if the marriage never existed. The law distinguishes between two types of annulled marriages – those that are void and those that are voidable. The distinction implies that – at least in theory – with the former there was never a marriage, whereas with the latter there was a marriage but it is defective. The provisions for annulment of a marriage in Danish law are found in the Marriage and Matrimonial Causes Act, Chapter 3, sections 23–28. In Danish law, a void marriage is defined as a marriage which does not fulfil the conditions of marriage and thus could not have been entered into. The voidable marriage is defined as the marriage which, although valid, because of a faulty marriage agreement between the prospective partners is rendered voidable. The only way in which a marriage can be annulled is by a court decision. There are only two grounds for declaring a marriage void in Denmark: if section 6 of the Act, which prohibits a marriage between closely related persons, or section 9 about bigamy, were infringed, when the couple was married. Court proceedings are initiated by: (1) the spouses themselves; (2) in the case of bigamy – by the spouse of the first marriage as well; and (3) by the Ministry of Social Affairs and the Interior (section 23). There is no absolute duty for the Ministry of Social Affairs and the Interiors to start court proceedings in the sense that these may be postponed, for example, in case of bigamy, if the first marriage is about to be dissolved by divorce.[34]

80. A marriage is voidable for the following reasons: (1) If the mental condition of one of the spouses made him/her unable to act rationally at the time when he/she was married. A person may be of unsound mind, because he/she was under the influence of alcohol, drugs or poison, in a high fever, hypnotized or the like. (2) If one of the spouses was coerced to enter into marriage. Thus he/she may have been under compulsion, because his/her life, health or welfare was threatened. Blackmail is another example. The partner or a third person may have exercised the compulsion. (3) If he/she was married to the wrong partner or did not want to enter into marriage at all. Multiple weddings may be a practical example, just as a person may misunderstand the nature of the ceremony because of language difficulties. (4) If he/she was misled to enter into the marriage by false information or fraudulent suppression of the truth about the identity of the partner or about the circumstances of his/her former life – all of which would have presented ample cause for him/her – had they been known – to refrain from entering into the marriage. The present significance of these circumstances must be such that the marriage cannot reasonably be upheld. In practice, the circumstances of the former life of the spouse must have been of a very serious nature for the marriage to be voidable, for example, if he/she earned a living as a prostitute or has served a prison sentence for a very serious crime. The grounds which are laid down in section 24 do not differ from the grounds which – if present – will normally invalidate a contract. Only the spouses themselves can start court proceedings. There are time limits, namely six months after the spouse was again of sound mind, the exercise of compulsion was stopped, he/she discovered he/she had married the wrong person or discovered the fraud. There is another time limit of three years after the voidable marriage was contracted. The legal effects of annulment are exactly the same as those of divorce (section 25(1)), this also applies to solving the problems of parental authority, maintenance contributions to the spouse and who is to keep the flat. When dividing up the assets, there is a greater scope for claiming assets in advance than in case of separation and divorce (section 25(2)). There is a special provision for compensation in section 26. If one of the spouses in a void or voidable marriage dies, before the marriage could be annulled, sections 27 and 28 safeguard the inheritance of the surviving spouse.

The provisions for annulment of void and voidable marriages are not in frequent use. In more recent years, however, the number of cases has risen. It is supposed to be due to the fact that bigamous marriages are more frequent now.

34. Ingrid Lund-Andersen et al., *Familieret (Family Law)*, 180 (5th edn, DJØF 2003), and Ingrid Lund-Andersen & Irene Nørgaard, *Familieret (Family Law)*, 65 (2nd edn, DJØF 2012).

§6. REGISTERED PARTNERSHIP

81. In 1989 Denmark was the first country in the world to introduce an Act of Parliament which allowed two persons of the same sex to enter into a registered partnership. Registered partnership was introduced to make it possible for persons of the same sex to enter into a relationship similar to marriage. Thus it is not possible for persons of opposite sex to enter into registered partnership.

According to section 1 of the Act, two persons of the same sex can register their partnership. A partnership certificate is issued instead of a marriage certificate. The effects of a registered partnership correspond to the effects of marriage as regards the rights and obligations of the spouses (section 3). Thus the partners have a mutual duty to maintain one another and the regulation of their financial circumstances corresponds to that of marriage. They have a mutual right of inheritance and one partner cannot disinherit the other. Similarly, the tax rules and the rules concerning entitlement to social benefits are identical to those which apply to married couples. A registered partnership is dissolved according to the same rules which apply to divorce in a marriage as regards grounds, procedure and effects.

Partners in a registered partnership can adopt a child together and a registered partner may adopt the other partner's child. Further, the partners can establish joint parental authority over a child. An exception in the Registered Partnership Act concerns provisions in international treaties which apply to married couples. The partners in a registered partnership are not put on an equal footing with the spouses in a marriage in this case, unless all the parties to the treaty agree to do this. A second exception concerns certain legal provisions which are linked to the sex of one of the spouses in a marriage. Such provisions do not apply to registered partnerships, for example, the provisions in the Legal Effects of Marriage Act according to which the husband is liable for certain debts incurred by the wife in connection with purchases for the household.[35]

82. In 2012 gender-neural marriage was introduced in Denmark and the new rules of the Marriage Act came into effect on 15 June 2012. After this date it is no longer possible to establish a new registered partnership in Denmark. The Registered Partnership Act was repealed as being no longer necessary. Previously registered partnerships may be converted into marriage if the partners want to do so. A registered partnership that is not converted remains in force.

35. Ingrid Lund-Andersen et al., *Familieret (Family Law)*, 181–183 (5th edn, DJØF 2003), and Ingrid Lund-Andersen & Irene Nørgaard, *Familieret (Family Law)*, 65–66 (2nd edn, DJØE 2012). For more details see Ingrid Lund-Andersen, *The Nordic Countries: Same Direction – Different speeds*, in *Legal Recognition of Same-Sex Relations in Europe: National, cross-border and European perspectives*, 3–18 (Katharina Boele-Woelki & Angelika Fuchs (eds), Intersentia 2012), (European Family Law Series, Vol. 32).

Chapter 2. Divorce

§1. Grounds

83. When a marriage (or a partnership) is no longer working properly, either, or both, of the partners may want to separate or perhaps put an end to the marriage (or partnership) by divorcing one another. Nowadays the law does not look closely at the conduct of the parties when a marriage or a partnership is failing. In the case of a failing marriage, one of the main considerations is to safeguard the welfare of any children in the marriage and to ensure that a dead marriage is not perpetuated as a sham. All that is said below applies to marriages and registered partnerships alike, but to avoid repetitions, only marriage will be referred to in what follows.

When a marriage is in trouble, most people immediately think of divorce as the obvious legal remedy, but in fact Danish law operates with three legal remedies: separation, divorce and in rare cases annulment. Annulment has been dealt with above in Chapter 1 under §5 and will not be referred to again in what follows.

A separation in Danish law is not vastly different from a divorce, most of the legal effects occur at the separation (§3 below). But the most significant difference between a separation and a divorce is that the marriage no longer exists, once the spouses have been divorced. Separation functions as an interval which can be likened to a 'trial divorce'; in other words, a period during which the partners can reflect on the possibilities of continuing their life together and make a decision about it. Separation may also be an option which the partners may have to choose, because the conditions for an immediate divorce are not fulfilled.

The provisions which regulate the conditions for separation are found in the Danish Marriage and Matrimonial Causes Act, Chapter 4, sections 29–31, for divorce in sections 29–30 and 32–36. Both separation and divorce presuppose that the grounds for obtaining either are present and that one of the partners or both file a petition either with the state administration or with the court to obtain it. Thus a separated couple may remain separated until one of them dies, unless they file a petition for a divorce, as the initiative is entirely theirs.

I. Separation

84. The spouses shall be entitled to a judicial separation if they are agreed on separation, cf. section 29. According to section 30(1) either one of the spouses has a right to separation, if he/she finds that it is no longer possible for them to continue living together. In other words a spouse has a unilateral, unconditional right to separation, regardless of the other spouse's attitude to it. The petitioning spouse need not give reasons for the petition and the authorities should not carry out any investigation of them. The only requirement is that the spouses follow up the petition by moving apart and thus end their life together. If the authorities get the impression that the spouses intend to continue living in their joint home beyond a reasonable transitional period, the grant of a separation license must be refused. Separation can be granted by administrative or court decision.

Once a separation has been granted, it lapses for the future, if the spouses resume their married life together (section 31). Whether or not a separation ever took effect, or whether it took effect and then lapsed, can be quite a difficult question to decide. Thus, if the spouses have continued living together, the separation is considered never to have taken effect. If the spouses have broken off their life together but later decided to resume it, the separation lapses. But since the transitional period may be quite long, it may obscure the facts so that it becomes impossible to decide the whole question of the effects of the separation. If the transitional period does not exceed two or three months, the separation license will stand. If it lasts longer, the separation may never take effect, unless the reason for the period's long duration is that the spouses have had difficulties in finding another suitable home for the one who is moving out. The decisive factor in all cases is whether or not the spouses have made a firm decision to stop living together. If the spouses have really moved apart into separate households, but later try resuming their life together, the separation will stand, if the attempt is of short duration, for example, if the spouses go on holiday together without this resulting in their afterwards moving back together.[36]

II. Divorce

85. The spouses shall be entitled to a divorce if they are agreed on divorce, cf. section 29. Further, there are six other grounds for which a divorce is obtainable: (1) after a period of separation (section 30(2)); (2) after living apart for a period due to disagreement between the spouses (section 32); (3) one of the partners was unfaithful to the marriage (section 33); (4) domestic violence (section 34); (5) bigamy (section 35) or (6) child abduction (section 36).

Any one of the spouses has a right to get a divorce after a period of only six months' separation. The time limits are reckoned from the date of the separation license. It does not affect the time limit, if the spouses have continued living together during the transitional period or have made attempts later at married life together. The spouses must agree about getting a divorce, but they need not agree about the conditions for obtaining it in order for them to obtain a divorce after six months' separation (section 30(2)).

Any one of the spouses have a right to divorce when the two have lived apart and had two separate households within the last two years. In order to obtain a divorce under this provision, it is required that the spouses have actually lived apart each in a separate household for the whole of the two years. Any attempts at resuming married life will interrupt the two-year period, so various shorter periods during which the spouses have lived apart cannot be added up, each time a new two-year period starts running. It is also a requirement that their living apart is caused by disagreement. Thus it does not count towards the fulfilment of the two-year period, if they have lived apart for work or education purposes or because one of the spouses had to serve a prison sentence (section 32).

36. Ingrid Lund-Andersen & Irene Nørgaard, *Familieret (Family Law)*, 69–71 (2nd edn, DJØF 2012).

Any one of the spouses has a right to a divorce, if the other spouse has been unfaithful to the marriage, that is, committed adultery, or has participated in a similar sexual relationship, unless the spouse consented to this, or renounced his/her right to obtain a divorce for this reason at a later stage. Adultery is defined as sexual intercourse with another partner, but not rape. A 'similar sexual relationship' is certain sexual relationships which are equal to sexual intercourse and indecent sexual behaviour towards children (section 33(1)). If the unfaithful spouse denies the adultery, the other spouse must prove that it took place. The adulterous spouse is not required to provide information about the identity of the third party.

86. Once the spouses have obtained a separation license, their duty to be faithful to the marriage lapses. Thus neither can obtain a divorce under section 33(1) after the grant of a separation license (section 33(2)). Application for a divorce on the grounds of adultery must be handed in, at the latest six months after the other spouse came to know about the adultery and within two years after the adultery took place (section 33(3)).

Any one of the spouses has a right to a divorce, if the other spouse is guilty of deliberate violence or engaged in sexual assault against the spouse, against the children of the spouses, against the next of kin of the spouse or of the spouses' children whom the spouse or the child of the spouses is attached to, or against other children. It is no excuse, if the violent spouse was under the influence of alcohol when violent (section 34(1)). Application for a divorce must be handed in at the latest within a year after the spouse came to know about the violence and three years after the violence was committed (section 34(2)).

Any one of the spouses has a right to a divorce, if the other spouse has married in contravention of the prohibition against bigamy in section 9 of the Act (section 35). This provision entitles the spouse of the first marriage to obtain a divorce from the bigamous spouse. There are no time limits in section 35, and a divorce is granted even though the bigamous spouse acted in good faith when contracting the bigamous, second marriage. The second bigamous marriage is liable to annulment under section 23 of the Act.

According to section 36, a spouse is entitled to a divorce when the other spouse has taken the child of the former illegally out of the country or illegally keeps the child abroad. This cause for divorce was introduced in 2003 due to the fact that in certain countries the authorities will not cooperate in getting a child back if said child has been abducted by the father, and the father and mother are still married or separated. In these countries, the authorities regard abduction as a conflict between spouses, and consequently they will not get involved. Section 36(2) requires that the divorce papers have been filed or an action instituted while the child, due to the abduction is still abroad or no later than one year after the child has been brought back.[37]

37. Ingrid Lund-Andersen & Irene Nørgaard, *Familieret (Family Law)*, 72–77 (2nd edn, DJØF 2012). See for further details Ingrid Lund-Andersen & Lise Krabbe, in *European Family Law in Action. Volume I: Grounds for Divorce*, (ed. Katharina Boele-Woelki, Bente Braat & Ian Summer, Antwerp, Oxford, New York: Intersentia 2003).

§2. PROCEDURE

87. In Denmark both separation and divorce can be obtained either in the form of an administrative license granted by the state administration or by a court judgment.

The detailed procedural provisions are laid down in Chapter 4, sections 42–43a and Chapter 5, sections 45 and 49–58(d). of the Marriage and Matrimonial Causes Act.

The spouses have to submit an application for separation or divorce to the state administration, where all divorce and separation cases are initiated. The application has to be digital, see section 58d(2) of the Act, unless special circumstances exist. Separation or divorce by administrative license is only granted in cases where the spouses agree about being separated or divorced by an administrative license (section 42(1)). If one of the spouses is without legal capacity to act, the guardian must give his/her consent. Furthermore, the spouses must agree about a number of terms and conditions for the separation or divorce. The terms and conditions about which there must be agreement – and an agreement which must continue until the license is granted – are the following: (1) the mutual duty of maintenance; the agreement must fix whether or not maintenance payments are payable, by whom and for how long; the spouses may refer the question of amount to the decision of the state administration; in the case where the spouses apply for a divorce after having been separated by court judgment and the question of maintenance was decided in the separation judgment, that decision stands and the spouses need not consider the question again in connection with applying for an administrative divorce; the spouses need not agree about maintenance payments to the children, since this question is regulated in the Children's Maintenance Act, which has empowered the state administration to make all decisions concerning this question; (2) the right to go on living in the spouses' flat; the spouses must agree about which of them is to take over the flat and on what conditions. The spouses need not agree about other conditions such as tax questions, or how their estate is to be divided between them, as long as they agree about obtaining either a separation or a divorce by administrative license. These provisions which deal with the terms and conditions of a separation or divorce are contained in sections 49 and 55 of the Act and will be referred to again below when describing the position, if the spouses cannot agree.

The spouses have no claim or right to be separated or divorced by administrative license. If the state administration finds that it is doubtful whether the conditions for a separation or divorce by administrative license are present, or if there is any doubt at all in connection with the license, the state administration may refer the spouses to the courts (section 43). The spouses must pay a fee of DKK 500 for the administrative license.

88. Before a license for a separation or a divorce is granted, the spouses must negotiate the terms and conditions. The state administration will summon the spouses to a meeting: (1) by request of one of the spouses (2) if the conditions, cf. section 42(1) are not fulfilled or (3) if special circumstances exist. The meeting is called a negotiation of terms (vilkårsforhandling), and both of the parties are required to attend.[38] In all other circumstances the application for divorce will then be dealt with in writing. If the spouses desire mediation by a clergyman of the Danish state church, this is arranged for them (section 40). This mediation used to be compulsory for the spouses, but it was made voluntary by the 1989 amendment of the Act. If the spouses cannot reach agreement about the conditions at the meeting, the state administration may offer the parties family mediation (section 41). Chapter 5, sections 45, 49–53, 55 and 58 of the Act deals exclusively with the terms and conditions of a separation and a divorce. It is a basic rule that terms and conditions which have been agreed upon or laid down in connection with a separation by court decision also apply to a divorce obtained on the basis of the separation, except for the question of maintenance payments where the court may refer this question to be considered again in connection with the divorce (section 45). The reasoning behind this is that the spouses should be able to adjust to their new life as soon as possible and already from the time when they are separated.

The provisions concerning maintenance contributions between the spouses are contained in sections 49–51. Provisions for amending already made agreements or court decisions in this area are found in sections 52–53. Maintenance contributions to the children of the marriage are not laid down in the Marriage and Matrimonial Causes Act but in the Children's Maintenance Act.

As already mentioned, the spouses must always reach an agreement about maintenance contributions to each other, if they want a separation or a divorce by administrative license. Only the question of the amount of the maintenance contributions may be referred to the decision of state administration. The spouses may refer the whole question of maintenance payment to the decision of the court, but they are free to reach an agreement by themselves, if they are able to do so. It must always be stated in the judgment, whether or not the question of maintenance payments is dealt with by the court, or the spouses have agreed on the issue by themselves. This has significance later, if it becomes necessary to amend the terms and conditions of the separation or divorce judgment. The spouses are free to make any agreement they see fit. If the decision has to be made by the court, the tendency is to be reticent in conferring a right to maintenance payments on a spouse, to limit the period during which maintenance payments must be made and to limit their amount. If the spouses cannot reach an agreement, the whole case is always referred to the court which decides, if there is to be a duty for one spouse to pay maintenance contributions to the other spouse and for how long. Unless special circumstances exist, the maintenance period cannot exceed ten years. The question of the amount of maintenance payments is always referred to the decision of the state administration. When deciding whether or not one spouse is to have the duty of maintaining the other after a separation or a divorce, the court takes into consideration the ability of the spouse who demands maintenance payments to maintain himself/ herself, and the financial ability of the other spouse to pay any such contributions. The duration of the marriage is also taken into consideration and whether or not the spouse who demands contributions is in need of support towards an education or any other similar purposes.

38. These rules were introduced in 2013.

A duty to pay maintenance payments lapses if one of the spouses dies or marries again. An agreement between the spouses about maintenance payments and their amount can be amended later by court decision, if the circumstances of either spouse have altered significantly, so that it would not be reasonable to uphold the agreement. If the original decision was made by the court, it may be amended later by a new court decision, if the circumstances have altered, and there are significant reasons for making a new decision. Similarly, the state administration may make a new decision about the amount of maintenance contributions, if this is indicated by the circumstances of the case.[39]

89. Provisions for other terms and conditions are laid down in section 55, provisions for amending agreements in this area laid down in section 58. These concern the question of which of the spouses is to continue in the matrimonial home in section 55 which, if it is a flat, is solved according to the provisions of the Tenancy Act. According to section 58, agreements about these terms and conditions may be amended by court decision or may be declared null and void, if it is considered to be unjust to one spouse at the time it was made.

§3. Effects

90. When the spouses have obtained a separation license or a separation judgment, most of the legal effects of the marriage lapse. Their mutual duty to be faithful to the marriage lapses. The assets included under community of property must be divided up between them. Their mutual duty to maintain each other and their mutual right to inherit each other lapse. It must be decided which of the spouses is to continue living in the matrimonial home, if this is a flat. It must be decided, if one spouse must pay maintenance contributions to the other. But the marriage still exists in the sense that the spouses cannot enter into another marriage. The separation will lapse, if they resume their married life together.

After the divorce, the marriage has been finally dissolved. The same questions are considered in connection with the divorce as at the separation. The former marriage does not revive, if the divorced spouses start living together again.

39. Ingrid Lund-Andersen & Irene Nørgaard, *Familieret (Family Law)*, 79–82 (2nd edn, DJØF 2012). See for further details Ingrid Lund-Andersen & Lise Krabbe, in *European Family Law in Action. Volume II: Maintenance between Former Spouses*, (ed. Katharina Boele-Woelki, Bente Braat & Ian Summer, Intersentia, 2003).

Chapter 3. Cohabitation without Marriage

§1. General Aspects

91. Since the beginning of the 1960s, it has become increasingly popular for couples to live together without being married in Denmark. Unlike marriage, when two persons start living together, this does not create several new duties and new obligations for the partners in the legal sense. Thus there is no parallel to the four effects of marriage: (1) the cohabiting partners do not have a mutual duty to support and maintain each other; (2) no community of property is established between them; (3) they do not have a mutual right of inheritance after one another without a will; (4) their relationship can be dissolved at will.

The Danish courts have been very reluctant to transfer the legal provisions for marriage to cohabitation and apply them by analogy. There are many reasons for this reluctance: cohabiting couples live together in a great variety of ways; the legal effects of marriage are many and enter into many legal relationships; the partners have deliberately chosen not to live by the legal rules which apply to marriage; it is a task for the legislator – not for the courts – to give rules for cohabiting couples.

This does not mean, however, that cohabitation in itself has no legal effects. Thus concepts like 'a joint household', 'a person living a common life together with somebody else' particularly of a certain (long) duration, 'a closely related person' have legal significance in, for example, the tenancy, social welfare, bankruptcy and administration of justice legislation. But in most of these cases the legal effects are not putting cohabitation on an equal footing with marriage, rather, the law operates with different entities altogether such as 'members of a household; persons either related by kinship, marriage or affinity; a common life together of more than one or two years' duration'. For example, in the tenancy legislation one person who has shared a household with another person for at least two years may continue in the lease when the other person dies. The child allowance from the state to a single person is stopped when the single parent establishes a household with a partner. Persons living in the same household cannot be required to testify against each other in court, etc.

In the following, some of those aspects which are particular to family law will be touched upon briefly concerning maintenance, tax, the possibility of joint ownership and continuing in the flat after the partners have stopped living together.[40]

§2. Family Law Aspects

92. Neither during their life together nor after a separation do cohabiting partners have a private law duty to maintain each other. The partners are regarded each as single persons. No duty to pay maintenance contributions for either partner can be imposed. This applies even though one of the partners has worked in the home during the couple's life together and may find it difficult to find work and maintain

40. Ingrid Lund-Andersen et al., *Familieret (Family Law)*, 675–680 (5th edn, DJØF 2003).

himself/herself, when their life together is discontinued. In this area, the only possible solution is for the couple to make an agreement according to which the partner who is able to support himself/herself after a separation undertakes an obligation to pay contributions to the other partner who is unable to do so at least for a transitional period. Such agreements are valid, as long as they have the necessary clarity.

In regard to the duty to pay tax, the main rule is that a cohabiting couple pays tax as two individuals of their income and capital, as if there were no relationship between them.

In regard to the question of transferring the provisions for the establishment of community property between married partners to cohabiting partners, this is regarded as a ruled out possibility. The fact that two persons live together does not affect their financial circumstances in the eyes of the law. Each partner preserves his/her full ability to dispose over his/her possessions, and he/she is liable to his/her creditors with all his/her possessions for any debt which he/she has incurred. Thus the legal position of a cohabiting couple is very similar to that of a married couple who has made a contract establishing separate property between them. A cohabiting couple can enter into contracts with one another without any difficulty, but there are no legal provisions which enable one partner to act on behalf of the other partner. Thus the provisions which apply to married couples in this respect cannot be used in case of cohabitation. To protect the economically weaker part after a separation, the Supreme Court has, based on a principle of unjust enrichment, established that the weaker part may be awarded an amount of money from the stronger part's property. In 1980, the Supreme Court created a new legal construction, based on a combination of property law and family law considerations. An amount will only be awarded if qualified family law circumstances exist. The cohabitation shall, thus, have lasted for a certain period of time, about three years. The amount will typically equal approximately one-fifth of the stronger part's fortune when substantial indirect contributions have been made, in general contributions to shared expenses. In extraordinary cases, emphasis may be put on housework and caring. It is worth noticing that normally importance is not attached to caring and housework inasmuch as these cases are normally instigated by women. There is, thus, a clear gender imbalance. Typically, working in the invisible economy is not valued and is not attached any importance except in extraordinary cases. In the particular situation where both have contributed equally to acquiring the property, but only one of the partners is listed as the owner, it is possible through substantial direct economic contributions to obtain that the other partner gets around half of the property.

As regards the flat, a tenant is allowed to let his/her partner move in without asking the permission of the owner; he/she needs the permission of the owner on the other hand, if he/she wants to take in a lodger. This follows from the Tenancy Act, according to which the tenant and his/her household may dispose freely of the flat; otherwise, the consent of the owner is needed. If a cohabiting couple rents a flat together, they are joint tenants, and one partner cannot in this situation terminate the lease without the consent of the other. If, on the other hand, only one of the partners signs the contract, he/she can dispose over the flat on his/her own without the consent of the partner. According to the Tenancy Act, in the case one of the partners dies, the other has a right to continue in the lease, if the partners shared a household for at least two years immediately before the death of the partner. It is a condition that the deceased person does not leave a husband or wife behind. If the partners stop living together for other reasons than the death of one of them, the partner who has not signed the contract may continue in the lease without the consent of the owner, if the other partner who is the tenant under the lease agrees. If the other tenant does not agree, it is a matter for the courts to decide who is to continue in the flat. The court will especially consider the welfare of children under 18, whether or not they are children in common or one of the partner's children from another relationship.[41]

41. Ingrid Lund-Andersen, Danish Report on Informal Relationships (www.ceflonline.net 2015) 35 pages. See also Ingrid Lund-Andersen & Irene Nørgaard, *Familieret (Family Law)*, 319–334 (2nd edn, DJØF 2012); Ingrid Lund-Andersen, *Familieøkonomien*, (*Financial Relations in the Family*) (DJØF 2011) and Ingrid Lund-Andersen, '*Legal Status of Cohabitation in Denmark*', in *Die Rechtstellng nichtehelicher Lebensgemainschaften, The Legal Status of Cohabitants*, 455–478 (ed. Jens M. Scherpe & Nadjma Yassari, Tübingen: Mohr Siebeck, 2005).

Chapter 4. Filiation

§1. Paternity

93. It was mentioned in the preceding chapter that at the end of the 1960s, many couples started living together without being married. The trend is still manifest, though perhaps with a somewhat diminishing vigour. This has had the obvious result that an increasing number of children are born out of wedlock. In 2008, 46% of all children in Denmark were born of unmarried parents.

On 1 June 2001, the Danish Parliament passed a new Children Act (Act No. 460 of 7 June 2001), in which a complete revision of the rules on paternity had been carried out. The Children Act is, in particular, based on the following principles: that married and unmarried parents shall be put on an equal footing regarding the determination of paternity, that each child shall, to the farthest possible extent, have both a father and a mother, that the administration of paternity cases shall be flexible, informal and citizen-friendly, and that paternity cases shall conform to the most recent legal genetic possibilities.

Due to the development within reproduction technology, the concept of paternity has, in recent decades, become less unequivocal. Consequently, it has also become relevant to talk about different kinds of paternity: Legal paternity describes a legal relationship between father and child: genetic paternity means that the child is developed from one of that man's sperm cells; and social paternity describing that the man in question – regardless of whether or not he is the legal/genetic father of the child – does in fact function as the child's father.

Rules regarding legal paternity are laid down in the Children Act. In certain cases, legal paternity has been assigned to the social father and not the genetic father. When legal paternity is determined, some of the effects are that: the father will have the obligation to provide for the child; child and father will have mutual right of succession; the father and mother will normally have joint custody; the father may get visitation rights; the father may get full custody either by agreement or a court order; the child can have the father's last name and can have the same citizenship as that of the father provided that the conditions for this are met.[42]

94. When a woman who is married to a man gives birth to a child, her husband will be regarded the father of the child, see the Children Act section 1(1), first sentence. This rule is a product of the reasoning that a married woman's husband will in general also be the genetic father of the child. The paternity is registered in connection with the registration of the birth of the child, see section 1(1), second sentence.

In three cases the father will not automatically be considered the father of the child and consequently paternity cannot be registered, see section 1(2). First, this is the case if at the time of the child's birth the spouses are separated inasmuch as a separation creates uncertainty regarding the paternity. Second, a husband will not be considered the father of the child in case the mother within the ten months before

42. Ingrid Lund-Andersen & Irene Nørgaard, *Familieret (Family Law)*, 28–29 (2nd edn, DJØF 2012).

giving birth has been married (without separation) to someone other than her actual husband. In these cases, it may be more likely to presume that the previous husband is the father of the child. Third, the husband will not be registered as the father if both spouses agree on filing a paternity action.

Access to a smooth registration of paternity has been introduced regarding children born by unmarried women. The rule is that a man will be regarded the father of the child if he and the mother declare in writing that they will jointly take responsibility and provide for the child, see section 2(1). The declaration is made by filling out a form called a 'care and responsibility declaration', which the midwife (physician) gives to the unmarried mother. The declaration is to be signed by both parents personally. The declaration is valid even though the parents do not live together or do not have the same address in Denmark. All that matters is that the parties have declared that they will henceforth jointly assume all responsibilities regarding the child. It is not required that the man in question is the genetic father to the child. Paternity can be registered based on a care and responsibility declaration, if submitted with the notification of the birth. According to section 2(2) paternity cannot be registered based on a care and responsibility declaration in case the mother within ten months before giving birth has been married to another man without having been separated. Registration can take place even if the mother, during said period, has cohabited with another man. The decisive factor is that she has not been married to him.

Parents can choose to recognize paternity with the state administration previous to the birth of the child, see section 3. This may be done by submitting a care and responsibility declaration, see section 14(1), or without submitting it, see section 14(2)(i) and (ii). On the basis hereof, it is possible to register the paternity in connection with the registration of the child's birth.

In consequence of submitting a care and responsibility declaration, the parents will automatically be granted joint custody, see the Parental Responsibility Act section 7(1).

Chapter 1 on registration of paternity has in 2014 been supplemented by a Chapter 1a titled registration of co-motherhood at the time of birth. The competent authority is not the civil registrar, as is the case of a male partner, but the state administration since the registration is combined with more paperwork. When a woman who is married to a woman or has a registered partner gives birth to a child, her spouse or partner will be registered as co-mother provided she has consented to the treatment and parentage in writing before the treatment took place, see the Children Act section 3a (1), first sentence. This rule is founded upon a contractual understanding of parentage directly linked to and based upon the consent given to the treatment. The co-mother who has not consented prior to the treatment can only establish parentage through adoption.[43] The situation is the same if the treatment has not taken place under the supervision of a health professional.

95. If paternity is not registered in connection with the birth, the state administration will institute affiliation proceedings. According to section 14(1), a man can

43. Christina G. Jeppesen de Boer & Annette Kronborg, *Parentage Laws – A comparison between Danish and Dutch Law*, Eur. J. Law Reform 232–246 (2015).

recognize paternity by declaring together with the mother that they will both provide and take responsibility for the child. In order to do so they both sign a care and responsibility declaration, which will also grant them joint custody. The declaration cannot be submitted in case the mother, within ten months previous to giving birth, has been married to someone else without having been separated, see section 14(1), second sentence. In which case the state administration shall, at the earliest possible date, notify the previous spouse in writing that the child has been born and inform him of his right to file an action for paternity, see section 6(3). According to section 14(1), acknowledgment cannot be accepted if it has been disclosed that the mother, during the time she got pregnant (the conception period), has had sexual relations to other men. If a couple does not want joint custody, paternity can be recognized pursuant to section 14(2)(i) provided that the mother, according to the information stated, has only had sexual relations with one single man at the time she got pregnant. If it has been informed that the mother, during the time of conception, has had sexual relations with other men, legal genetic tests shall be performed. If it turns out that the man in question is undoubtedly the father of the child, he may recognize paternity, see section 14(2)(ii). The legal genetic tests shall prove the man in question to be the father on a scale of 10,000 to 1 or more. If the mother has had sexual relations with two or more men during the period she got pregnant, one of these men may acknowledge paternity by filing a care and responsibility declaration together with the mother, see section 14(3). Such an acknowledgement is possible even though if the legal genetic tests have established that he cannot be the genetic father of the child. The acknowledgment is even possible when the tests prove another man to be the genetic father of the child. The rule is based on an acceptance of the fact that social paternity can as decisive for the legal status of the child. It is, however, a condition that none of the other possible fathers want to assume paternity. Each of these men are thus to sign a special form to declare that they accept that the man in question assumes the paternity.

Special rules concerning recognition of co-motherhood are laid down in section 14(5)-(6).

96. The state administration has an obligation to institute affiliation proceeding in case paternity or co-motherhood has not been established in connection with the child's birth, and in case no one has filed an action for paternity or co-motherhood, see section 7(1). If a case is closed in pursuance of section 14(1), that is, when a man assumes paternity by filing a care and responsibility declaration, there is no need for further information. The legal situation is the same if the co-mother who has consented to the treatment and parentage in writing assumes co-motherhood by filing a care and responsibility declaration. Otherwise the mother has a duty to disclose whom she has had sexual relations with during the time she got pregnant or whether assisted reproduction has taken place and the child could have come into being as a result of the treatment, see section 8(1). All paternity or co-motherhood cases start in the state administration. The administration is given access to all relevant information from and about the parties and access to procure proof in the shape of legal genetic tests. The state administration shall encourage the parties to take the genetic tests, see section 11, but the administration cannot force the tests to be taken.

The possible parties to a paternity or co-motherhood case are enumerated in section 9(1)(i–v). To be a party to the case influences whether the man or the mother may be encouraged to undergo legal genetic tests, and whether said person is entitled to file an action, see section 13(1). The parties to the case are the child (or its estate) and the mother (or her estate). In case paternity or co-motherhood has been registered or acknowledged, the father/co-mother (or his/her estate) will also be a party to the case. In addition to this, a man (or his estate) who, according to the information stated by the mother, is or may be the father of the child will also be party to the case. A man (or his estate) who make use of the right, laid down in section 6, to have tested whether he is the father of the child will also be regarded a party to the case. And lastly, a woman (or her estate) who has consented to the treatment and parentage in writing so that she can have tested whether she is the child's co-mother.

In section 6(1), a new rule has been introduced granting a man who has had sexual relations to the mother at the time of conception the right to file an action. A request shall be submitted in writing within six months from the birth of the child, unless there is already a pending suit at the time of the request. According to section 6(2), first sentence, the right of action is limited to apply only to cases where no one has been registered as father or co-mother of the child, sections 1, 2, 3, see section 14(1). If a mother rejects having had sexual relations to a man who intends to file an action, the state administration will have to bring the case before a court of law, see section 13, No. 2. A man can be precluded from paternity if the child has come into being as a result of a criminal offence, see section 10. The provision concerns incest and rape.

97. As the point of departure, the mother has an unconditional obligation to disclose who is or may be the father or co-mother of her child, see section 8(1). An important exception is the rule in section 8(2), first sentence, which states that the disclosure obligation does not apply if paternity or co-motherhood has been acknowledged by filing of a section 14(1) care and responsibility declaration, regardless of whether it is filed before or after the child is born. In these cases, the father or co-mother who has joint custody with the mother, is expected to take part in the upbringing of the child immediately, and the parents will typically be cohabiting. Thus, the main importance is put on social paternity or co-motherhood. The mother and the men which the state administration summon to appear at the administration office will, when of importance to the case, be encouraged to undergo legal genetic tests, see section 11(1).

Today paternity diagnostic is based on DNA-tests. By testing the mother, the child, and a specific man's genetic profile, it is possible, in practically all cases, to establish proof on a scale of no less than 10,000 to 1, corresponding to a probability of 99.99% for or against a tested man being the father. The calculated weight of the test results is called a paternity index. Real doubt regarding paternity will only occur if the man in question cannot be tested, for example, because he is dead or he has disappeared without leaving any suitable material for a legal genetic test, or in the particular situation that the mother has had sexual relations with two identical twins. The state administration may decide that a man shall no longer be party to the case if his paternity can be excluded with a certainty of 99.99% inasmuch as he is certainly not the father of the child, see section 12.

For the legal genetic tests, two drops of blood are normally taken from the mother, the child, and that or those men who are parties to the case. If it is not possible to procure a blood sample, a DNA-analysis can be made on other kinds of genetic material – for example, hair or saliva.

When paternity or co-motherhood has been registered or acknowledged with the state administration, the mother, father, the co-mother or guardian of the child are, within six months from the child's birth, entitled to file an action, see section 5(1). This is clearly an annulment right inasmuch as there is free access, and there is no requirements regarding the probability of someone else having fathered the child. If action is filed in pursuance of section 5, the person who is registered as the father or co-mother or has acknowledged fatherhood or co-motherhood will be regarded as father of the child or co-mother until the state administration or the court has come to a different decision.

98. A paternity or co-motherhood case can only be brought before the court by the state administration, see section 15. The court will then decide the case. The state administration will bring the case before the court if one of the parties to the case requests it, or if the state administration finds it inadvisable to continue the treatment of the case.

According to section 16, the mother is obliged to appear before the court to testify who is, or might be, the father of her child or whether assisted reproduction has taken place and the child could have been a result of the treatment and if so who has consented to the treatment. The men or women party to the case are likewise obliged to appear before the court. These rules are sanctioned through the provision on the duty to give evidence, for example, by imposing a fine. If it may influence the case, the court will, in pursuance of section 18, decide that legal genetic tests shall be performed. The court can impose blood tests to be performed, however, not by the use of mechanical force.

The court will establish paternity if, according to the result of the legal genetic tests, one particular man is undoubtedly the father of the child. The legal genetic test shall prove that man to be the father on a scale of 10,000 to 1 or more (99.99%). It is beside the point whether the mother at the time of conception has had sexual relations to other men whom it has not been possible to test. Likewise, with a so significant level of hereditary biological certainly, it can in general be ignored that the man in question refuses to have had sexual relations with the mother at the time of conception.

In certain situations, it is not possible to perform legal genetic tests. These situations are covered by section 20(2). There are no special requirements regarding the assessment of evidence. Attempts may thus be made at establishing that the man in question was impotent, or that the relationship between the parties was so poor that sexual relations are out of the question.

If it is then established that the mother has had sexual relations to one man only, he will be declared father of the child provided that there are no circumstances that make it unlikely that he could be the father of the child, see section 20(2) first sentence. If the court finds that the mother, at the time of conception, has had sexual relations to more than one man, it is not possible to declare a man who has not undergone legal genetic tests to be the father of the child unless legal genetic tests have excluded the possibility that the other men have fathered the child, i.e., paternity has been excluded on a scale of 10,000 to 1, and circumstances which make it unlikely that he is the father of the child have not been disclosed, see section 20(2), second sentence, (i). In case it has not been possible to perform legal genetic tests on two or more men, one of these men may be declared father of the child provided that circumstances which make it unlikely that he is the father of the child have not been disclosed, and it is highly unlikely that one of the other men has fathered the child, see section 20(2), second sentence, (ii). According to section 20(3), importance shall also be put on whether the mother has been married to or cohabited with one of the men at the time of conception.

99. When reopening a paternity or co-motherhood case, the question will either be tried again after the six-month statute of limitation laid down in sections 5 and 6, or after the court has decided the case. The decision as to whether a case should be reopened in pursuance of sections 21–26 is made by the state administration. This decision may be brought before the court.

The rules on reopening a case are of tremendous practical importance and apply to a number of very different situations. Therefore, the Children Act contains 5 rules on reopening. First, there are rules governing the situation where paternity or co-motherhood has not been registered or established by acknowledgement or court order. According to section 21(1), there is no statute of limitation for reopening a case if the mother (or her estate), the child or its guardian (or his/her estate), a man entitled to file an action in pursuance of section 6 or a woman entitled to file an action in pursuance of section 6 a, requests the case reopened. There is, however, the condition that it shall be presumable that one specific man or one specific woman may become the father or co-mother of the child, see section 21(2). Second, a reopening is possible in cases where the parties (or their estate) agree on wanting the case reopened, see section 22. The rule applies without any statute of limitation. It is a precondition that the probability that a man or a woman may become the father or co-mother of the child is demonstrated; see section 22(3).

Third, a reopening is possible if, in connection with the registration of paternity or co-motherhood, an error has been committed influencing which person has been registered as the father or co-mother. Within three years from the birth of the child, an action may be filed by the mother (or her estate), the child's guardian (or its estate), the registered father/co-mother (or his/her estate), or the man or woman who, due to an error, has not been registered as the father or co-mother, see section 23(1). As an exception, it is decided that the father/co-mother (or his/her estate) is not entitled to file an action if he/she, although he/she was aware of or suspected that an error had been committed, has acknowledged the child by treating it as if it was his/her own. Likewise, the mother will be debarred from filing an action if she, although she was aware of or suspected that an error had been committed, has let the father/co-mother treat the child as if it was his/her own.

Fourth, a reopening is possible after paternity or co-motherhood has been registered or established by court order if new information has appeared regarding circumstances which supposedly would have led to a different outcome of the case, or there are particular reasons to believe that the case would have been had a different outcome, see section 24(1). Within three years from the birth of the child, an action may be filed by the mother (or her estate), the child's guardian (or his/her estate), or the registered father/co-mother (or his/her estate). The decision as to whether or not a case will be re-opened is based on an overall assessment. The wish for having a DNA-profile analysis performed on the ground that the scientific develop has made it possible to establish or reject paternity with a near certainty is not sufficient for a reopening. In section 24(2) a number of circumstances, which will especially be emphasized, are enumerated: (1) how much time has passed since the child was born; (2)(3) was the father/co-mother aware of or suspected those circumstances which give reason to question the fatherhood/motherhood he/she has acknowledged by treating the child as if it was his own; (4) has the mother, though aware of or suspecting those circumstances mentioned in (point 2 and 3), let the father or co-mother treat the child as if it was his/her own; (5) has a party, though aware of or suspecting those circumstances which give reason to doubt who the father or co-mother of the child is, not in due time requested a reopening; and (6) will the child be expected to get a father or co-mother in case of a reopening.

The so-called principle of acknowledgement, which has been developed through legal practice, is put into statutory form in section 24(2) Nos (2) (3) and (34– likewise in section 23(2) – of the Children Act. The principle of acknowledgement was based on the notion that the father or a mother should not arbitrarily be in a position to deprive a child the status of being the child of one specific man. The parties could therefore be bound by actual acknowledgement of said man as the father, if they had been aware of or suspected that the man in question was not the genetic father to the child.

Fifth, a reopening may be allowed after the three year statute of limitation, laid down in sections 23 and 24, has expired if there are particular reasons in favour hereof, see section 25.[44]

§2. New Problems

100. The number of couples – married or unmarried – who cannot have children, even though they want to, is considerable and increasing. If only one of the partners is infertile, modern technology now makes it possible for the couple to have children all the same. There are several possibilities now, for example, insemination either from the husband or an anonymous donor, surrogacy, in-vitro fertilization, etc.

Artificial insemination performed by a physician or at the responsibility of a physician is only to be offered, if the woman who is going to give birth to the child is not be more than 45 years old, see section 6 of the Act on Assisted Reproduction in Connection with Medical Treatment, Diagnostics and Research, etc. (Consolidation

44. Ingrid Lund-Andersen et al., *Familieret (Family Law)*, 6–27 (5th edn, DJØF 2003), and Ingrid Lund-Andersen & Irene Nørgaard, *Familieret (Family Law)*, 29–36 (2nd edn, DJØF 2012).

Act No. 93 of 19 January 2015). Further, in order to perform an artificial insemination legally, the ovum shall come from the woman who is going to give birth to the child, or the sperm cell from her partner, see section 5.

When a woman has been artificially inseminated by a physician or someone acting under the responsibility of a physician, her husband, her registered partner or partner is regarded the father or co-mother of the child provided that he/she has consented to the treatment, and that the child, presumably, has come into being as a result of the treatment, see section 27 of the Children Act. The consent to the treatment shall be in writing and in it shall be declared that the man will be the father of the child or that the woman will be the co-mother, see section 27(2). The spouse or partner can be registered as the father or the co-mother, or he/she can acknowledge paternity or co-motherhood before the state administration in accordance with the rules described above regardless of whether the sperm cell used for the insemination derives from the man or a donor. Likewise, it will be possible to have paternity or co-motherhood established by court order.

In 2012, new rules on assisted reproduction were introduced and the former principle of sperm donation being wholly anonymous was changed. The new rules make it the choice of the woman or couple receiving fertility treatment whether the donor is to be anonymous or known. This meant that a known sperm donor under certain circumstances would become the legal father, see sections 27a and 27b of the Children Act. Apart from situations described in sections 27, 27a (1) and 27b paternity cannot be imposed on a sperm donor when the sperm is donated for the purpose that a physician uses it in connection with assisted reproduction or it is donated to a public or private sperm bank that meets the requirements for handling sperm laid down by the health authorities, see section 28. In general, legal maternity does not cause any problems inasmuch as it is the mother who gives birth to the child. In section 30 of the Children Act this has been established especially for children who have come into existence through assisted reproduction. The rule is of importance in connection with donation of ovum where the ovum from which the child has developed is derived from another woman. By surrogate mother is understood that the woman who gives birth to the child shall not keep it. From section 31 of the Children Act it appears that an agreement stating that a woman who gives birth to a child shall deliver the child to someone else is not valid.

Chapter 5. Adoption

§1. Background

101. According to the legal definition, adoption is the creation of an artificial kinship between the adopted child (the person who is adopted) and the adopting parents (the persons who adopt). Adoption is granted by permission, issued by the state administration, see section 1 of the Adoption Act (Consolidation Act No. 1094 of 7 November 2014).

Adoption permissions were originally issued so that the adopted child preserved some of its ties to its biological parents, while other, new ones were established to the new, adopting parents. In other words, adoption was based on a 'two-family principle'. This principle was incorporated in the 1923 Adoption legislation, but was abolished by the 1956 Act and replaced by the 'single-family principle', according to which the ties between the child and its biological kin lapsed entirely, and the adopted child became in every respect as the natural child of the adopting parents.

The present adoption legislation dates back to 1972, when the former legislation was amended, and new provisions which allowed for compulsory adoption (i.e., adoption without the consent of the biological parents or of the child) were introduced. In 1974, the new 'county adoption joint councils' (henceforth: joint councils) were established in each local county authority for the purpose of approving persons as to their capacities as adopting parents. In 1976, the National Adoption Board (Adoptionsnaevnet) was set up in order to deal with complaints over decisions made by the joint councils. The Adoption Act has been amended many times since then, most recently in 2014.

An adoption can either be anonymous or open. If the adoption is anonymous, the biological parents are not informed about the identity of the adopting parents. If the adoption is open, the biological parents know the adopting parents, which is the case of adoptions within the family. Usually adoptions of children from abroad are anonymous adoptions. In 2014, 124 adoptions permissions concerning foreign children were issued. In 2009, the number was 497. Many of the foreign children came from South Africa, China or Thailand and were under the age of two at the time of the adoption. There are only a very limited number of anonymous adoptions of Danish children. Most adoptions of Danish children are family adoptions, typically the husband in a new marriage adopting the wife's child of a former marriage.

It is forbidden for a private person to act as an intermediary and a private person can be punished with a fine or imprisonment, if he/she makes arrangements to establish contact between prospective adopting parents and children for adoption. It is also prohibited for a private person to give other assistance than legal assistance and assistance with the contact to public authorities. The only assistance which private persons may give is thus legal assistance and help with contacting public authorities. However, one private non-profit organization has permission to act as intermediary between Danish adopting parents and foreign children, namely Danish International Adoption.

Just as it is forbidden to act as in intermediary in the case of adoptions, so it is forbidden to act as an intermediary by establishing contact between foster parents and children, or between a surrogate mother and a woman who desires to have a child in this way. Both are criminal offences.

On 2 July 1997, Denmark ratified the Hague Convention on Protection of Children and Co-operation in Respect of Intercountry Adoption of 29 May 1993.[45]

§2. The Adoption Requirements

102. For an adoption permission to be issued, the adoption requirements must be fulfilled according to sections 2–15 of the Adoption Act. According to section 2, the result of the adoption investigation must indicate that the adoption will be of benefit to the person adopted. Today, the Minister of Social Affairs and the Interior sets up one or more Joint Councils which decide, following an inquiry, carried out by the state administration, whether an applicant may be approved as a prospective adoptive parent (section 25 a). It is a condition that the child will be brought up by the adopting parents or has already been brought up by them. A formal approval of the adopting parents, issued by the joint council, is required, if the adopted person is under 18, but not if he/she is over 18, or if he/she is adopted within the family. Thus a formal approval is usually required when parents adopt a foreign child, but only rarely when the child is Danish, in fact only in case of anonymous adoptions of Danish children, which are rare indeed.

103. By an amendment in 1999 of the Adoption Act, a revision of the rules on investigation and approval of future adopters was introduced. The aim was to grant the adopters more responsibility and co-determination in connection with the adoption, and to make the authorities' controlling function tone down. Consequently a three-phase course of action was introduced. In phase 1 it is assessed whether the applicant meets the general requirements for being approved as adopter. The first requirement is that the applicant's age does not, at the time of applying, exceed the age of the child with more than 40 years. Second, for couples there are requirement regarding their status and the length of their life together. Only married couples and unmarried cohabitants (since 1 January 2015) are permitted to adopt jointly. In order for a married couple or an unmarried couple to be approved as adopters, they shall, at the time of applying, have lived together for at least 2.5 years unless particular circumstances are presented. A single applicant may adopt if he/she is found qualified to raise a child on his/her own. Third, the applicant shall be able to document living in sound social conditions. Phase 2 consists of a pre-adoption counselling course. The main purpose of the course is to give the applicants knowledge on the central issues in connection with an adoption so that the applicant is in a better position to assess whether he/she has the resources to adopt a foreign child. Participation is mandatory for applicants who have not previously applied for adopting a child from a foreign country. The course consists of two weekend sessions. When an applicant has participated in a preparatory adoption course, phase 3 may be initiated, here an individual assessment of whether the applicant can be considered qualified as an adopter will be made. At the end of the third phase, a home study

45. Ingrid Lund-Andersen et al., *Familieret (Family Law)*, 33–35 (5th edn, 2003).

report about the applicant is put before the joint council and the final decision on arrival is made. In those cases where no formal approval by the joint council is required, namely in the case of family adoptions, the state administration is in charge of investigating the circumstances of the applicants. In the cases where one spouse/cohabitant is adopting the other spouse's/cohabitant's child from a former marriage/relationship, permission is granted without any difficulty by the state administration. In other cases of family adoptions, the administration will carry out the following two checks: (1) Does the applicant have a criminal record?; (2) Does the applicant fulfil the requirements laid down by the social services department of the local authority for taking a child into care? These requirements are far less strict than those which prospective adopting parents who need the approval of the joint council must fulfil. This is because there is already a family relationship between adopting parents and child. In these situations, for example, grandparents may obtain permission to adopt a grandchild. Permission to adopt ones own child is never granted, since the child's legal position will be unaltered (section 3). This applies to all children, whether born in or out of wedlock, but adoption by an aunt or uncle and their spouses is permitted. An applicant must normally be over the age of 25 in order to adopt a child. If the applicant is under 25 but over 18, the applicant must be approved by the joint council (section 4). Applicants who are married or are cohabitants can only adopt jointly. Only in case the other spouse/cohabitant has disappeared or is unable to act rationally because of a mental disability or a mental illness or another similar condition, will permission be granted to one spouse/cohabitant only. A spouse/cohabitant can adopt alone, if he/she adopts the other spouse's child of a former marriage/relationship. There is nothing in Danish adoption legislation to prevent a child from being adopted twice. When adoption is granted second time, the first adoption lapses (section 22).

104. The state administration must always check whether either a fee or compensation for lost earnings is payable by the adopting parents to the biological parents (section 15(1)). If this is found to be the case, adoption is refused. Permission to adopt is granted only if the child and its parents consent to it. The child's consent is normally required, if it is over twelve years of age, unless it would cause damage to the child. If the child is over 18, its consent is obligatory in all instances. The consent, which must be unconditional, may be given in writing or orally during a meeting in the state administration. Before giving the consent, the child must be advised about the legal effects of the adoption. The consent may be withdrawn until the moment the adoption permission is issued (sections 6(2) and 7). When a child is under the age of 12, information on its attitude towards the adoption shall be available but only to the extent that the child's level of maturity and the circumstances of the case make is reasonable (section 6(3)).

105. If the child is under 18, both parents must consent to the adoption. If one parent has disappeared or suffers from a mental disability or illness, the consent of the other parent is sufficient. If both parents are in this situation, the child's guardian must consent (section 7). The parental consent must fulfil the same requirements as that of the child. Parental consent is only valid if given three months after the birth of the child unless special circumstances apply (section 8).

In those cases where parental consent is not required, the parents must make a declaration, unless this is considered to be harmful to the child, or there are other special circumstances in the case (section 13). If the parents object to the adoption in this declaration, it is a matter for the state administration to decide whether or not adoption is still to be permitted. If the child and its biological parents have established a relationship and the parents object, because they will lose touch with the child, permission to adopt will normally be refused.

Compulsory adoptions may be granted under section 9(1)) of the Act, in those cases where a consent was given, but the parents withdraw it later. Permission to adopt, despite the withdrawal, is granted out of consideration for the welfare of the child, and if the withdrawal is considered unreasonable. Similarly, permission to adopt is granted without parental consent in special circumstances, if the welfare of the child definitely indicates this, see section 9(3) of the Act. If the child has been housed in a place other than its family home, the National Social Appeals Board must consent to the adoption, see the conditions of section 9(4).[46]

§3. The Legal Effects of Adoption

106. Once a permission to adopt is granted, the legal relationship which the child had with its biological kin lapses, and new legal ties are established between the child and the adopting parents, so that the child obtains exactly the legal position of a biological child of the adopting parents. If terms such as 'children', 'descendants', 'brothers and sisters', or similar expressions are used in legal terminology, they will apply equally to the adopted child. If a spouse/cohabitant adopts the other spouse's/cohabitant's child from a former marriage, the other spouse/cohabitant and his/her kin retain the legal ties with the child (section 16). Thus the duty to maintain the child, the parental authority and guardianship are all transferred from the biological parents to the adopting parents. In very special cases, at request of the child's biological relatives contact rights can be granted to the relatives, see section 20a of the Parental Responsibility Act. If the adopting parents separate, divorce or die, the same rules as for biological children concerning the division of parental authority and guardianship apply. The child loses its right of inheritance from its biological parents and kin and will inherit the adopting parents and their kin, as if it had been their biological child. A foreign child under the age of 12 will normally acquire Danish citizenship at the adoption.[47]

§4. The Annulment of Permissions to Adopt

107. Provisions for the annulment of permissions to adopt are found in the Adoption Act, sections 18–24. The Ministry of Social Affairs and the Interior may grant an annulment, if the adopted child and the adopting parents agree, and the

46. Ingrid Lund-Andersen & Irene Nørgaard, *Familieret (Family Law)*, 36–38 (2nd edn, DJØF 2012).
47. Ingrid Lund-Andersen et al., *Familieret (Family Law)*, 46–47 (5th edn, DJØF 2003).

child is over 18. If any of the parties to the agreement is under guardianship according to section 5 of the Guardianship Act or is deprived of his/her legal capacity to act, the guardian must consent to the annulment. The parties to the agreement have no right to the annulment, because the Ministry may refuse it, if the agreement between the parties is considered unreal. If the adopted child is under the age of 18, an annulment can only be granted, if the biological and adopting parents agree, and the annulment is considered to be in accordance with the welfare of the child. Both biological parents must consent, it is of no importance in this respect that only one of the parents consented to the adoption. If the child is over 12, it must also consent. When a child is under the age of 12, its attitude shall be informed. If both the adopting parents have died, the Ministry may grant an annulment at the request of the biological parents on condition that the annulment is best suited to the welfare of the child. Both the biological parents must agree, and the child must consent, if it is over the age of 12.

An adoption may be annulled by court order, if the adopting parent has offended grossly against the child or has neglected his/her duties imposed by the adoption to a considerable extent, or if the court order is considered to be in the best interests of the child, see section 19 of the Adoption Act. Only the child can request that court proceedings be started. If the child is under guardianship or incapable of acting rationally due to a mental disability or illness or a similar condition, court proceedings can be initiated by either the child's guardian or its biological father or mother, or by the Ministry of Social Affairs and the Interior or any other person authorized by the Ministry. If the child is adopted a second time, the first adoption lapses automatically. If a married or unmarried couple has adopted jointly, annulment is also granted jointly, unless they have divorced, or one of them has died. All the legal ties between the adopted child and the adopting parents and their kin lapse. The annulment has legal effects only for the future, and the adopted child retains his/her entitlement to carry the surname of the adopting parent. The legal ties between the child and its biological parents are only re-established, if the biological parents have agreed to or applied for the annulment.[48]

48. Ingrid Lund-Andersen et al., *Familieret (Family Law)*, 47–49 (5th edn, DJØF 2003).

Chapter 6. Parental Authority

108. According to section 1 of the Parental Responsibility Act (Consolidation Act No. 1095 of 7 October 2014), children and young persons below the age 18 are subject to parental authority unless they have married. Young persons under 18 who live with somebody in a stable relationship, or who have children themselves are still subject to parental authority. In all matters relating to the child, the child's own views must be taken into consideration, depending on the child's age and maturity (section 5).

Parents who are married to one another or marry later have joint custody (section 6(1)). If the parents have separated at the time of the birth of the child, the mother has sole custody, unless the separated husband is recognized as the father of the child or his paternity is established by court judgment *or* the parents have submitted a declaration according to section 7(1)(1); see, however, section 7(2) (section 6(2)). If the parents have been married to each other within the ten months immediately preceding the birth of the child, they have joint custody (section 6(3)).

Parents who are not married to each other have joint custody if they, according to the Children Act section 2(1), section 14, subsection (1) or (3), or section 19, see section 14, subsection (1) or (3), have submitted a declaration that they will jointly care for and assume responsibility for the child, *or* they have made an agreement about joint custody according to section 9 (section 7(1)). This shall not, however, apply if the declaration in subsection (1) has submitted without the fulfilment of the conditions of section 448(f) of the Danish Administration of Justice Act regarding the processing of the cases of custody in Denmark (section 7(2)). If a man is considered to be the father of a child by recognition or because paternity has been established by court judgment, the parents have joint custody if they have or have had a joint address according to the Danish national register within the ten months immediately preceding the birth of the child section 7(3)). In all other cases the mother has sole custody (section 7(4)).

In case of parents separating or divorcing or if their marriage has been annulled or they have ceased marital relations, the joint parental authority continues (section 8). Parents who have not submitted a declaration that they will jointly care for and assume responsibility for the child can agree to have joint custody (section 9). The state administration must be notified of the agreement in order for it to be valid. If a custody case has been brought before the court, notification can be made to the court. The procedure is the same, if parents who have joint custody but do not live together can agree that one of them is to have sole custody (section 10). If non-cohabiting parents with joint custody disagree about custody, the court will decide whether joint custody is to continue or whether one of the parents is to have sole custody (section 11). The court can only terminate joint custody if there is reason to assume that parents cannot cooperate. A decision will be based on the child's best interests (section 4). If the parents have joint custody and disagree about which parent the child should live with, the court can decide the matter (section 17(1)).

If parents have joint custody but disagree about custody, they both have to give their consent for the child to leave the country, including travel to Greenland or the Faroe Islands (section 3). The parents also have to give their consent if the child's stay abroad is extended beyond the agreed, unless an agreement has been made according to section 17(1), second sentence, or section 25. The court can decide that the child can live with a parent who lives, or want to live, abroad or in Greenland or the Faroe Islands (section 17(1)(2)). Further, the state administration can decide that one of the parents can take the child abroad or to Greenland or the Faroe Islands for a short period (section 25). If the parents have joint custody and a risk exists that one of them will take the child out of the country and thus pre-empt a decision about custody, the Minister of Social Affairs and the Interior or a person authorized by the Minister, can temporarily grant sole custody to the other parent (section 27). This provision applies to flight situations and it cannot be applied if one of the parents has sole custody. Nor can it be applied in kidnapping within the Danish borders. According to section 18, a parent who intends to change his/her place of residence or that of the child to another location in Denmark or abroad is required to inform the other parent of this intension not later than six weeks before the impending move.

In case of custody being conferred on one parent, joint custody is resumed, if married or separated parents who have stopped living together start living together again (section 12). In case of unmarried or divorced parents resuming their life together, they do not obtain joint custody, unless they make an agreement about it, see section 9. The separated or divorced parents may make a new agreement according to which the custody is transferred to one of the parents alone (section 13). The state administration must be notified of the agreement in order for it to be valid. If a custody case has been brought before a court, notification can be made to the court. Custody can also be transferred to an individual or individuals other than the parents, by agreement approved by or the state administration. For example, the custody may be transferred jointly to one of the parents and spouse in a second marriage by agreement between the parents. If a custody case has been brought before a court, the court can approve the agreement. On the request of a parent who does not have custody, the court can order joint custody or transfer custody to this parent (section 14).

If parents have joint custody and one of them dies, custody remains with the other parent (section 15(1)). If that parent who has sole custody dies, the state administration decides to whom it should be transferred. If the surviving parent applies for custody, the application will be granted unless it is not considered to be in the child's best interests (section 15(2)). Parents should indicate to whom custody should be transferred in case of their death (section 16).

The final question here concerns the duties which the holder of custody has. First of all, according to the Act's section 2(1), to have custody means that its holder must care for the child and make decisions about its personal circumstances based on considerations of the interests of the child and its needs. This care of the child is different from the duty to maintain the child financially is regulated separately in the Children's Maintenance Act.[49] Second, the child is to be treated with respect for its personality and not subjected to corporal punishment or other sorts of humiliating treatment (section 2(2)).[50] Parents with custody can use the child's income from

49. The financial duty of parents to maintain their child will be dealt with in the text under No. 112.
50. The provision in s. 2(2) was introduced in the Act in 1997.

any capital for its maintenance to the extent suitable in consideration of their position and the position of the child (section 2(3)). This provision only allows parents to spend the income from the capital but not the capital itself.[51]

109. If parents make the wrong decisions about their child, not much can be done about it in today's legislation. Only in the case of financial decisions does the state administration exercise supervision. If on the other hand, parents neglect their duty to look after the interests of the child and its personal circumstances, if the child is treated in a humiliating way or lives under circumstances which endanger its health or development, any person who comes to know about this must inform the local authority office. The parents' serious neglect of their duty to look after their child may lead to the child being taken into compulsory care, for example, if the parents are violent or drug addicts, or if the child is involved in crime or suffers significant harm. Compulsory child care is initiated by a special committee in the local authority social welfare office, 'The Children's and Young Persons' Committee'. A child can be removed from its home under these rules without the consent of the parents.

§1. CONTACT

110. It is a principle of the Parental Responsibility Act that the child should preserve his/her relationship with both parents even though they do not live together. This means that attempts should be made to maintain the child's connection with both parents by ensuring that the child has contact with the parent with whom the child does not live (the non-resident parent). Both parents are responsible for ensuring that the child has contact (section 19(1)). The parent who does not have the child living with him/her has the right to be with his/her child every now and again. A formal decision about this can be made by the state administration according to what is in the best interests of the child. Such decisions may be altered for the same reasons, namely, the best interests of the child. In special cases, the state administration may also make decision about contact between the parent and child who are not living together in the form of phone calls, exchange of letters, emails and the like (section 22). The parent with joint custody may enforce this with the help of the state administration, in case the other parent who has the child living with him/her tries to prevent their seeing each other. A different situation is the one where the parent without custody is granted a right to be given information about the child's circumstances in school, day care and in relation to the social services (section 23). If one or both parents are dead, contact rights can be granted to the nearest relatives to whom the child is closely attached (section 20(1)). Where the child does not have contact with the non-resident parent or has only extremely limited contact

---

51. Ingrid Lund-Andersen & Irene Nørgaard, *Familieret (Family Law)*, 39–50 (2nd edn, DJØF 2012), and Stine Krone Christensen, *Forældreansvarsloven med kommentarer*, 51–296 (2nd edn, Thomson Reuters 2014).

with this parent, contact rights can be granted to the child's nearest relatives (section 20(2)).[52]

§2. Contracts for Personal Work

111. Section 43 of the Act of the Parental Responsibility has a provision according to which a child or a young person may undertake a service or other personal work with the permission of the holder of custody. If this enables him/her to maintain himself/herself, he/she may after his/her 15th-year resign and undertake other work of similar nature without the permission, unless the holder of custody decides otherwise. However, all agreement about service or personal work which a child or young person has made on his/her own may be revoked by the holder of custody out of consideration for the upbringing or welfare of the young person. The employer must be given suitable warning and may be entitled to reasonable compensation (section 44). The provisions in sections 43 and 44 must be seen in connection with sections 42 and 43 in the Guardianship Act, described in Chapter 1. The holder of custody is normally also the guardian.

§3. Financial Maintenance

112. Chapter 2 of the Children's Maintenance Act (Consolidation Act No. 1100 of 7 October 2014) deals with the civil law duty of parents to maintain their child financially. A parallel to the civil law duty is the public law duty, according to which a man and a woman have to maintain themselves, their spouse and their child under 18, which is laid down in the Active Socialpolicy Act (Consolidation Act No. 806 of 1 July 2015).[53] Chapter 2 of the Children's Maintenance Act applies to all children whether born within or out of wedlock. The duty to maintain a child rests on the parents and the parents alone. A second wife cannot be obliged to maintain children from her husband's first marriage. The maintenance duty applies independently on how the question of parental authority is solved. Each one of the parents must maintain the child. The child should be maintained, brought up and educated in consideration of the parents' circumstances in life and the welfare of the child. In case a parent neglects his/her duty to maintain the child, the state administration

52. Ingrid Lund-Andersen & Irene Nørgaard, *Familieret (Family Law)*, 50–54 (2nd edn, DJØF 2012), and Stine Krone Christensen, *Forældreansvarsloven med kommentarer*, 297–418 (2nd edn, Thomson Reuters 2014).
53. Section 2 of the Active Socialpolicy Act. The public law duty of parents involves that the parents have primary responsibility towards the social welfare authorities to maintain their child. This means that the social welfare authorities will only grant means-tested assistance to a child as part of the means-tested assistance to the parents, in cases where the parents are unable to maintain their child or themselves.

may enjoin on the neglectful parent to contribute towards the maintenance of the child in cash. The maintenance contribution is fixed according to the welfare of the child and the financial circumstance including the earning ability of the parents (sections 13 and 14).[54]

54. Ingrid Lund-Andersen & Irene Nørgaard, *Familieret (Family Law)*, 54–58 (2nd edn, DJØF 2012).

Chapter 7. Guardianship

113. Guardianship is regulated by the Guardianship Act (Consolidation Act No. 1015 of 20 August 2007). Children under the age of 18 years who have not entered into marriage, are considered to be underage. Only under special circumstances is the ward allowed to enter into agreements concerning property rights. The same applies to adults who are declared incapable of acting in legal matters. A guardian will act on their behalf, see the Guardianship Act section 1. The guardian must have the consent of the state administration if the contract concerns dealings of a more unusual nature. Securities and money must also be administered by an approved administration office which is connected to a financial institution, see in detail below.

The rules concerning guardians are to be found in the Guardianship Act. These rules are connected with the rules in the Act concerning parental authority and residence orders (the equivalent to the Children Act) as the possessor of the parental authority is normally also the guardian.

The question of guardianship is also referred to in Part I, Chapter 1, §2. This chapter will only deal with some specific aspects of the question of guardianship.

§1. Disposal on Behalf of Minors and of Adults Who Are Incapable to Act in Legal Matters

114. As mentioned above, the disposal on behalf of the legally incompetent is conducted as a collaboration between the guardian, the state administration and the state. According to the Guardianship Act section 1(3), the guardian has the right to act on behalf of the minor. This is only valid within certain limitations. It is stated in the Guardianship Act section 35(1) that cash assets, shares, bonds, mortgages and other securities which are incorporated under the guardianship, have to be administered by an administration office approved by the Ministry of Justice. Amounts below a level fixed by the Ministry of Justice, can still be administered by the guardian, see the Guardianship Act section 35(2)(2). Assets which fall within the scope of the Guardianship Act section 35(1) are not administered by the Ministry of Justice but by the guardian, see the Guardianship Act section 35(2)(1). Real estate, personal belongings and claims of natural disbursements are examples of such assets administered by the guardian.

The guardian's administration is not free, though. Dispositions that are beyond what is accepted as normal can only – to the extent that it can be done at all – be administered on approval by the county office. It is explicitly stated in the Guardianship Act section 39 that the guardian must have the approval of the state administration, if he/she intends to spend part of his/her ward's capital which is incorporated under the guardianship. This applies regardless of how the assets are administered. Certain assets can also be removed from the administration of the guardian, partly by the ward having the right to spend it himself/herself and partly by certain assets being removed from the guardian's administration according to special regulations, see below.

According to the Guardianship Act section 27, the ward cannot be held responsible for a guarantee or any other form of security for a third party's debt. This restriction is absolute in the sense that the guardian cannot make the minor responsible for a third party's debt not even with the consent of the authorities. This rule is modified in certain situations, for example, if the minor as a beneficiary undertakes the responsibility for the debt of the deceased person or takes out a mortgage loan.

Although the minor does not have the disposal of his/her capital there are exceptions to this rule. For example, the minor disposes of what he/she has earned by his/her own work after the age of 15. This also applies to what he/she has received for his/her own use as a present or as a free inheritance by way of a will, see the Guardianship Act section 42. The indefeasible share cannot be given to the minor to dispose of freely, though. The power of disposal can be taken away from the minor by the guardian with the approval of the state administration, if it is deemed necessary because of the behaviour of the minor, see section 42(3) of the Act.

115. The administration of the monetary assets and securities of the ward is normally handled by an approved administration office. Smaller sums below a set minimum level are excluded.

The guardian may keep those sums of money over which he/she has the right of disposal by him/her in cash, as long as the sum does not exceed a certain minimum level fixed by the Ministry of Justice, see the Guardianship Act section 35(2)(2). Amounts which are above this limit must be paid into a special account in a financial institution or placed in accordance with the rules laid down for this purpose, see the Guardianship Act section 36.

As mentioned above, presents and the part of the estate which is in excess of the legitimate portion can be placed at the free disposal of the ward, but these items can also be brought under the administration of the guardian, but without the limitations that apply to the administration of assets carried out by an administration office, the Ministry of Justice or which must be accounted for to the state administration according to the rules concerning placement of assets, see the Guardianship Act sections 37 and 38. Because presents are typically given to the minor for him/ her to dispose of freely or are made subject to the administration of the guardian with no restrictions concerning placement an Act of Parliament has been passed according to which supervision rules, accountancy rules, administration rules and placement rules only apply if it is the explicit wish of the giver. A similar rule has not been made concerning excess inheritance, but a testator can decide in his/her will whether or not the excess inheritance is to be excluded from the rules. Whether the assets are excluded from the placement and administration rules and belong to the administration of the guardian, or whether they are at the free disposal of the ward, depends on the wishes of the giver of the present or the testator. If specific regulation in this matter is lacking, the question must be decided after assessment of the particular situation, where the amount and (concerning minors) the age and maturity of the individual in question is included in the evaluation. It must also be specified which assets are excluded from the normal rules.[55]

§2. Placement of the Assets

116. As mentioned above, the following assets are administered in an administration office according to the Guardianship Act section 35: cash assets, shares, bonds, mortgages and other securities. The administration office is connected to a financial institution, which the Ministry of Justice has approved, whereas the assets and amounts below a certain minimum limit are administered by the guardian himself/herself. Assets which are acquired as a present or excess inheritance by the minor can be kept in the form in which they were received, see the Guardianship Act section 34. Otherwise, the placement of assets included in the guardianship must be done by transferring them to an administration office or a financial institution in order to be invested in assets which are reasonably secure. This applies chiefly to certain bonds, but the placement may also be within certain limits in share and investment companies or as a loan against a mortgage in real estate. As already mentioned, the assets can remain in the original form, but if they get 'transformed' into liquid assets, the placement must be done in accordance with the rules of placement. Amounts below a certain sum fixed by the Ministry of Justice, can be administered by the guardian as cash assets, see the Guardianship Act section 35(2)(2).

A present or inheritance in excess of the legal portion of the estate can be given in such a way that the regulations concerning placement, supervision, administration and accountancy do not apply. The assets will then have to be administered in accordance with the rules stated in the will or stated when the present was given. A present can, for example, be given in the form of shares, which are to be under the administration of the guardian or another person, whereby the individual receives a voting right over the shares. A similar situation can be accomplished with the excess inheritance.

If no specific rules concerning placement are laid down, the guardian or the individual responsible for administration must make sure, in accordance with the Guardianship Act section 25, that the fortune is maintained and gives a reasonable profit. Parents acting as guardians of their children may use the profits towards the child's upbringing within reasonable limits, and if necessary use some of the capital towards this purpose. Assets which are not excluded from the normal administration rules may, where the capital is concerned, only be used when the state administration has given its approval, see the Guardianship Act section 39.[56]

55. See Svend Danielsen, *Værgemålsloven med kommentarer*, 373 et seq (DJØF 2006).
56. See Svend Danielsen, *Værgemålsloven med kommentarer*, 491 et seq (DJØF 2006).

Chapter 8. Kinship and Relationships of Affinity

117. In Danish Family Law, the concept of the family is defined as the marriage relationship and the relationship between parents and children.[57] This concept is also reflected in the provisions for the status of a person and personality rights in their broadest sense. Thus it is found in the provisions concerning minors and guardianship, legal incapacity as well as parental authority and residence orders. The acquisition of a surname and of nationality by birth is also bound up with this concept of the family. The concept is found in the provisions governing filiation for children born in wedlock. In addition, the provisions for adoption are more lenient in cases of family adoption. The relationship between spouses is the main topic of matrimonial property law. At the present moment, the concept of the family covers marriage and registered partnership between persons of the same sex and to some extent unmarried cohabitation irrespective of the sex of the partners.

On the other hand, persons living together in a community or persons living with a family in the family home are not regarded in law as family or kin, even though they may be related to the family as distant relatives such as cousins, aunts, uncles, nephews and nieces.[58] In Danish Succession Law, distant relatives do not come into consideration as beneficiaries, if the deceased person has a living spouse or children, *see* Part 4 Succession Law.

Danish Social Law has a different concept of the family, which operates on the basis of three principles: one is based on individuality, which means that the financial circumstances of a person are estimated independently of those of the partner and of the other persons living in the household; the second principle is based on marriage and to some extent on cohabitation, thus an overall assessment is made of the spouses' or cohabiting couples financial situation; the third principle is based on the household, which is wider than the traditional family concept, because assistance is granted according to the individual person's kinship with another person or with members of the household.[59]

Danish Law is based on a principle of unity of the family in the sense that the members of a family have a right to be together and to live together. This means, on the one hand, that the family cannot be split up, for example, by deportation, and on the other hand, that they have a right to be reunited if they have been separated for various reasons. Many circumstances in people's daily life may cause periodical separation such as illness or business travel, but such separations do not require special legal provisions.

---

57. The relationship between parents and children covers all persons in the direct ascending line (i.e., between grandparents, great-grandparents and great-great-grandparents). Similarly it covers all persons in the direct descending line (i.e., grandchildren, great-grandchildren and great-great-grandchildren).
58. All the European legal systems are based on this family concept as opposed to the Muslim countries which are centred on the mother and are based on collective family principles. See Inger Dübeck, *Personers Rettigheder (The Rights of Persons)*, 179 (1st edn, DJØF 1996).
59. The concept of closely related persons is used for a spouse, a cohabiter, a parent, a child and other closely related persons who look after a seriously ill or handicapped person in the home for the purposes of granting care-payment.

In three situations, special legal provisions have been introduced to cover family separation for a longer time, namely in the case of commitment of children into care by the courts, in the case of imprisonment or deportation of a family member and if the family member is a foreigner or a refugee. In such cases, the rights of parents and children as well as brothers and sisters to be together, which is a fundamental right in the European Human Rights Convention,[60] indicates that, for example, the commitment of a child into care is ordered only if this is absolutely necessary out of consideration for the welfare of the child, because by such a commitment the unity of the family is destroyed.[61]

---

60. The European Human Rights Convention adopted in Denmark by Act No. 285 of 24 Apr. 1992.
61. The Danish Social Services Act, ss 58 and 75.

Part III. Matrimonial Property Law

Chapter 1. Rights and Obligations of Spouses

§1. General Principles

118. The property rights derived from marriage are primarily embodied in Act of Parliament No. 56 of 18 March 1925 governing the legal effects of marriage, as subsequently amended. This Act now appears as Consolidation Act No. 37 of 5 January 1995 as amended. The Marriage and Matrimonial Causes Act also contains a few rules which are significant to the economic effects of marriage. The Legal Effects of Marriage Act is aimed at ensuring equal rights for the spouses in regard to the law of property by, in sections 2 and 3, imposing on the spouses a mutual obligation to contribute towards maintenance according to one's means, and in section 11 by the right to make contracts, for which the spouses are jointly liable, to obtain the necessities of life. Moreover, one attempts to achieve equal rights through the principles of separate ownership and separate liability for one's debts in that each spouse can independently deal with the property he/she has acquired before – as well as during – the marriage, so that each spouse is personally liable for this property to his/her own creditors. These principles of separate ownership and separate liability seem, on the face of it, to be at odds with the community property settlement. However, the community property settlement of the Legal Effects of Marriage Act is peculiar to this. As long as the community exists, each spouse can deal freely with the property he/she has contributed to the marriage, within certain limits. The true significance of the term community property can only be seen where the community is terminated, in which case the statutory share of the community property is divided equally between the spouses or their heirs. The exact rules governing the division of community property between spouses are to be found in Act No. 594 of 14 June 2011, the Division of Family Assets Act, as subsequently amended.

§2. The Household Expenses

119. According to the Legal Effects of Marriage Act section 2, 'man and wife shall, according to their individual means, contribute towards maintenance of the family in a fashion appropriate to the spouses' living conditions.' A spouse must deal with his/her statutory share of the community property and his/her separate property in such a way that complies with the duty to maintain, see sections 3 and 4.

Should the duty to maintain be neglected, maintenance can be provided for by the regional state administration, see sections 5 and 8. This, however, will hardly be relevant as long as the spouses still live together. However, what is relevant is that the duty to maintain remains even after separation on grounds of disagreement, and that in such cases maintenance can be provided for by the regional state administration, see section 6 of the Legal Effects of Marriage Act. The size of this maintenance is largely stipulated pursuant to the rules governing legal separation and divorce, and the maintenance is terminated in case of legal separation and divorce. Where the public authorities are concerned, the spouses have a mutual obligation to maintain one another. If welfare benefits are necessary to maintain one of the spouses, it will be provided according to section 8 in the Social Assistance Act in which the right to claim benefits is stated.

Traditionally, the husband has had the largest income – and in previous times the only income. To make sure that the wife is able to purchase the everyday necessities, section 11 of the Legal Effects of Marriage Act stipulates joint liability for purchases made on credit. Under this section, each spouse is entitled to make such contracts as to obtain the necessities of life and to provide for the children, and be jointly liable for it when still in marital cohabitation. The other spouse is, however, not liable if any third party knew or should have known that the contract, according to the nature of the case, was unreasonable.

This rule covers what can be termed usual contracts to the maintenance of the aforementioned needs. The interpretation of 'usual contracts to the maintenance of aforementioned needs' depends on the family in question, its ordinary living conditions and consumption. It has been argued whether the rule can be said to comprehend once-only purchases of items ordinarily used in modern households. There are, as yet, no decided cases in which section 11 has been used for once-only purchases of such items. A number of decisions have specified the extent of the joint liability rule. If, for example, only one spouse has signed the lease on the family flat the other spouse is neither liable for rent, nor for repair expenses when the premises are vacated. Also, charges for heating, which are paid in addition to the rent, are not covered by section 11. Case law has it, however, that heating oil for the heating of family premises is covered by section 11. Electricity, gas and water are similarly comprehended by this section.

The section does not comprehend the raising of loans, not even if the money is used in purchases for the household or to repay debts. If the purchase has been made with an account card, the liability can be extended with the specific rules governing account cards.

The necessaries needed to maintain children include food, clothes, and, to a certain extent, toys and expenses to cover leisure activities and the like.

120. The wife's rights under section 11 are more wide-ranging than that of her husband in that she may make it his duty as well as hers to maintain her special needs. The wife's special needs include clothing, hairdressing, necessary medical and dental treatments, but probably not extensive cosmetic surgery, special courses or the like.

In case any one spouse abuses his/her right to make contracts under the provisions in section 11, the other spouse is still liable if the contracting party neither knew nor should have known that the content of the contract was unreasonable according to the nature of the case, see section 11(3). This means, in effect, that both spouses usually will be liable for the claim if the purchased item is included in section 11, even though it is put to different use in the specific case since the contracting party usually makes the contract in good faith, in cases such as these.

In case of irretrievable separation due to disagreement the authorization under section 11 is terminated. It is assumed, however, that a spouse must notify the local shopkeepers of the separation if he/she wants to avoid liability for the purchases. Similarly, it will be assumed, under the ordinary rules of identification that any person who accepts that another person poses as his/her spouse will be liable for contracts made by the latter.

Section 11 of the Legal Effects of Marriage Act is a statutory authorization given to the spouse. The other spouse may not, therefore, unilaterally deprive the other of this authorization. In case of abuse, the Legal Effects of Marriage Act does provide a certain degree of protection in that the regional state administration may, on request, deprive one spouse of the right to make contracts for which the other spouse is liable, see section 12.

The provisions of section 11 are merely rules of authorization and identification. Which of the spouses of the mutual relationship shall pay the expenses is not specified under section 11. The spouses may freely decide between themselves who shall pay the expenses. The specific rules governing the mutual obligation to maintain one another in sections 2 and 3 of the Legal Effects of Marriage Act might be of significance inasmuch as a spouse without an income may demand that the other spouse pay the expenses.[62]

§3. The Matrimonial Home

121. The Danish matrimonial property regime is, as we have seen in section 1 and Chapters 2–4, a special system of community property in which each spouse, in principle, himself/herself deals with the assets he/she has contributed to the community. It is a common phenomenon, therefore, that only one of the spouses owns the property designated as matrimonial home, even though the property is a part of the so-called community property. This principle also applies to furniture and household effects within the matrimonial home. Sections 18 and 19 of the Legal Effects of Marriage Act therefore contain rules to protect the matrimonial home from the situation where the spouse who holds the relevant assets deals with these without the consent of his/her spouse. These rules which impose limitations upon

62. See for more details Anitta Godsk Pedersen & Hans Viggo Godsk Pedersen, *Familie- og Arveret (Family and Succession Law)*, 80 et seq. (8th edn, Karnov Group 2013); Ingrid Lund-Andersen & Irene Nørgaard, *Familieret (Family Law)*, 202 et seq. (2nd edn, DJØF 2012), and Linda Nielsen, *Familieretten*, 113 et seq. (6th edn, Gjellerup 2012), See also Ingrid Lund-Andersen & Ingrid Magnussen, *Danish Report*, in *European Family Law in Action. Volume IV: Property Relations between Spouses*, (ed. Katharina Boele-Woelki, Bente Braat & Ian Summer Antwerp, Oxford, New York 2009), 5 et seq. can be seen in www.ceflonline.net.

the spouse's dealings with assets contributing towards maintenance of the matrimonial home apply where the assets belong to the so-called community property. If, on the contrary, the spouse holds the property separately, *see* Chapter 3 *below*, these rules do not apply. If this is the case the spouse concerned can deal freely with the assets.

I. Real Property

122. Where a property used as matrimonial home belongs to the community property, the spouse who owns the property cannot deal freely with it. According to section 18 of the Legal Effects of Marriage Act, a spouse may not dispose of or mortgage real property which belongs to the community property, if the property is used as matrimonial home, or if the other spouse or both the spouses use it in the course of business.

The expression 'real property used as matrimonial home' does not only include single-family houses, but also larger properties in which the family occupies a flat, as well as cottages used only on weekends and holidays.

As for business enterprises, section 18 only applies where a business is run by one of the spouses, or by both spouses jointly. Moreover, section 18 does not apply where the other spouse occasionally assists in running, or occupies a subordinate position in, the business.

Disposal not only includes sale, but also bestowal. A part of the property may presumably be disposed of without the consent of the other spouse, unless the property, as a result of this, becomes less suited for its purposes as matrimonial home or business enterprise.

The injunction preventing a spouse from mortgaging property also comprehends wilfully made mortgages. However, refinancing, reissuing of exceptionally redeemed mortgages, as well as owner's mortgages issued with consent are not included in the injunction. Moreover, assumption of debt and mortgages secured to Vendor in connection with purchase of property do not come under the provisions of this section.

The consent of the other spouse is also needed in the event that the property is leased so that the property becomes less suited to serve as matrimonial home or as home of the business enterprise. Easements, although these are not mentioned in section 18, may probably not be granted without prior consent if the easements are pronouncedly excessive.

When a property that is meant to serve as matrimonial home belongs to the community property, the spouse who does not own it has the option of administering it when separating. This, according to section 63 of the Division of Family Assets Act, implies that the property is important to the spouse in question and his/her maintenance of the household. The protection inherent in section 18 must also be applicable after separation, legal separation, and divorce until a division of the property has established who shall administer it, in order that this joint right of spouses to select assets for personal use prior to division of community property is not merely academic.

Consent is normally given by co-signing the document with which the right to the property is asserted, but there are no specific rules. Consent may be given *in blanco.* Has consent not been given, the interested party, who should be familiar with the terms, must sanction the contract. That the interested party offers to take possession of the property at a fixed price cannot be regarded as giving his/her consent to sale of the property at a higher price.

If a contract has been made contrary to the provisions under section 18, it may be annulled by decree in case the contracting party acted in bad faith when the contract was made. Proceedings must, however, be commenced within three months on and after that day when the interested party has, or should have with reasonable duty of care, become acquainted with the terms of the contract. Still, proceedings must have been commenced a year after the contract was lodged for registration, at the latest.[63]

II. Furniture and Household Effects, Etc.

123. The furniture, etc., which belongs to the matrimonial home is subject to similar rules. According to section 19 of the Legal Effects of Marriage Act, a spouse may not dispose of or mortgage chattels which belong to the community property without the prior consent of his/her spouse – provided the chattels belong to the matrimonial home, or are necessary to the other spouse for use in his/her business, or are used personally by the children.

Furniture and household effects of the matrimonial home include common household effects like pieces of furniture, radios and televisions used in the home or in a weekend cottage. Specific collections of coins, paintings or books, etc., are, however, not included under this provision.

Section 19, as well as section 18, must be considered to be effective – even after separation – until the property has been wound up.

If a contract concerning chattels, as is the case with real property, has been made contrary to the provisions under section 19, it may be annulled by decree.

Both section 18 and 19 can be serious obstacles for the spouse who needs to procure available funds by selling or mortgaging chattels comprehended by these sections. This is the reason why section 20 of the Legal Effects of Marriage Act authorizes the government office to sanction a contract if it does not show cause to the contrary.

63. See for more details Anitta Godsk Pedersen & Hans Viggo Godsk Pedersen, *Familie- og Arveret (Family and Succession Law),* 76 et seq. (8th edn, Karnov Group 2013); Ingrid Lund-Andersen & Irene Nørgaard, *Familieret (Family Law),* 188 et seq. (2nd edn, DJØF 2012), and Linda Nielsen, *Familieretten*, 96 et seq. (6th edn, Gjellerup 2012). See also Ingrid Lund-Andersen & Ingrid Magnussen, *Danish Report* in *European Family Law in Action. Volume IV: Property Relations between Spouses*, 18 et seq. (ed. Katharina Boele-Woelki, Bente Braat & Ian Summer Antwerp, Oxford, New York 2009), can be seen in www.ceflonline.net.

III. Tenancy

124. Section 18 of the Legal Effects of Marriage Act only protects the spouse who lives in a property owned by his/her spouse. This is why section 81(2) of the Rent Act has a rule with basically the same effects as those of section 18 of the Legal Effects of Marriage Act. According to this rule, no spouse may terminate the tenancy without the consent of his/her spouse, if the tenancy is used for matrimonial home or if one or both the spouses use it in the course of business. The consent of the other spouse is also needed if the tenancy is subleased, provided that the tenancy thereby becomes less suited for its use as matrimonial home or as home for a business enterprise, see section 72 of the Rent Act.

As for expressions like 'matrimonial home' and 'business enterprise', the reader is referred to the comments on section 18 of the Legal Effects of Marriage Act above. In the event of separation, legal separation or divorce consent is still needed, as described in section 81, until it has been decided which of the spouses has the right to continue to hold the tenancy. A spouse may annul, by decree, the termination of the tenancy under the same provisions as those of section 18(2). This, however, calls for prompt reaction – for example, by notifying the landlord when separating – since the rights of the spouse are defeated as soon as the flat is subsequently leased.

Section 81 is, in a sense, more far-reaching than section 18 of the Legal Effects of Marriage Act in that it even applies where rent and share are paid with funds derived from the separate property of the spouse concerned. Where cooperative flats are concerned, section 81 of the Rent Act may presumably be applied in a similar way.

§4. Transactions between Spouses

125. Since spouses are independent individuals with respect to the property law, they may enter into ordinary property contracts with each other. In section 29 of the Legal Effects of Marriage Act, statutory basis is explicitly provided for spouses to 'enter into contracts with each other regarding property which one or both of them control, and be mutually liable for these'. Certain formalities must be observed regarding transactions free of charge from one spouse to the other, *see* paragraph 2 *below.*

I. Ordinary Bilateral Contracts

126. A spouse can sell an asset to his/her spouse in accordance with existing rules. If the transfer is made for a monetary consideration appropriate to the value of the asset, the transfer is good between the spouses and against the creditors in the sense that, although the transferor is unable to meet his/her creditor's demands, the creditors cannot take legal action for the asset. The spouses, however, must be able to prove that transfer was made for a money consideration appropriate to the value of the asset. This is based on section 32 of the Legal Effects of Marriage Act which stipulates that it is for the spouses to prove that a transfer does not contain a gift, and that gifts can only be accepted if certain formalities are observed. Where the kinds of assets which are only protected from the transferor's creditors if properly perfected, for example, by means of a land registration when transferring real property, are concerned, an act of perfection must obviously be undertaken to protect these when the transfer is from one spouse to the other. In most cases transfers between spouses do not have fiscal consequences.

If one spouse runs a business enterprise in which his/her spouse helps, an actual contract of employment may be drawn. In that case the contract could have fiscal consequences in the sense that the pay is deductible as business expenditure for the spouse running the business, and regular income from employment for the other. This could be significant in that the overall burden of taxation decreases on account of the progressive tax system when income is divided between two people instead of one. Specific rules, then, make it possible for the spouse running the business to transfer any business profit to the spouse who helps out around the business, and he/she will be taxed instead.

Danish law acknowledges that a spouse may be the creditor of his/her own spouse. That is, if it is evident that a loan agreement really exists, the agreement must be recognized by any third party. A spouse may, therefore, act as an ordinary creditor if his/her spouse is subjected to insolvency proceedings.[64]

II. Gifts

127. According to section 30 of the Legal Effects of Marriage Act, gifts are only acceptable by marriage settlement. This has to be so, not only with respect to the relationship with the creditors, but also with respect to the relationship between the spouses. In section 32 of the Legal Effects of Marriage Act, a rule of burden of proof is added to this relationship with the creditors. According to section 32, it is for the spouses to prove that a transaction between them did not have to be done by marriage settlement. The burden of proof thus rests with the spouses who shall be able to prove that a transfer required to be done by marriage settlement is not, in fact, a gift, or that the transfer is not otherwise possible without settling marriage. A contract between the spouses to the effect that community property is to become separate property, or that separate property is to become community property, also has to be made by registered marriage settlement if it is to be valid, se effect that community property is to become separate property, or that separate property is to become community property, also has to be made by registered marriage settlement if it is to be valid, see section 28 and section 28(b) of the Legal Effects of Marriage Act. With the exception of stamp duty and court fees on registration of property, there are no legal taxes involved in transferring a spouse's assets from the statutory share of the community property to his/her separate property. Some cases may be

64. See for more details Anitta Godsk Pedersen & Hans Viggo Godsk Pedersen, *Familie- og Arveret (Family and Succession Law)*, 91 et seq. (8th edn, Karnov Group 2013); Ingrid Lund-Andersen & Irene Nørgaard, *Familieret (Family Law)*, 105 et seq. (2nd edn, DJØF 2012); Linda Nielsen, *Familieretten*, 223 et seq. (6th edn, Gjellerup 2012).

excepted from the marriage settlement requirement. Ordinary gifts which are not out of proportion to the donor's circumstances do not require marriage settlement. Whether a gift can be donated without a marriage settlement is particularly relevant in connection with enforcement proceedings and division of community property.

The restrictions imposed on the expression 'ordinary gifts' are limited in that the interpretation of it depends on the general relations between the spouses. The key element of the provision is whether a gift can be said to be out of proportion to the donor's circumstances, the determination of which depends on a specific evaluation of the donor's circumstances compared with the value of the gift. Basically, this evaluation must be carried out in the same way both in cases where community property is divided and where legal action is taken. When fairly expensive gifts are donated by an insolvent or a person in an otherwise bad position financially, it will be assumed that the gift is out of proportion to the donor's circumstances.

Gifts comprising life insurance, death benefit insurance or other means of maintenance may also be donated without adherence to the rule of marriage settlement. Not all appointments of beneficiaries to a life insurance policy can be considered to be gifts since the policyholder may abolish the policy and be paid the surrender value or deal with the insurance in any other way, see section 108(1) of the Insurance Contracts Act. If the appointment has been made irrevocable, the policyholder will not be able to deal with the policy in any way which is contrary to the rights of the beneficiary, see section 108(2). Provided that the appointment was not made for a money consideration, such an irrevocable appointment will be considered a gift, but the appointment may happen without settling marriage.[65] Formerly, a spouse was to pay gift tax for gifts donated to his/her spouse if the gift were to become part of the donee's absolute separate property – a tax that was easy to dodge by simply making the gift into property contributed to the marriage and subsequently held by the donee. However, according to section 22(3) of the Estate and Gift Tax Act (IHT) gifts between spouses are no longer subject to gift tax. The donor spouse does not have to consider a donation to his/her spouse as a disposal subject to gift tax, *see* paragraph 3.1 *below.*

128. Section 31 of the Legal Effects of Marriage Act contains an important exception from the rule that gifts between spouses are only valid by marriage settlement. This exception is often referred to as 'the surplus rule'. According to section 31, a spouse who has accumulated a surplus during a calendar year may gratuitously transfer as much as half of this surplus to his/her spouse within the following year, without making a deed of gift between spouses. This rule is probably not used very much in practice, and that gives food for thought inasmuch as the rule provides a spouse with the possibility of continuously transferring amounts of money to his/her spouse without registration of the marriage settlement. The reason why this has been overlooked might be that the position of the property does not seem very important when it is possible to make use of section 31.

---

65. See for more details Anitta Godsk Pedersen & Hans Viggo Godsk Pedersen, *Familie- og Arveret (Family and Succession Law)*, 86 et seq. (8th edn, Karnov Group 2013); Ingrid Lund-Andersen et al., *Familieret (Family Law)*, 482 et seq. (5th edn, DJØF 2003), Linda Nielsen, *Familieretten*, 118 et seq. (6th edn, Gjellerup 2012).

It is a condition for the validity of the transfer, with respect to the donor's creditors, that the donor executes a document in which he/she specifies the amount of the surplus when transferring it. Another element of a valid transfer should be that the donor, without a doubt, has withheld sufficient funds to maintain his/her obligations. Being solvent after the donation is not enough; he/she must have been in possession of sufficient available funds to satisfy the creditors when due. The phrasing of these provisions makes it clear that it is for the spouses to prove that these rules have been observed.

The relationship between the spouses does not require that the document has been executed. It is therefore, in principle, possible that a gift donated without deed of gift between spouses may be valid under section 31. Has a document not been executed, the donee will have difficulties proving that the gift received was within half the surplus of the calendar year preceding the transfer, if the donor spouse or the heirs state anything to the contrary.

III. Invalid Gifts and Annulled Transfers

129. If the spouses have transferred an asset from one spouse to the other by means of a valid contract, the creditors, as a rule, shall adhere to this, provided that the spouses also have undertaken an act of perfection – e.g., registration of real property – as might arise from protecting the contract against enforcement proceedings. The creditors do not, on the contrary, have to adhere to a sham transfer.

As mentioned in paragraph 2, a transfer free of charge from one spouse to the other requires that certain formalities – like a deed of gift between spouses or an execution of a document in accordance with the provisions of section 31 of the Legal Effects of Marriage Act – are observed. Since, according to section 32 of the Legal Effects of Marriage Act, it is for the spouses to prove that a given transfer could take place without a deed of gift between spouses, they consequently should be able to show that the transfer was made for a full monetary consideration.

Even though a valid transfer has been made from one spouse to the other, it may, depending on the circumstances, be made subject to annulment. Where personal insolvency is not involved, the transfer can be annulled under section 33 of the Legal Effects of Marriage Act, and in case of personal insolvency the transfer can be annulled with reference to the specific rules governing gifts donated to the debtor's associate.

Annulment under section 33 is significant where gifts which are to be donated and have been donated by registered marriage settlement. Ordinary gifts that may be donated outside the marriage settlement are excepted from this, see section 33(2). Other gifts not donated by marriage settlement are repealed under section 30 of the Legal Effects of Marriage Act, see section 32. If a gift is to be annulled under section 33, it requires that the donor is unable to satisfy his/her creditors, and that he/she did not – when donating the gift – withhold sufficient funds to satisfy his/her creditors. This does not merely mean that he/she was not or did not become insolvent by donating the gift, but also that he/she withheld sufficient available funds to satisfy the creditors when due. It is for the spouses to prove that this was the case. The spouses' concordant evidence to this effect in judgment U 1962.738 was not presumed to be sufficient evidence. In this connection it is irrelevant whether the donee spouse acted in good faith upon receiving the gift.

Section 33 of the Legal Effects of Marriage Act is a unique rule of annulment in that it does not benefit all the creditors; it only benefits those creditors who had a claim on the donor when the transfer was made, that is, when the marriage settlement was registered. The older creditors will not even rank equally among the other creditors since the spouse is entitled to satisfy his/her individual creditors as they make their claims due. When the spouse has deposited what amounts to the value of the transfer, he/she is excluded from liability.

The right to pay individual creditors as they make their claims due, however, must cease in the event of personal insolvency because – unless this right is transferred to the insolvent estate – the equal ranking of all the debtor's creditors aimed at during insolvency proceedings cannot be obtained.

Where an annulment is made under the provisions of section 33 of the Legal Effects of Marriage Act, the spouse is excluded from liability when he/she has deposited the value of the transfer, or if the transfer has been lost through no fault of his/her, for example, by an accident. If the spouse knew or should have known the circumstances by which a gift may be annulled under section 33, he/she will probably be liable for the transfer even though it was lost through no fault of his/her.

130. If the spouse who has transferred an asset to his/her spouse becomes personally insolvent, the transfer may be annulled under Chapter 8 of the Bankruptcy Act. In the relationship between spouses such an annulment will particularly relate to gifts (section 64) and compensations which, compared with the donor spouse's economy and the work performed by his/her spouse, will be considered unreasonable (section 66), but can naturally be applied under different provisions, depending on the circumstances of the case. Moreover, the rules of annulment apply where restructuring proceedings are initiated, and where an order of rescheduling of debts has been made, see sections 12(i) and 221 of the Bankruptcy Act.

Spouses are comprehended by the rules of the Bankruptcy Act governing associates, see the delimit in section 2(1) of this Act. A spouse can also be an associate with a company with which his/her spouse is an associate, see section 2(2) and (3) for further particulars.

Section 64 of the Bankruptcy Act deals with annulment of gifts. Under the provision of subsection 1, gifts executed later than six months before the specified date of notice are annulled. This rule is an objective one, so that a gift may be annulled even though the debtor – as an exception – was solvent when executing the gift, and despite the fact that the donee spouse acted in good faith. Section 64(2) contains an objectified rule with a time limit of one year. The time limit is, however, two years for gifts donated to associates. In the relationship between spouses, therefore, gifts executed later than two years before the specified date may be annulled, unless it can be proved that the debtor neither was, nor became, insolvent when executing the gift.

Gifts between spouses are not considered to be executed until the marriage settlement has been registered. If registration of the marriage settlement is also required on a property registration or needs to be otherwise recorded to establish the owner's right to obtain protection against insolvency proceedings, the gift is not considered to be executed until the property, or the record has been registered, see section 73 of the Bankruptcy Act.

An annulment can be made under the rules governing gifts, even though the gift on the face of it appears to be a bilateral contract, for example, a sale where the consideration is not equal to the value of the gift. This bears no real significance with respect to transfers between spouses in that a gift contained in such a transfer very often will be invalid when it has been donated outside the marriage settlement.

A whole or partial renunciation of one's statutory share of the community property after division may be regarded as a gift, see Supreme Court judgment U 1986.89 H. In this case the husband let his wife keep a house, with a certain equity and other less valuable assets, while he himself merely withdrew a business enterprise of very little value. During the husband's subsequent personal insolvency proceedings this division was annulled as a gift.

If spouses make their statutory shares of the community property into separate properties immediately before division in order to avoid that a solvent spouse has to surrender half his/her statutory share to his/her (insolvent) spouse, and thereby the creditors, it could probably be regarded as a gift as defined in the Bankruptcy Act.

Occasional gifts and donations that are not out of proportion to the donor's situation, see section 33(3), are excepted from the provisions of section 64 of the Bankruptcy Act, as they are from section 33 of the Legal Effects of Marriage Act.[66]

66. See for more details Anitta Godsk Pedersen & Hans Viggo Godsk Pedersen, *Familie- og Arveret (Family and Succession Law)*, 107 et seq. (8th edn, Karnov Group 2013); Ingrid Lund-Andersen & Irene Nørgaard, *Familieret (Family Law)*, 222 et seq. (2nd edn, DJØF 2012); Lars Lindencrone Petersen & Anders Ørgaard, *Konkursloven*, 558 et seq. (12th edn, Karnov Group 2013); Linda Nielsen, *Familieretten*, 126 et seq. (6th edn, Gjellerup 2012), and Anders Ørgaard, *Konkursret*, 100 et seq. (11th edn, DJØF 2014).

Chapter 2. The Marriage Settlement

131. In Denmark marriage does not necessitate the formation of special contracts regarding property. The general law of community property will be applied where no contracts are formed. This law is dealt with in more detail in Chapter 3 below. A contract pertaining to the matrimonial property regime, on the other hand, must be formed by marriage settlement in order to be valid. This does not only apply to relations with any third party, but also as between the spouses.

As it has been mentioned already in section 4 of Chapter 1, gifts between spouses require a formal marriage settlement to be valid. However, ordinary gifts that are not out of proportion to the donor's economic situation are excepted from this rule.

A marriage settlement is a written contract between the spouses which deals with the matrimonial property regime or a transfer of a gift. It must be signed by both spouses, and it has to be lodged for registration. A marriage settlement may be formed prior to the marriage itself or during the marriage. Finally, the rule of marriage settlement must also be observed where a gift donated from one spouse to the other requires that the spouses actually are married, see section 30 of the Legal Effects of Marriage Act.

A marriage settlement cannot be revoked without adherence to certain requirements as to form. However, it may, at any time, be changed or abolished by another registered marriage settlement. A marriage settlement governing separate property can incidentally be limited in time.

§1. Separate Property Contracts

132. Previously, a contract for separate property included division of matrimonial property both in the spouses' lifetime (on legal separation or divorce) and in the event one of the spouses died. On the assumption, however, that many spouses would want it so, it was made possible, effective as from 1 October 1990, to enter into contracts for separate property which are only to be effective on division of matrimonial property in both spouses' lifetime. However, the possibility of making contracts for separate property to be effective also in case one of the spouses dies remains.

Under section 28(1) of the Legal Effects of Marriage Act spouses may agree by marriage settlement that (1) each spouse keeps his/her property after dividing property on legal separation or divorce (divorce separate property), but that community of property applies where the administration of estates of deceased persons are concerned; and (2) that, in connection with an agreement governing separate property, the property from an estate of deceased persons goes to a spouse or his/her heirs (absolute separate property). However, the terms of this section do not provide that the estate of a deceased person can be made into separate property, but that the property in case of legal separation or divorce can become community property.

A contract for separate property, incidentally, may be made to take effect only in case one of the spouses dies, see section 28(2) of the Legal Effects of Marriage Act. It may be stipulated that all assets or a fraction of them are held as separate property, or that specific assets are held as separate property so that the assets are held as partly separate property and partly community property. It is not uncommon that one or both of the spouses want a marriage contract providing for separate property at the time of the marriage to be abolished after a few years. It has now been made possible, therefore, to make a fixed-term marriage contract providing for separate property, see section 28(2) of the Legal Effects of Marriage Act.

It may be provided by marriage settlement that absolute separate property can only be granted in case one of the spouses dies, a specifically designated spouse or 'the surviving spouse'. On the other hand, separate property may not otherwise be made subject to conditions, for example, in such a way that it is applied only on legal separation or divorce caused by specific circumstances or on the request of one of the spouses. A marriage settlement to this effect will in all probability be denied registration. If a (unconditional) marriage settlement has been registered, it must be presumed to be applicable even though the parties of a subsidiary unregistered contract have decided otherwise.

According to the provisions of section 28(3) of the Legal Effects of Marriage Act, a contract for separate property also comprehends income earned from the separate property, unless otherwise agreed. That which takes the place of separate property is also separate property, for example, in case an object of the separate property is disposed of and replaced by another object. This question will be dealt with in more detail in Chapter 3 below.

Spouses may decide by marriage settlement that separate property is to be community property, unless this is contrary to a third party's directions, see section 28(b) of the Legal Effects of Marriage Act. If the separate property is the result of a testamentary direction, it can only be made into community property where the testament authorizes this. If it is a gift which, in accordance with a third party's direction, belongs to the separate property, it may be made a part of the community property with the donor's consent or under the authority of the deed of gift. A sum of money belonging to the separate property in accordance with a third party's direction might be used to cover the continuing requirements, in which case the third party's direction becomes insignificant.

A marriage contract providing for separate property is terminated in the event of divorce. The contract cannot be made effective again even though the divorcees remarry each other. Legal separation, on the other hand, does not terminate a contract.[67]

67. See for more details Henrik Dam, *Ægtepagter*, 60 et seq. (DJØF 1997); Anitta Godsk Pedersen & Hans Viggo Godsk Pedersen, *Familie- og Arveret (Family and Succession Law)*, 58 et seq. (8th edn, Karnov Group 2013); Ingrid Lund-Andersen & Irene Nørgaard, *Familieret (Family Law)*, 129 et seq. (2nd edn, DJØF 2012); Noe Munck & Finn Taksøe-Jensen, *Særeje*, 61 et seq. (GadJura 1996); Linda Nielsen, *Familieretten*, (6th edn, Gjellerup 2012), 131½ et seq. and Irene Nørgaard, *Formueordninger*, 44 et seq. (DJØF 2001). See also Ingrid Lund-Andersen & Ingrid Magnussen, 'Danish Report' in *European Family Law in Action. Volume IV: Property Relations between Spouses*, 7 et seq. and 27 et seq. (ed. Katharina Boele-Woelki, Bente Braat & Ian Summer, Antwerp, Oxford, New York 2009), can be seen in www.ceflonline.net.

§2. Other Ways of Making Contracts for Separate Property

133. Third-party performances may be made into separate property by the third party himself/herself when the spouse is under no obligation to make a consideration for these. This is significant where gifts and testamentary successions are concerned. Separate property can be considered a gift when it has been given by a third party on the condition that the transfer is to become separate property, see section 28(a) of the Legal Effects of Marriage Act. A third party may not, by contrast, stipulate by means of a bilateral contract that the transfer is to become separate property. That would make it possible for one spouse to make the property he/she contributed to the marriage a separate property without regard to the other spouse.

If the transfer is made for a consideration by the donee, or if the donee takes over an asset with an obligation to pay interest on or repay an amount outstanding, it should be impossible that an amount exceeding the value of the gift could become separate property. In case law, however, it has been assumed that the whole asset may be made into separate property according to a third party's direction, even though the donee to a certain extent obligates himself/herself to pay interests and repay amounts outstanding with funds from the community property. If the separate property is to be acknowledged as such, the transfer must be seen as a gift in one way or the other.

Where the gift bears no significance, the transfer as a whole will hardly be acknowledged as separate property, but the sum of money transferred as a gift can be regarded as separate property. Since it is emphasized that all circumstances surrounding the transfer should be made subject to specific evaluations, a lowest limit – neither a relative nor an absolute one – for transfers to be acknowledged as separate property cannot be specified.

134. In 1990 when the Act was amended, it was not decided whether the right to hold 'fractions of assets as separate property' can be presumed to be of significance to question whether an asset may be held as separate property when partly given as a gift. On the assumption the donor wants as large a part as possible to be held as separate property, it will be reasonable to assume that a fraction of the asset corresponding to the value of the gift may be held as separate property. This, however, is not certain before legal decisions regarding this have been published.

A testator can put as a direction in his/her will that the testate succession descended to a beneficiary – including indefeasible shares – is to be held by the beneficiary as separate property, see section 28(a) of the Legal Effects of Marriage Act. If the testator died before 1 October 1990, leaving a testamentary disposition for separate property, it means that this is to be held as absolute separate property. If the testator died after this date, testamentary dispositions for separate property will only take effect in case of legal separation or divorce, unless otherwise stipulated, see section 17 of Act No. 396 of 13 June 1990. Even if the will provides that the testate succession is to be held as separate property, an advancement will become part of the community property, unless the advancement is specifically designated as separate property, see judgment U 1975.473.

If a will provides that the testate succession is to be held as separate property, and if the beneficiary compensates with cash funds from the community property in order to appropriate certain assets, these assets will usually become separate property. However, a testamentary disposition to this effect may, depending on the circumstances, substantiate a claim for consideration, see judgment U 1975.1144, but to make such a claim requires that the cash funds are of little importance compared with the value of the succession.

A donor or a testator may provide for the property to be settled. Property may be settled by will. A gift must be settled at the time when the gift is donated. For the purpose of proof, it will usually be necessary to include the settlement in a gift of deed. Settled gifts belong to the community property. In connection with the donation of a gift, the donor may also make it a provision that the gift is to be held as separate property. Property settled by will by a testator is held as absolute separate property, unless otherwise stipulated in the will, see section 62(3) of the Inheritance Act.

When appointing a beneficiary to a life insurance policy in accordance with section 103 of the Insurance Contracts Act, the policyholder may decide that the insurance money is to be the recipient's separate property. The policyholder may, however, also put as a direction in his/her will that the insurance money is to be the beneficiary's separate property. A testamentary disposition to the effect that the insurance money going to the spouse is to be held as separate property can only be significant to his/her subsequent marriages.[68]

68. See Anitta Godsk Pedersen & Hans Viggo Godsk Pedersen, *Familie- og Arveret (Family and Succession Law)*, 64 et seq. (8th edn, Karnov Group 2013); Ingrid Lund-Andersen et al., *Familieret (Family Law)*, 386 et seq. (5th edn, DJØF 2003); Ingrid Lund-Andersen & Irene Nørgaard, *Familieret (Family Law)*, 149 et seq. (2nd edn, DJØF 2012). Noe Munck & Finn Taksøe-Jensen, *Særeje* 135 et seq. (GadJura 1996), and Linda Nielsen, *Familieretten*, 154 et seq. (6th edn, Gjellerup 2012).

Chapter 3. The Legal Matrimonial Regime

§1. General Principles

135. Danish law takes community of property in marriage to be the statutory basis. This has actually been the case for a very long time, but the contents of this community property settlement have gone through material changes. As will be seen in more detail from the following sections, the concept of community property has no bearing upon which spouse gets to deal with specific assets, nor does it concern the creditors' right to satisfy their claims on the assets. Here the principles of separate liability and separate ownership apply in the relations with the creditors. The spouses are thus independent individuals with respect to the law of property, in spite of their marriage and no matter whether the spouses have agreed on separate property or community of property. Although an asset is a part of the community property, the spouse who has contributed it still has the ownership of the asset.

The essential meaning of community of property only shows when one of the spouses dies, or in the event of legal separation or divorce. Where the community is terminated, each spouse is to cede that half of the community property which he/she owns, while receiving half of his/her spouse's share of the community property in return. Since a spouse is not liable for his/her spouse's debts, only half of a favourably balanced share of the community property may be ceded. The rules governing these aspects will be dealt with in more detail below.

Basically, all of the spouses' possessions form part of the community of property. This includes both the property the spouses own at the time of the marriage and the property acquired by them during the marriage, see section 15(1) of the Legal Effects of Marriage Act. The Danish community of property is thus a very wide-ranging one. Since community of property is considered to be the statutory basis of marriage, special documents will be needed if an asset is to be held as separate property and not as community property. Possible documentation include, for example, a special registered marriage settlement, a documentary disposition or a deed of gift. If assets originally held as separate property are disposed of and replaced by other assets, proof should be given that the new assets have been acquired by using the previously separate property items. Otherwise, the new assets will form part of the community property.

Even though the most significant differences between community of property and separate property only show when the community is terminated, the differences do have a bearing upon the community while it still exists. Under the community property the spouses between themselves have a claim to statutory shares of the community property; this gives justification to the rule that a spouse must not abuse the right to deal with the property he/she has contributed to the marriage in a fashion detrimental to the other spouse, see section 17 of the Legal Effects of Marriage Act (see section 4 below for more details). Furthermore, sections 18 and 19 of the Legal Effects of Marriage Act contain rules that prohibit the spouse to whose contributory property the matrimonial home, its household effects, and trade tools of the other spouse belong from making certain transactions without his/her spouse's consent. This protective measure is, with certain variations, further developed in section 63(2) of the Division of Family Assets Act governing the joint right of spouses to select certain assets for personal use prior to division of community property (see section 3 of Chapter 1 for more details); and in section 91 of the Inheritance Act governing the right to deal with assets from the community property by will; and, to a certain extent, in section 63 of Administration of Estates Act governing extension of inheritance (see Part 4 below for more details). These limitations do not apply where the property is held as separate.[69]

As far as community property are concerned, the surviving spouse will often retain undivided possession of the estate from the predeceased spouse, but that does not apply to the predeceased spouse's absolute separate property. Since divorce separate property means that community of property applies where the administration of estates of deceased persons are concerned, the surviving spouse will also have the opportunity to retain undivided possession of the estate of this part of the predeceased spouse's property.

§2. Personal Possessions and Rights

136. Section 15(2) of the Legal Effects of Marriage Act contains a provision that limits the effects of the community of property with respect to particular rights. The provision runs as follows: 'The rules of community of property can, however, only be applied to non-transferable or otherwise personal rights to the extent they are consistent with the specific rules governing these rights.' The provision has caused considerable practical difficulties in connection with case law, and has been the subject of extensive discussions in the legal community.[70] The following examples may be used to show the difficulty in applying this provision.

A business which one of the spouses runs may often include some goodwill. It can, however, be difficult to include goodwill in a division of matrimonial property. Assuming that the owner often will have to undertake a (non-)competition clause in order to realize the goodwill, goodwill may, to a certain extent, be said to be connected with the person who owns the business. Goodwill connected with a business enterprise as such – e.g., the location of the business – must be included in the estate as an asset, see judgment U 1948.961. However, where it is possible to say that the goodwill is connected with the person who owns the business, the goodwill may be separated from the estate in accordance with the provision of section 15(2).

Particularly the professions have had a tendency to regard goodwill as personal so that it could be separated from the estate under section 15(2). In these cases, it

69. See Anitta Godsk Pedersen & Hans Viggo Godsk Pedersen, *Familie- og Arveret (Family and Succession Law)*, 58 et seq. (8th edn, Karnov Group 2013); Ingrid Lund-Andersen & Irene Nørgaard, *Familieret (Family Law)*, 101 et seq. (2nd edn, DJØF 2012), and Linda Nielsen, *Familieretten*, 79 et seq. (6th edn, Gjellerup 2012). See also Ingrid Lund-Andersen & Ingrid Magnussen, 'Danish Report' in *European Family Law in Action. Volume IV: Property Relations between Spouses*, 11 et seq. (ed. Katharina Boele-Woelki, Bente Braat & Ian Summer, Antwerp, Oxford, New York 2009), can be seen in www.ceflonline.net.

70. See in general Anitta Godsk Pedersen & Hans Viggo Godsk Pedersen, *Familieog Arveret (Family and Succession Law)*, 122 et seq. (8th edn, Karnov Group 2013); Ingrid Lund-Andersen et al., *Familieret (Family Law)*, 525 et seq. (5th edn, DJØF 2003), and Linda Nielsen, *Skilsmisseret*, 114 et seq. (2nd edn, Karnov Group 2012).

has apparently been emphasized that the owner must undertake a competition clause in order to realize the goodwill.

It will often be possible to dispose of some of the business' goodwill by taking somebody into partnership, without denying the owner his/her right to exercise his/her profession in any way. If that happens, the goodwill must be included in the estate, see Western High Court judgment of 10 October 1984 on a dental practice (division 3, No. 2268/83).

Particularly goodwill connected with medical practices has caused problems. Owing to the agreement between the National Health Service and the general practitioners (GPs), the right to establish a medical practice is limited in most areas. The implication of realizing goodwill (in a medical practice) is that the GP in question will be prevented from running a practice in that area again. This may speak in favour of excluding goodwill from the estate. However, goodwill will often have been, partly, purchased with property contributed to the marriage by a spouse, just as that contributory property may have been mortgaged to acquire the goodwill. Purchased goodwill can hardly be considered to be connected with the person in question. In case law, the goodwill will normally – by the Court's discretion – be divided into personal goodwill which may be excluded from the community property, and non-personal goodwill which is to be included in the community property, see judgment U 1995.771 in which, by the Court's discretion, DKK 300,000 of a maximum goodwill of about DKK 553,000 attached to a specialist practice had to be included.

In closed areas, there are difficulties in characterizing an average goodwill of the area, like the goodwill connected with a person; the goodwill is rather connected with the ordinary property a practice situated in the area represents, which speaks in favour of including the goodwill in the estate. Recent theory has it that goodwill is to be included fully as an asset, but in such a way that a modest liability is included as well to reflect that the goodwill is in fact tied and cannot be sold or mortgaged. This liability must, therefore, be fixed according to the person's age and professional situation (the older the person is, the shorter the term will be, and this makes for a smaller liability). However, there are, as of yet, no reported decisions based on this point of view.[71]

137. Copyright is included in the estate of an author, but it is not included in the estate after divorce or legal separation. This is so because the author during his/ her lifetime solely decides whether – and if so, how – such a right as that is to be used. Spouses or creditors cannot force an author to publish his/her manuscript. However, if the right has been used financially, the profit goes into the community property. If the materials for an unexploited work carry a financial value themselves, they must be included in the estate.

In the case of life insurances, the question of whether a sum of money is to be included in the estate usually depends on whether the beneficiary may be paid a sum

71. See Anitta Godsk Pedersen & Hans Viggo Godsk Pedersen, *Familie- og Arveret (Family and Succession Law),* 123 et seq. (8th edn, Karnov Group 2013).; Ingrid Lund-Andersen et al., *Familieret (Family Law)*, 566 et seq. (5th edn, DJØF 2003), and Linda Nielsen, *Skilsmisseret*, 122 et seq. (2nd edn, Karnov Group 2023).

of money to have at his/her free disposal. If no beneficiary has been appointed to a life insurance, or if the beneficiary's appointment is revocable, the policyholder may sell or mortgage the insurance policy, or demand that he/she be paid the surrender value, see section 108(2) of the Insurance Contracts Act. Since the policyholder may deal freely with the surrender value, this value is included in a division of the property. However, where the beneficiary's appointment is irrevocable, or where the insurance policy has been assigned, the policyholder cannot deal freely with the policy, see section 108(2) of the Insurance Contracts Act. Thus, no sum of money is included in the property. Even though the other spouse has been appointed irrevocably to the insurance, he/she cannot deal with it, see section 109. The insurance policy will therefore not be counted as an asset belonging to his/her property contributed to the marriage. If, on the other hand, the insurance policy has been assigned to the spouse, he/she may deal with it, see section 111 et seq. The surrender value must therefore be counted as an asset belonging to the spouse's property contributed to the marriage.

Pension schemes[72] which are comprehended by the Act guaranteeing widows' pensions in case of legal separation or divorce, that is, public servants' pensions and other pension schemes which guarantee widows' pensions, are not included in the estate. However, if the pension scheme is abolished, the spouse is guaranteed one-third of the surrender value or of the compensation for retirement, see section 2(7) of the Act for details. If the widow's pension is a death benefit insurance, it may be provided that the insurance is passed on to the wife, see section 1(3) of the Act. When a widow's pension is due, incidentally, it will have to be split between several beneficiaries. This does not apply to personal pension schemes, see judgment U 1990.457.

Each spouse is entitled to his/her own reasonable pension rights prior to the disposition of the community property in case of divorce or legal separation, see section 16(b) of the Legal Effects of Marriage Act. Ordinary occupational pension schemes is to be seen as reasonable pension rights. On the other hand if a spouse has a pension right in addition to an occupational pension right the additional pension right cannot be seen as a reasonable pension right unless the other spouse has a similar pension right. The right of priority also applies to an amount from capital pension rights or supplementary one-off payments that have already been paid, to the extent that such rights are not regarded as having been exhausted. Pension rights which are not seen as reasonable are to be included in the estate after divorce or legal separation. However, if the marriage has been of shorter duration, each spouse is entitled to all pension rights prior to the disposition of the community property, see section 16(c) of the Legal Effects of Marriage Act.

72. Pension schemes have caused considerable difficulties; see Anitta Godsk Pedersen & Hans Viggo Godsk Pedersen, *Familie- og Arveret (Family and Succession Law)*, 127 et seq. (8th edn, Karnov Group 2013); Linda Nielsen, *Skilsmisseret*, 157 et seq. (2nd edn, Karnov Group 2012), and Irene Nørgaard, *Pension Schemes by Legal Separation, Divorce and Death* (DJØF 2007). See also Ingrid Lund-Andersen & Ingrid Magnussen, *Danish Report* in *European Family Law in Action. Volume IV: Property Relations between Spouses*, 13 et seq. (ed. Katharina Boele-Woelki, Bente Braat & Ian Summer, Antwerp, Oxford, New York 2009), can be seen in www.ceflonline.net.

In spite of the main principles, the Legal Effects of Marriage Act contains two sections (16(d) and 16(e)) to the effect that a spouse who only has a reasonable pension right shall pay an amount to the other spouse. The Probate Court can decide that one spouse shall pay an amount to the other spouse if: (1) during the marriage the latter spouse has made smaller savings that would amount to a reasonable pension scheme for that spouse, and (2) this is because, out of regard for the family or the other spouse, the spouse in question has, in whole or in part, not been in active employment, has been on leave or has worked reduced hours. The amount to be paid may be a maximum of half the difference between the values of the pension savings which each spouse has made during the marriage from the means of the community property. The Probate Court can also decide that one spouse shall pay an amount to the other spouse to ensure that the latter is not unreasonable situated with regard to a pension if: (1) the marriage has been of longer duration and (2) there is a large difference in the values of the spouses' pensions rights.

Amounts to be paid in accordance with section 16(d) and (e) shall be paid in cash, see section 16(f). Further details are stipulated in the section with regard to cases where a spouse cannot pay the amount in cash.

According to section 16(h) the spouses may agree, by marriage settlement, that a pension right shall be separate property. Spouses may also agree, by marriage settlement, that the value of a capital pension or annuity pension scheme shall be included in the division of the community property upon administration in the event of divorce or legal separation. To the extent that pension rights may not be taken prior to the disposition of the community property the spouses shall take their own pension rights, unless the rights can be terminated, see section 16(g).

138. According to section 18(2) of the Civil Liabilities Act, compensations for personal injury and for loss of dependency do not form part of the community of property between spouses in case of division of property on dissolution of marriage, separation, or during the marriage. But it is a condition that the sum of money is found not to have been spent. The compensations do, however, form part of the community property where the spouse dies sometime after the compensations has been awarded, unless the compensations have been held as absolute separate property through marriage settlement.

This arrangement is slightly different from that of divorce separate property. If the beneficiary is alive when dividing the property, the compensations will not form part of it; compensations for loss of dependency to the surviving spouse, for instance, are not included in an undivided estate if the estate is administered in the survivor's lifetime. However, where an undivided estate is divided following the survivor's death, the compensations belong with the undivided estate.

According to section 18(3) of the Act, section 18(2) does not apply to claims for compensations for loss of earnings. Compensations for loss of earnings do, therefore, form part of the estate. It is held, on the contrary, that compensations for pain and suffering cannot be included in the estate.

The damages and compensations under section 18(2) also comprehend compensations from the insurance company of the person causing the loss. However, the provision does not comprehend direct payments from life insurances or accident insurances. It is made clear in the provision that one cannot act contrary to it, and the principles of it will probably also be applied to payments from accident insurances; benefits received under the Act governing industrial industries insurance; and payments from a life insurance in case the policy-holder dies.

§3. Ways of Holding Separate Property

139. Danish law has traditionally had it that a contract for separate property signified that assets held as separate property were not included in a division of matrimonial property whether on divorce or legal separation. Since the Danish divorce rate was (and is) fairly high, it was considered reasonable to make provisions against losing one's property in the event of divorce or legal separation, but contracts for separate property often had undesired effects. If one of the spouses died after a long marriage in which property had been held separately, the surviving spouse would be deprived of a number of those 'spousal advantages' a spouse from a marriage with ordinary community of property had. It was considered particularly unfortunate that the spouse was unable to take advantage of the, in Danish law, common practice of retaining possession of undivided property, which is dealt with in more detail in Part 4 below. Basically, this practice makes it possible for the surviving spouse to go on controlling the entire community property after the death of the predeceased spouse, so that the division of community property is postponed until the surviving spouse dies or wants to remarry.

All this meant that a right was provided for spouses to enter into a so-called contract for divorce separate property as from 1 October 1990; a contract by which property is held as separate on divorce but as community property where the marriage is terminated with the death of one the spouses. The rules governing this are to be found in section 28(a) and (b) of the Legal Effects of Marriage Act.

According to section 28, spouses may agree by marriage settlement that each spouse retains the property he owns when it is divided on divorce or legal separation but that the property is held as community property when administrated as an estate of deceased persons, and that the possessions of an estate of deceased persons are to be reserved to a spouse or his/her beneficiaries in connection with a contract for separation of property on divorce (absolute separate property). A contract for separate property can apply to all or specific possessions of a spouse. It will be possible to provide that a fraction of specific assets or all the spouse's assets are to be held as separate property (property regime whereby a fraction of family assets is held as separate property).

Separation of property on divorce or legal separation and absolute separate property may be combined in various ways. One or both of the spouses may have assets which form part of the community property; assets which are to be separated on divorce; and assets which are held as absolute separate property. It may also be provided that a contract for separate property only becomes effective if a designated spouse is the first to die, or it may have it that the surviving spouse's assets are held as absolute separate property. Under the latter agreement, the surviving spouse gains an advantageous position over the predeceased spouse's beneficiaries.

A contract for separate property may, however, be made subject to a limitation in time. This is so because it used to be fairly common to enter into marriage contracts providing for separate property when marrying, and then dissolve the contract after a few years.

The rules mentioned here make it fairly easy to organize the property in a way which adapts it to the spouses. A marriage contract may, however, not otherwise be made subject to conditions. It may, for instance, not be provided that a contract providing for separate property only becomes effective in case of divorce granted on the ground of infidelity. The spouses are entitled to alter the existing property settlement between them by means of another registered marriage settlement at any time. This is, however, subject to the restriction that a third party testamentary disposition, or a deed of gift, regarding separate property cannot be altered unless the contract provides it or without the donor's subsequent consent, see section 28(b) of the Legal Effects of Marriage Act.

§4. The Control of the Property

140. Under section 16(1) of the Legal Effects of Marriage Act each spouse during his/her lifetime holds and controls all property he/she has contributed to the community property. This control is an exclusive one in the sense that a spouse is denied control over assets belonging to the other spouse. Similar rules apply to the spouse's separate property. Generally, the control is restricted so that it does not conflict with the spouses' mutual duty to maintain, mentioned in §2 of Chapter 1 above. While the control over separate property merely is restricted to the extent it does not conflict with the mutual duty to maintain, the control over community property is subject to additional restrictions, such as the special rules of sections 18 and 19 of the Legal effects of Marriage Act governing consent to control real property and chattels which provide the framework of the matrimonial home. These rules are described above in §3 of Chapter 1. Section 17 of the Legal Effects of Marriage Act, however, contains a general rule governing the duty to deal responsibly with property contributed to the marriage by a spouse. The rule is phrased thus: 'A spouse shall exercise his right to deal with the community property in a way which does not waste the property or is damaging to his spouse.' Apart from being an admonition the rule in itself does not carry much weight, but other rules make the admonition more tangible.

Under section 38 of the Legal Effects of Marriage Act, a spouse may demand that the community property be divided during marriage when the other spouse 'has significantly wasted the share of the community property he controls by failing to manage his financial affairs, or abusing his control over community property, or behaving otherwise irresponsibly'. Division of community property during marriage is a special legal concept under which the matrimonial property is divided between the spouses, and after which all assets are held as absolute separate property. The original intention with this was that, in these cases, the marriage was just to continue without community of property. This legal concept is not used like that in practice, but only to set an earlier date of completion by dividing matrimonial property on legal separation or divorce. Today, it would be almost unthinkable for spouses to continue the marriage when the right to division of community property during marriage has been invoked.

More importantly, a spouse may demand to be paid a consideration when dividing community property, if the other spouse has significantly wasted the property he/she has contributed to the marriage by failing to manage his/her financial affairs or by abusing his/her control over community property, see section 23 of the Legal Effects of Marriage Act. The consideration shall as far as possible make the waste of property immaterial to the spouse in question. Since the provision also contains 'other adjustment options', it is described in its whole under §6 below.

If a spouse deals with assets belonging to another spouse, it will, as a point of departure, be considered an abuse of control as if it were a third party's assets the spouse had dealt with. In accordance with the general principles of Danish law, the spouse will therefore be entitled to try to recover assets from a third party if his/her spouse has sold or mortgaged those assets to the said third party. Similarly, a spouse may not sign for payments which are due to the other spouse. It is a different matter with the third party who normally will not be involved, unless the marriage is about to be terminated, in that the transaction usually will be liable to punishment.

Since Danish law takes the concept of exclusive control in its strictest sense, one spouse will often authorize his/her spouse to make certain transactions in accordance with the general rules of agency. Section 13 of the Legal Effects of Marriage Act, incidentally, contains a rule under which a spouse – during married life – may do that which cannot be postponed without causing the other spouse inconvenience, including collecting income, if the other spouse is unable to manage his/her affairs due to absence or illness. Case law, however, makes it so demanding to show that a person is unable to manage his/her affairs that the provision is not applied. It is far simpler to make an authorization or – in cases where this is necessary – be appointed a guardian *ad litem.*

§5. The Relationship with the Creditors[73]

141. Under section 25 of the Legal Effects of Marriage Act, each spouse is liable to property contributed to the marriage and separate property for his/her obligations. As it has been mentioned already as a general rule, only the spouse who has entered into a contract or has committed a wrongful act is liable for the subsequent claims. The rule (mentioned in §2 of Chapter 1 above) governing joint liability for household debts is an exception in that a spouse, under this provision, may be made liable for his/her spouse's transactions.

A spouse can obviously also be liable for his/her spouse's debts by providing a guarantee or a mortgage in security of the debt or the spouses may undertake a joint obligation to do so. Furthermore, a spouse can be obligated by acting as himself/herself, even though the other spouse should have been the agent.

73. See in general to this paragraph Anitta Godsk Pedersen & Hans Viggo Godsk Pedersen, *Familie- og Arveret (Family and Succession Law)*, 102 et seq. (8th edn, Karnov Group 2013), and Linda Nielsen, *Familieretten*, 113 et seq. (6th edn, Gjellerup/Gads Forlag 2012).

Section 12 of the Act concerning collection of pubic debt contains a special exception from the rule of separate liability for one's debts. If it has proven impossible to collect the debt from the liable spouse, possessions belonging to the other spouse may be collected instead. This rule almost works as a statutory guarantee.

This provision is a rule governing secondary liability for the cohabiting spouse. A futile collection must therefore have been carried out during marital cohabitation if the claims against the other spouse are to be allowed. However, it is not a condition that the income has been obtained during the marriage. Nevertheless, the liability does not comprehend income earned in the years prior to the marriage.

Since a creditor may only take enforcement proceedings against possessions belonging to the prosecuted spouse, it becomes important to determine to which of the spouses the assets in question belongs during enforcement proceedings. In principle, the spouses should be able to deal with their property during enforcement proceedings in the same manner as during division of property. However, during enforcement proceedings it usually does not matter whether an asset is held as the separate property of the spouse in question, or whether it belongs to the property he/she contributed to the marriage. But on division of matrimonial property it matters greatly whether an asset forms part of the community property or whether it is held as separate property. It should, furthermore, be noted that the spouses share a mutual interest, when involved in enforcement proceedings, in trying to explain that the asset belongs to the spouse who is not prosecuted, so that is not made subject to enforcement. An explanation on the part of the spouses to the effect that the asset belongs to the spouse who is not prosecuted will therefore hardly be sufficient under enforcement proceedings; for example, judgment U 1988.278H in which the spouses' explanation was not considered credible. There will, therefore, be cases in which the decisions vary depending on whether it is a case involving enforcement proceedings or division of matrimonial property.

The spouses shall be able to prove that the spouse to whom the asset allegedly belongs has possessed funds for which he/she could have obtained the asset. It should be noted here that production of an invoice bearing the spouse's name, or the vendor's explanation, may not necessarily be based on realities in that the funds for which the asset was obtained might easily have belonged to the other spouse.

142. Although both spouses had available funds, it is not very likely that their explanation alone will be sufficient evidence; but in a case like that, it can hardly be demanded that it be rendered probable that it was not the prosecuted spouse who obtained the asset, see judgment U 1971.335. When the husband had lost his possessions due to enforcement proceedings, the spouses' solicitor advised them to let the wife accumulate and obtain assets with her salary. It was held that the spouses acted on the solicitor's advice so that those assets were considered to belong to the wife. A list of which assets belonged to each spouse drawn up by the spouses in accordance with section 22 of the Legal Effects of Marriage Act might have the same effect. However, such lists probably do not exist in great numbers.

If one spouse has registered title to a property, his/her creditor will be entitled to enforce the security thereby created even though the other spouse is the real owner of it. If a purchased asset is jointly owned by the spouses, enforcement proceedings will probably be limited to one share of the asset. If the asset has not been purchased to be jointly owned by the spouses, or has joint ownership not been agreed on, case law has been reluctant to hold the asset as jointly owned.

If claims are made as between the spouses, the claims – provided there is sufficient evidence – can normally be made subject to enforcement proceedings by the justified spouse's creditors. Further, the justified spouse can – still provided there is sufficient evidence – enforce his/her security on equal terms with the debtor's other creditors.

If one of the spouses is unable to pay his/her debts – e.g., after personal insolvency – the spouses will often let the other spouse purchase assets or new business in order to avoid that these are enforced as security for the debtor's debts. As to the relationship with the creditors, placing the assets with the contributory property of the spouse who is solvent is, in the short run, sufficient to be secured, but the assets are usually made to be held as separate property.

When dividing matrimonial property it matters greatly whether the assets form part of property contributed to the marriage by a spouse or whether they are held as separate property. If the assets form part of the property contributed to the marriage, both spouses will get a share of them, which they may want if both are solvent or their debts to the community property are limited at the time of division. However, if the debtor (still) cannot pay his/her debts, the property he/she contributed to the marriage will go to his/her creditors. In other words, the protection from the creditors achieved by placing the assets with the contributory property of the spouse who is solvent is terminated. This will often happen when a spouse dies. A part of the debtor's debts, however, could possibly be limited in respect of the claims at this time. If a continuation of the protection is desired, it will be necessary that the assets are held as absolute separate property. However, the spouse from whom creditors' protection is wanted hereby disclaims the possibility of getting a share of the assets in case of division of property.

§6. Division of Matrimonial Property [74]

143. Where the community is terminated, the community property shall be divided. As a rule, each spouse cedes half the net property he/she has contributed to the marriage in return for his/her spouse's. In the case of division of matrimonial property between spouses living, the property is divided in accordance with the specific rules in Chapter 6 of the Division of Family Assets Act. In the case of division of property in the event one of the spouses dies, the estate is administered under the specific rules in Chapter 5 of this Act.

74. See in general to this paragraph Anitta Godsk Pedersen & Hans Viggo Godsk Pedersen, *Familie- og Arveret (Family and Succession Law)*, 117 et seq. (8th edn, Karnov Group 2013); Ingrid Lund-Andersen & Irene Nørgaard, *Familieret (Family Law)*, 257 et seq. (2nd edn, Jurist- og Økonomforbundets Forlag 2012), and Linda Nielsen, *Skilsmisseret*, 87 et seq. (2nd edn, Karnov Group 2012). See also Ingrid Lund-Andersen & Ingrid Magnussen, *Danish Report*, in *European Family Law in Action. Volume IV: Property Relations between Spouses*, 20 et seq. (ed. Katharina Boele-Woelki, Bente Braat & Ian Summer, Antwerp, Oxford, New York 2009), can be seen in www.ceflonline.net.

Separate property does not enter into the division of property. Separate property is characterized by the fact that the other spouse cannot claim a share of the separate property after division. In the case of division of matrimonial property between living spouses, it does not matter whether assets are held as separate on divorce or held as absolute separate property, whereas the separation of property in case of divorce is treated as community property if one of the spouses dies. In some cases, the assets have become so mixed that it cannot be determined who owns the assets or whether the assets are the joint property of the spouses. In that case, the assets shall be treated as community property, see section 1 of the Division of Family Assets Act. Furthermore, in special cases, a spouse may be ordered to donate a part of the separate property to his/her spouse in order that that spouse is not subjected to grave financial hardship, see section 67 of the Division of Family Assets Act(see §7 below for more details).

As a starting point, the spouses divide the property privately – if necessary with expert assistance – by entering into an agreement on property division. The terms agreed on do not have to correspond with those of a court administration. An agreement on property division will probably often contain diverging agreements in practice. All the same, the rules governing administration by the court have much bearing on an agreement on property division in that each spouse may demand that the property be administered by the court. If the spouses disagree on individual aspects of the agreement, these may be brought before the Probate Court.

As mentioned above, each of the spouses may request that the estate be administered by the Probate Court, see section 64 of the Division of Family Assets Act. Even though the property is administered by the Court, each spouse still controls the property he/she contributed to the marriage. A spouse may, however, be deprived of this control if it is presumed that he/she will rearrange it, see section 66 of the Division of Family Assets Act.

For tax purposes, the assets, as well as income and expenses connected with them, remain with the spouse who controls them during division. And the joint taxation of spouses ceases on legal separation or divorce, but is obviously reapplied if separated spouses resume marital cohabitation. Transfers of property in connection with division of property are not taxable. Payments in accordance with section 56 of the Division of Family Assets Act, or lump sums instead of maintenance payments, are not taxable either.

I. Grounds for Division During Marriage

144. The community property is divided where the marriage is terminated due to divorce and annulment, as well as legal separation and division of community property during marriage, see section 16(2) of the Legal Effects of Marriage Act. The majority of divisions of matrimonial property arise due to legal separation or divorce. The division of community property during marriage is a special legal concept in which the consequence of the division is that the statutory share of the property will be held as the spouse's absolute separate property, while the marriage is continued, see section 42 of the Legal Effects of Marriage Act. Division of community property during marriage is often a forerunner of legal separation or divorce in that a spouse who applies for it can see to it that assets he/she acquires in future will not form part of the community property. Since, in fact, this legal concept merely is applied in cases such as these, it has been suggested that it should be abolished. Abolishment is virtually of no significance, but the special way of dividing property is indirectly significant in that this concept has a bearing on the division of community property after short-lived marriages. Whereas legal separation, divorce and annulment of marriage occur independent of the matrimonial property, the right to apply for a division of community property during marriage is often based on (abuse of) the matrimonial property. Since division of property during marriage, as mentioned, is a special legal concept in which the consequence of the division is that the statutory share of the property will be held as absolute separate property while the marriage is continued, the specific grounds for application of division during marriage in section 38 of the Legal Effects of Marriage Act must be present. The spouses do not have the right to make unregistered marriage contracts providing for separate property.

A spouse may demand that the community property be divided when the other spouse has significantly wasted, or made such a waste possible, the share of the community property he/she controls by failing to manage his/her financial affairs, or abusing his/her control over community property, or behaving otherwise irresponsibly. A failure to manage one's financial affairs is particularly connected to the mismanagement of financial interests, but is also connected to an unjustified consumption. Abuse of control over the community property is particularly connected to the donation of gifts to next of kin and other associates, as well as to the acquisition of significant special rights funded by property contributed to the marriage by a spouse. The acquisition of less significant special rights will, however, not be a ground for division of property during marriage. That a transaction is sound financially does not rule out that it may be a ground for division during marriage if it is detrimental to the other spouse.[75]

145. Irresponsible behaviour is connected to very rash or injudicious transactions. In judgment U 1985.990, in a case where the husband had been sentenced to imprisonment for serious tax fraud and to pay a considerable extra fine, an application for division of community property during marriage was granted, in that it was held that it would be in the wife's interest to have her acquisitions removed from the community property after applying for the division during marriage. Ordinary business speculation, however, is not included under this provision. If a transaction causes a waste of the property contributed to the marriage by a spouse, the right to apply for division of community property during marriage in itself does not provide for compensations for the loss, but section 23 of the Legal Effects of Marriage Act contains specific rules governing considerations, under which the spouse in question, provided the estate contains sufficient funds, will be restored to the position held prior to the transaction.

75. See judgment U 1971.516 in which an application for division of property during marriage was granted because it was held that the husband's attempt at consolidating his own personal business by converting it into a limited company was intended to be detrimental to his wife prior to a division of community property.

Division of community property during marriage may also be required when the other spouse's property has been made subject to insolvency proceedings. The consequence of this will primarily be that the spouse who is solvent will have to cede half of the property he/she has contributed to the marriage to his/her spouse's creditors. Personal insolvency, therefore, is not a significant ground for division of property during marriage.

Finally, division of property during marriage may be required in cases where the other spouse illegally withdraws from matrimonial cohabitation. Division of property during marriage must, however, be applied for before a certain time limit, see section 38(3).

As mentioned above, the division of community property during marriage is often used as a forerunner of legal separation or divorce in order to terminate the community at an earlier stage. Such an application must have been granted and set down for judgment before the community is terminated by legal separation or divorce in that the Probate Court may not by order terminate a community previously terminated by legal separation or divorce.

II. Assets and Liabilities of the Estate

146. A number of problems may arise in connection with a liquidation of community property, partly with deciding which assets and liabilities are to be included in the estate, and partly with determining the value of the assets.[76]

Assets and liabilities, which form part of the property contributed to the marriage at the time the community is terminated, are included, so that acquisitions and obligations which are of a later date, as a rule, are excluded from the division.

By separation and divorce the community of property terminates at the end of the day when submitted request for divorce or separation to The state administration, see section 51 of the Division of Family Assets Act. In case of separation of estates the community of property terminates by the end of the day when filing for separation of estates to the Probate Court. By reversal of marriage the community of property terminates at the end of the day when applying for reversal. During the division of estate the spouses can in writing agree on another time of terminating the community of property. As well as the Probate Court can decide another time of terminating after recommendation from 'bobehandlere' (a lawyer who is appointed to assist with the liquidation). As mentioned above, it is of the greatest importance to determine to which of the spouses an asset belongs with respect to the relationship with the creditors. As for the relationship between the spouses, it is often more important whether an asset forms part of the community property or whether it is held as separate property since the standards laid down in division of property only have a bearing on community property. If one spouse is subjected to insolvency proceedings, or if both spouses want to recover the same asset, it does, however, matter with whose property the asset belongs.

---

76. See Anitta Godsk Pedersen & Hans Viggo Godsk Pedersen, *Familie- og Arveret (Family and Succession Law)*, 117 et seq. (8th edn, Karnov Group 2013), and Ingrid Lund-Andersen & Irene Nørgaard, *Familieret (Family Law)*, 257 et seq. (2nd edn, Jurist- og Økonomforbundets Forlag 2012).

In the case of division of matrimonial property, a spouse's registered title to an asset will obviously favour the assumption that the asset belongs to this spouse. Since the specific rules of extinguishment for creditors such as section 1 of the Registration of Property Act are not applied to the relationship between the parties, it will, however, be possible to take a position on the ownership of the asset independent of the formal title to it, see for example, judgment U 1958.438 in which it was held that the house to which the husband held the deed belonged to the wife.

If, in accordance with section 22 of the Legal Effects of Marriage Act, the spouses have made up a list of the community property and which parts of it each spouse controls, as well as which parts of the property that belong with each spouse's separate property, such a list may be taken into account when dividing, unless it is proven that it is a sham list, contains an invalid gift, or is otherwise invalid under the rules of contract law. Such lists are hardly made up in great numbers in actual practice. The same applies where the spouses have agreed on owning an acquisition jointly or if they have made a partnership agreement or the like. It will, however, not matter greatly on which of the spouses' tax return the asset is listed in that a tax return serves an entirely other purpose.

147. As to assets acquired during marriage, it will often not have been made clear to whom the asset is to belong, or if it is to be owned jointly. If both spouses have paid a share of the original cost or a share of the down payment, it will probably be held that the asset is owned jointly by them. However, a spouse's contribution to the payment of interests and repayment of capital on an asset acquired by the other spouse will not normally be sufficient to constitute joint ownership of the asset if special arrangements have not been made.

The liabilities are the debts which rest on the property contributed to the marriage when the community is terminated. If a spouse has property part of which is held as community property and part of which is held as separate property, it must be determined which items of the liabilities rest on the property he/she has contributed to the marriage and which items rest on the property held separately. To take a loan secured on the separate property does not necessarily mean that the debt concerns the separate property. If, for instance, a mortgage in an asset of the separate property is provided as security for opening a cash credit to be used with the property contributed to the marriage, the debt concerns the contributory property. If, on the other hand, the separate property is mortgaged for purposes of consumption, the separate property will probably have to be considered wholly or partly spent so that the debt does not concern the property contributed to the marriage. If, after the division, the separate property contains more liabilities than assets, the liabilities rest on the property contributed to the marriage. If the spouses disagree as to the division of the liabilities, the Probate Court will decide in the matter, see section 56 of the Division of Family Assets Act.

If both spouses are liable for an item of debt, they may both require that the other spouse pays or provides security for that share of the debt he/she will have to pay. In case a spouse cannot pay the share which rests with him/her, the other spouse is entitled to set off that share against the claims made on the former spouse's statutory share of the community property. If these claims are not covered by this, they may be raised at a later date.

In decision U 1980.646, it was held that an as yet unassessed outstanding tax of the tax year prior to separation may be included as a liability in the property the spouse liable to pay the outstanding tax has contributed to the marriage. Overpaid taxes can, similarly, be included as an asset. An asset or a liability may, presumably, also be included in the property contributed to the marriage by a spouse if, in the course of that income year, too much or too little advance tax has been paid, even though the actual tax to be paid cannot be determined until the end of the income year; if the advance tax deviates from the actual tax to be paid, the size of the property contributed to the marriage will be different on the date of completion.

The assets shall be included in the estate at their market value, and each spouse is entitled to demand that the assets be re-valued in case he/she disagrees with the valuation already made, see section 48 of the Division of Family Assets Act. Case law has it that, unless an asset has been executed earlier or if the spouses have agreed otherwise, the valuation must be based on the value of the assets when the division has been completed.

Income derived from assets of the estate is included in the estate, but a spouse who has incurred expenses for an asset, on the other hand, shall be entitled to coverage for these. Earnings acquired during the division, however, are not included in the estate. Since earnings acquired during the division do not belong with the estate, it may be justified to grant a spouse entrepreneur's compensations in case he/she has run a business in the course of the division. The principles of including in the estate income derived from assets of the estate and of basing the valuation on the value of the assets when the division has been completed do imply that a spouse shall normally be answerable for the use of the assets of the estate during the division. As for household effects, etc., the division of property will in practice often be based on a valuation which has taken place at the beginning of administration, since the spouse who has had to execute such an asset has made use of it during the division he/she will be held answerable for any waste of the value of the asset.

If the disposal of an asset is to be answerable by a tax liability, a regulation liability will have to be included in the estate, just as answerable accounts containing latent tax liabilities need to be adjusted. The establishment of a liability for a tax liability must be based on an estimate. In several case decisions on the establishment of liabilities, the liability has been established with regard to spouses' individual interests. In principle, it is necessary to estimate when a latent tax liability, and the amount of money involved, will be realized, just as the interest-free credit will have to be taken into consideration until the liability is realized. While some capital allowances may turn out to be a liability, it could, depending on the circumstances, happen that a tax liability is not meant to be realized. A liability, therefore, will often be valued fairly roughly.

III. Rules for Unequal Division of Community Assets

148. If a spouse cannot select from the share of the property which falls to him/her the necessary furniture and household effects to the maintenance of the matrimonial home, and if he/she cannot procure the necessaries in any other way, he/she may, if applying for it, be granted a larger share of the community property, see section 62 of the Division of Family Assets Act. This rule only concerns very small community properties. If the other spouse holds separate property, section 62 is supplemented with section 67 of the Division of Family Assets Act, see §7 below. If the spouse in question himself/herself holds separate property or has a large income, he/she thus has means of acquiring the necessaries in other ways. Likewise, the rule is probably not applicable where the spouse can repay the value of the assets under section 64 of the Division of Family Assets Act.

When a marriage is annulled, the matrimonial property is divided in accordance with the specific rule under section 60 of the Division of Family Assets Act. Very few marriages, however, are annulled. The rules themselves are therefore not used very much in practice. In the cases of short-lived marriages, similar rules may, however, be applied. The rules governing division of community property in case of annulment are thus made applicable in practice.

In the case of annulment of marriage, each spouse selects in priority that which he/she contributed to the community property at the time of the marriage, inheritance, gifts, as well as the assets he/she has transferred from his/her separate property to the community property. Subsequently, the remaining property is divided equally between the spouses. If the funds of the estate are insufficient for the selection in priority, the property is divided in accordance with the funds each spouse would have had priority of, had the estate held sufficient funds.

In the case of division on divorce or legal separation, it is now possible to apply similar rules under section 61 of the Division of Family Assets Act if an equal division of the property will be considered to be obviously unfair. In order that the unequal division may happen in accordance with this rule, one of the spouses must have contributed most of his/her property to the community property as described in section 60, that is, contributed property at the time of the marriage; acquired inheritances or gifts during the marriage; or transferred assets from his/her separate property to the community property. Furthermore, an equal division must be found obviously unfair, particularly where the marriage has been short-lived and without any significant economic community. Even though it is not possible to set a specific time limit, a marriage will hardly be considered short-lived if it has lasted about five years. Not only will the duration of the marriage be taken into consideration in this connection, but probably also any previous cohabitation. If the other spouse has contributed to the preservation or to an increase of the funds contributed by his/her spouse, the marriage cannot normally be found to have been without a significant economic community. Case law also seems to take into consideration how onerous an equal division would be to the spouse who wants selection in priority. The standards of an equal division of property may be derogated from, to a great or small extent. The standards are derogated from to the extent it can be substantiated, for example by excluding a specific asset from the equal division. The rules of section 60 of the Division of Family Assets Act governing annulment do, however, impose limits on the extent to which one may derogate from the standards of equal division. In judgment U 1992.311, unequal division was applied wholly in a case where the couple merely had been cohabitants the first six weeks of the period of a year and a half which passed prior to the separation. The general rules governing the distribution of assets are applied even though unequal division is applied also.[77]

IV. Claims for Compensation

149. If a spouse has used funds from his/her separate property to improve or conserve the property he/she has contributed to the marriage, he/she may select in priority compensations from that property; if the property he/she has contributed to the marriage does not hold sufficient funds, the claim for compensation is lost, see section 23(3) of the Legal Effects of Marriage Act. In contrast with this, section 23(2) of the same Act contains a rule governing claims for compensation where a spouse acquires special rights. Compensations may be claimed where the other spouse has used funds from the property he/she has contributed to the marriage to acquire property to be held separately or to improve such property, or to acquire rights under section 15(2) of the Legal Effects of Marriage Act. The provision thus makes it possible to adjust the property contributed to the marriage (and subsequently held) by a spouse when funds from the community property have been used to acquire or improve rights which may be excluded wholly or partially from the division.

If a spouse has wasted the property he/she has contributed to the marriage by abusing his/her control over it, the other spouse may make a claim for compensation pursuant to section 23(1) of the Legal Effects of Marriage Act. In section 23 of this Act abuse is defined as failure to manage one's financial affairs; abuse of one's control over the community property; or other irresponsible behaviour which has significantly wasted that share of the community property he/she controls. This is almost identical to the grounds for division of community property during marriage under section 38(1) of the Legal Effects of Marriage Act. Whereas division of community property during marriage can be demanded when there is a risk of waste, claims for compensation can evidently only be raised where the property contributed to the marriage by a spouse has actually been wasted.

150. If cohabitation no longer takes place, or if the spouses separate in preparation for divorce or legal separation, a spouse might be tempted to spend or give away a share of the property he/she has contributed to the marriage in order to avoid ceding half of this to his/her spouse. Gifts donated to family or a person with whom the spouse intends to live with in the future, may easily appear disloyal, which may substantiate a claim for compensation. Since, in the case of a division of matrimonial property on divorce or legal separation, advancements are not included in the property the donor has contributed to the marriage, an advancement made prior to the division may also appear disloyal, which may substantiate a claim for compensation, depending on the circumstances.

---

77. See Anitta Godsk Pedersen & Hans Viggo Godsk Pedersen, *Familie- og Arveret (Family and Succession Law)*, 138 et seq. (8th edn, Karnov Group 2013); Ingrid Lund-Andersen & Irene Nørgaard, *Familieret (Family Law)*, 275 et seq. (2nd edn, Jurist- og Økonomforbundets Forlag 2012).

In the case of a division on the death of the spouse entitled to inherit, his/her beneficiaries may raise the claim for compensation. Pursuant to section 23 the compensation is withdrawn from the remaining community property. If this does not hold sufficient funds, half of the amount will be withdrawn from the spouse's separate property.

Claims for compensation may only be raised in case of division of property, and if the required compensation cannot be covered, the claim is extinguished, see section 24 of the Legal Effects of Marriage Act. If one spouse has given away the majority of the share of the community property he/she controls, and if this also makes up the majority of the total community property, under the rule governing claims for compensation in section 23, the other spouse cannot be compensated so as to be put in the position he/she had prior to the abuse. The Legal Effects of Marriage Act does not, however, authorize annulment of a gift which has wasted an estate. Nevertheless, it must presumably be supposed that a gift may be annulled in case the donee knew or should have known that the donor donated the gift with the purpose of rendering futile his/her spouse's claim for a statutory share of the community property.[78]

V. The Qualitative Division

A. *General Principles*

151. During division, each spouse may demand possession of the property of the estate after a valuation, see section 63 of the Division of Family Assets Act. If the spouses demand possession of the same asset, the spouse to whose property that asset belonged when it was contributed to the marriage is entitled to possess it. If it cannot be determined to whose property contributed to the marriage the asset belongs, or if it is the joint property of the spouses, it may be determined by lot which of the spouses is to take possession of the asset. Unlike an estate of deceased persons, authorization for drawing lots may not be granted if a special agreement has not been worked out. For want of such an agreement the asset must be sold so that the proceeds of the sale can be included in the estate, see section 63(3).

Normally, each possession must be considered an individual asset. Several possessions may belong together so that they may be considered one asset. A business enterprise, for instance, will often have to be considered one asset, even though it obviously can consist of a large number of 'individual assets'. Similarly, a block of shares must also be seen to consist of a number of shares which, in principle, may be possessed individually. However, a block of shares might also be seen as a whole. A minority of shares which does not have an influence on a 'business run by one

78. See Anitta Godsk Pedersen & Hans Viggo Godsk Pedersen, *Familie- og Arveret (Family and Succession Law)*, 139 et seq. (8th edn, Karnov Group 2013); Ingrid Lund-Andersen & Irene Nørgaard, *Familieret (Family Law)*, 180 et seq. (2nd edn, Jurist- og Økonomforbundets Forlag 2012), and Linda Nielsen & Annette Kronborg, *Skilsmisseret*, 145 et seq. (2nd edn, Karnov Group 2012). See also Ingrid Lund-Andersen & Ingrid Magnussen, *Danish Report*, in *European Family Law in Action. Volume IV: Property Relations between Spouses*, 21 et seq. (ed. Katharina Boele-Woelki, Bente Braat & Ian Summer, Antwerp, Oxford, New York 2009), can be seen in www.ceflonline.net.

person' is usually not attractive and often virtually unsalable; a block of shares is only valuable where it forms part of a whole and should, therefore, probably be possessed as such.[79]

A spouse may take possession of an asset even though it is more valuable than the spouse's statutory share of the community property, but in that case the spouse shall make a cash payment of the surplus to his/her spouse, see section 64 of the Division of Family Assets Act. Since it often will be very difficult to obtain a loan of sufficient funds, the provision provides the Probate Court with the possibility of ordering the loan to be repaid with an interest fixed by the Probate Court, and that the loan is adequately secured on the matrimonial property. Such an extension of payment is particularly settled with a view to the continued running of a business enterprise, but it may also be applied where single-family houses, furniture and trade tools are concerned. Apart from business enterprises, cases where the spouse who selects an asset has been granted parental responsibility might particularly call for a settlement for repayment as regards real property.

B. Joint Right of Spouses to Select Assets Prior to Division

152. Section 63(2) of the Division of Family Assets Act provides that spouses, depending on the circumstances, can select assets which belong with property the other spouse has contributed to the marriage, even when both spouses demand possession of the asset. Like the rules in sections 18 and 19 of the Legal Effects of Marriage Act, the purpose of this rule is to make maintenance of the matrimonial home or the business enterprise possible. The provision consists of five headings:

(1) Real property which is used exclusively or mainly as matrimonial home may be taken into possession by one of the spouses if the property is found to be necessary for the maintenance of the matrimonial home to this spouse. The criterion for demanding one of the spouses' possession of the matrimonial home is that it is found necessary for the maintenance of the matrimonial home to this spouse. This is particularly the case where the spouse in question is granted parental responsibility, but it is, however, not a condition. In the case of joint parental responsibility, it will presumably be significant if the spouses have agreed that the children primarily are to live with one of the spouses. The provision will normally not be applied where it is possible for spouse in question to obtain another suitable home; where the spouse is unable to manage the financial obligations connected with possessing the matrimonial home; and where the other spouse has a special connection with the property.
(2) Real property which has been used as a summer cottage by the family may be possessed by one of the spouses if it is found to be of great importance to this

79. See Anitta Godsk Pedersen & Hans Viggo Godsk Pedersen, *Familie- og Arveret (Family and Succession Law)*, 137 et seq. (8th edn, Karnov Group 2013); Ingrid Lund-Andersen & Irene Nørgaard, *Familieret (Family Law)*, 287 et seq. (2nd edn, Jurist- og Økonomforbundets Forlag 2012), and Linda Nielsen & Annette Kronborg, *Skilsmisseret*, 104 et seq. (2nd edn, Karnov Group 2012).

spouse. As opposed to houses which are suitable for use all the year, the property must have served as the family's summer cottage. Summer cottages which have not yet been in use are, therefore, not included in this provision which covers the same rules as section 18 of the Legal Effects of Marriage Act.

(3) A spouse may demand possession of a business enterprise if this has been run exclusively or primarily by this spouse. Joint business enterprises are not comprehended by this in that it must be held as a condition that the contributions of the spouse to the running of the business have been of minor importance. The provision may be applied even though the business enterprise has been run as a public or private limited company, if, however, it has also been run as a 'one person business'. In that case the shares make up the asset.

(4) Trade tools and other business chattels may be possessed by the other spouse to the extent this is found necessary for the continuation of his/her business. If the said chattels are of great importance to the user spouse, it will hardly be considered necessary to demand they be possessed by the other spouse.

(5) Furniture and other household effects which have belonged with the matrimonial home may be possessed by the other spouse where this is found necessary for the maintenance of the matrimonial home or where the effects have been of importance to the spouse in question. In this connection it seems only natural to take into consideration which of the spouses has been granted parental responsibility, as well as a spouse's chance of obtaining similar furniture and household effects.

The joint right of spouses to select assets for personal use prior to division may be applied even though the spouses hold a fraction of the assets as separate property. This, however, does not apply where the asset in question is specifically held as separate property.[80]

If neither spouse demands possession of the assets of the estate, the assets will be put up for public sale unless the spouses agree to sell privately, see sections 63 and 25 of the Division of Family Assets Act for more details.

VI. Agreement Modifying a Contract

153. If spouses have made a contract for division of the matrimonial property, the maintenance obligation, or other terms in case of divorce or legal separation, the contract can be ordered modified or not binding if the terms of the contract are found unfair to one of the spouses at the time the contract was made, see section 58 of the Marriage and Matrimonial Causes Act. However, under section 58, the contract cannot be modified due to circumstances which arise after the contract was

80. See Anitta Godsk Pedersen & Hans Viggo Godsk Pedersen, *Familie- og Arveret (Family and Succession Law)*, 144 et seq. (8th edn, Karnov Group 2013); Ingrid Lund-Andersen & Irene Nørgaard, *Familieret (Family Law)*, 188 et seq. (2nd edn, Jurist- og Økonomforbundets Forlag 2012), and Linda Nielsen & Annette Kronborg, *Skilsmisseret*, 112 et seq. (2nd edn, Karnov Group 2012). See also Ingrid Lund-Andersen & Ingrid Magnussen, *Danish Report*, in *European Family Law in Action. Volume IV: Property Relations between Spouses*, (ed. Katharina Boele-Woelki, Bente Braat & Ian Summer, Antwerp, Oxford, New York 2009), 23 et seq. can be seen in www.ceflonline.net.

made. However, under section 52 of the Marriage and Matrimonial Causes Act, contracts providing for maintenance obligations may be modified if the circumstances of the contract have changed significantly. Previously, section 52 provided a one-year limit, but this has now been abolished.

When judging whether a contract is unfair, all the terms of the contract must be considered as a whole. If, for instance, one of the spouses has renounced his/her statutory share of the community property, this will, if the contract is not considered as a whole, be found unfair. If, however, the marriage was short-lived so that the property could be divided unequally under section 60 of the Division of Family Assets Act, a contract for renunciation of the statutory share of the community property may be made and not found unfair if it resembles an unequal division. Furthermore, such a contract for renunciation of the statutory share of the community property might be countered by other advantages. This, for instance, is the case where one spouse's funds are locked-up with a business enterprise or other assets from which they hardly can be made available; here it would be natural that the other spouse partly renounces his/her statutory share of the community property on the right to a larger maintenance than he/she would otherwise have been entitled to, and that he/she is insured in case his/her spouse dies, for example by being made the beneficiary under an irrevocable life insurance policy or under an irrevocable will. Such an arrangement is almost an alternative of the rule of extension of payment under section 64 of the Division of Family Assets Act. It would, on the other hand, be possible for a spouse to renounce maintenance on having a larger share of the community property.

If the contract is based on a wrong valuation of the size of the estate, the contract will normally be found unfair; see for example, judgment U 1980.222 V in which the wife was granted an amount of money because it was held that she was misinformed about the size of the community property and the financial affairs as such; and judgment U 1985.1104 V in which the wife's application for having the division administered by the court was granted even though an agreement on property division had been made in that she had not been informed of a capital payments scheme when making the arrangement. This will normally also be applied even though the spouse did not know her statutory rights.

If a spouse renounces his/her statutory share of the community property partly or wholly although he/she is familiar with the size of the estate, the renunciation will, prima facie, be considered. But under section 58 of the Marriage and Matrimonial Causes Act it is taken into consideration that the spouse may have been mentally unbalanced on entering into the contract so that he/she has accepted terms which he/she would not accept under normal circumstances. Such contracts may therefore, to a certain extent, be set aside.

Contracted terms are not only voidable under section 58 of the Marriage and Matrimonial Causes Act, but also under the general rules of contracts. Under these rules, a contract made under wrongful conditions will particularly be subject to invalidation. If one of the spouses has made his/her spouse enter into the contract on wrongful conditions, the contract will be voidable under section 30 of the Contracts Act governing fraud.

Section 36 of the Contracts Act may also be applied to agreements on property division. Even though section 36 of the Contracts Act can be applied also where circumstances arise after the contract was made, it will not necessarily have a significant bearing on case law. The test of reasonableness as regards setting aside contracts due to new circumstances is based on a risk assessment; setting aside a contract will, by implication, place the risk with the other spouse. It will probably very rarely be reasonable to set aside an 'originally' fair contract and thereby place the risk of new circumstances with the other spouse.[81]

§7. Claims Raised against Separate Property on Division

154. Separate property is not included in a division. Separate property may, however, be included in the estate to the extent it is necessary for a spouse's satisfaction of claims for compensation under section 23 of the Legal Effects of Marriage Act. Furthermore, the assets may have been blended so thoroughly that it is difficult to determine which of the assets are held as the separate property of a spouse. In these cases the assets will be treated as community property pursuant to section 1 of the Division of Family Assets Act.

If the spouses have enjoyed a certain standard of living by virtue of one of the spouses' separate property, the other spouse will be subjected to financial hardship in the case of divorce or legal separation. This can to a certain extent be alleviated if it is provided that one spouse is obligated to maintain the other. Under the authority of section 67 of the Division of Family Assets Act, a spouse may be obligated to donate an amount of money to his/her spouse to ensure that the latter is not subjected to grave financial hardship following legal separation or divorce. This may be authorized if the spouses' matrimonial property, the duration of the marriage and other circumstances particularly favour it.[82] This provision may also be applied if one of the spouses has rights governed by section 15(2) of the Legal Effects of Marriage Act, and if these rights can be excluded from the division itself.

In case of disagreement, the claims must be raised before the ordinary courts during legal separation or divorce. The claim must be raised before the Court of First Instance in that new allegations, according to the rules of the Danish Administration of Justice Act, may only be raised before the Court of Appeal if the Court of Appeal finds it excusable that these were not raised before the lower court.

A standard for judging whether a spouse will be exposed to grave financial hardship cannot be determined. It must be taken into consideration whether a spouse will be made subject to grave financial hardship compared with his/her spouse in the

---

81. See Anitta Godsk Pedersen & Hans Viggo Godsk Pedersen, *Familie- og Arveret (Family and Succession Law)*, 154 et seq. (8th edn, Karnov Group 2013); Ingrid Lund-Andersen & Irene Nørgaard, *Familieret (Family Law)*, 95 et seq. (2nd edn, Jurist- og Økonomforbundets Forlag 2012), and Linda Nielsen & Annette Kronborg, *Skilsmisseret*, 287 et seq. (2nd edn, Karnov Group 2012).
82. See Anitta Godsk Pedersen & Hans Viggo Godsk Pedersen, *Familie- og Arveret (Family and Succession Law)*, 157 et seq. (8th edn, Karnov Group 2013); Ingrid Lund-Andersen & Irene Nørgaard, *Familieret (Family Law)*, 276 et seq. (2nd edn, Jurist- og Økonomforbundets Forlag 2012), and Linda Nielsen & Annette Kronborg, *Skilsmisseret*, 145 et seq. (2nd edn, Karnov Group 2012).

sense that a significant difference between the spouses' financial situations will be a ground for raising the claim.

The duration of the marriage cannot alone give cause for a claim pursuant to section 67 of the Division of Family Assets Act, but a long marriage will favour that an amount of money be granted to one of the spouses. The reference to the duration of the marriage does, on the other hand, exclude that an amount of money can be granted to a spouse if it has been a short-lived marriage.

Typical cases in which it may be reasonable to grant an amount of money to a spouse pursuant to section 67 are mentioned in the explanatory statements of the provision. If both spouses have contributed to one of the spouse's separate property, either by saving up money during the marriage or by a spouse's direct efforts in the other spouse's business enterprise, this favours granting an amount of money to one of the spouses pursuant to section 67.

If granting a spouse an amount of money is necessary for the spouse to be established in a suitable home or to be vocationally rehabilitated by means of training or an additional education, this will also be a sufficient ground.

Part IV. Succession Law

Chapter 1. Intestate Succession

§1. The Opening of the Succession

I. Death

155. The burial authorities or any other Danish authorities which receive notification of a death are to notify the Probate Court of the judicial district in which the deceased resided as soon as possible, see section 4 of the Administration of Estates Act. Since the burial authorities are not entitled to perform the burial without a death certificate issued by a doctor, it is guaranteed that the Probate Court will be notified about the death. In the unique cases where it has been established for sure that a person is deceased, but where a death certificate cannot be issued, the Probate Court may order that the person in question is to be presumed dead at the request of anybody who has cause of action. In the ruling, the probable time of death is indicated, see section 5 of the Administration of Estates Act. A court declaration of death may be issued if, for instance, the person in question has crashed with a plane. If it turns out that the person in question is not dead after all, he/she is entitled to recover his/her possessions pursuant to the rules governing missing persons and absentees, see below. Since hard evidence is required for a court to declare a person dead, it is almost impossible that the person should turn out to be alive.

II. Missing Persons and Absentees

156. If a person is missing, a declaration of death, depending on the circumstances, may be issued after ordering a summons. An order of summons may normally not be issued until five years after the missing person was last known to have been alive. If the missing person's life was in danger, or if there are other reasons why the missing person almost certainly is dead – e.g., because the ship or aircraft the person was on board is missing – the time limit is merely six months, see section 6 of the Missing Persons Act. When a declaration of death has been issued, the missing person's estate will be administered as the estate of a deceased person, see section 6 of the Missing Persons Act.[83]

83. See Ernst Andersen, *Arveret (Succession Law)*, 257 et seq. (Juristforbundets Forlag 1967), and Finn Taksøe-Jensen, *Skifte af dødsbo*, 173 et seq. (DJØF 1998).

If it turns out that the person in question is alive when the declaration of death has been issued, he/she is entitled to try and recover his/her possessions from the recipients within ten years thereafter.

§2. THE HEIR

I. Capacity to Succeed

157. According to section 94(1) of the Inheritance Act, the person who has the right to succeed is the one who is alive when the intestate is dead, or who has been conceived prior to the intestate's death and subsequently born alive. That the beneficiary under the intestacy is not alive when the inheritance is actually paid is, thus, not decisive under Danish law. If a beneficiary dies in the period between the intestate's death and the payment of the inheritance, the inheritance will form part of the beneficiary's estate so that it, where necessary, may be used to satisfy the creditors and so that a potential surplus will go to the beneficiary's beneficiaries. That a child has been born before the intestate's death is not a condition for the child to inherit, as the provision states. The only requirement is that the child is conceived prior to the intestate's death, and subsequently that the child is born alive, which only matters where the father dies before the child has been born.[84]

II. Commorientes

158. As mentioned in subsection I, a beneficiary will be an inheritance link even though he/she dies between the intestate's death and the payment of the inheritance, provided, however, that it can be determined that one of them lived longer than the other. If two persons have died, and if it is not known which of them died first, neither will be found to have survived the other, see section 94(2) of the Inheritance Act. If, for instance, a father and his son die in an accident and the father dies instantly while his son dies later, the estate of the father is inherited by the son so that the surplus, after satisfying the creditors, is devolved upon the son's spouse and children. If it cannot be determined which of them survived the other in this case, the son will not inherit, and after him his heirs, but the inheritance will be devolved directly upon the grandchildren.[85]

---

84. See Rasmus Kristian Feldthusen, Ingrid Lund-Andersen & Linda Nielsen, *Arveretten (Succession Law)*, 13 et seq. (4th edn, Gjellerup/Gads Forlag 2014), Anitta Godsk Pedersen & Hans Viggo Godsk Pedersen, *Familie- og Arveret (Family and Succession Law)*, 238 et seq. (8th edn, Karnov Group 2013), and Irene Nørgaard, *Arveret (Succession Law)*, 38 et seq. (6th edn, Jurist- og Økonomforbundets Forlag 2013).

85. See Rasmus Kristian Feldthusen, Ingrid Lund-Andersen & Linda Nielsen, *Arveretten (Succession Law)*, 13 et seq. (1st edn, Thomson 2007); Anitta Godsk Pedersen & Hans Viggo Godsk Pedersen, *Familie- og Arveret (Family and Succession Law)*, 238 et seq. (8th edn, Karnov Group 2013), and Irene Nørgaard, *Arveret (Succession Law)*, 38 et seq. (6th edn, Jurist- og Økonoforbundets forlag 2013).

III. Unworthiness to Succeed

159. Has a person through an intentional violation of the Criminal Code caused the death of another, it can through a verdict be sentenced that the violator's right to inherit the killed, to insurance sums, pensions or other sums which depended on the death of the deceased, as well as it can be sentenced, that his/her inheritance, part of insurance sums or other sums shall not be increased as a result of his/her violation of the Criminal Code, see section 48(1) of the Inheritance Act. This section is discretionary. It is at the court's discretion in each case to decide whether a disqualification of the right to inherit shall occur or not. Disqualification can only occur when the perpetrator intentionally has violated the Criminal Code, although it is not necessary that the ensuing death was the desired effect. On the other hand, negligence cannot lead to the forfeiture of the right to inherit. Typically, disqualification will occur in cases involving wilful murder although violence resulting in death can also lead to the disqualification of the right to inherit. If the perpetrator was mentally incompetent, case law has shown that disqualification does not usually occur.

Disqualification affects only the perpetrator personally. His/Her descendants take his/her place when he/she has been denied the right to intestate succession. In the motifs of this section, it has been assumed that this is not only true in cases with intestate succession but also in cases where a will has been made. Furthermore, it is assumed that the right to retain undivided possession of estate is included in this section.

Disqualification of the right to inherit can also happen to the person who has tried to kill a relative in ascending line, has exercised violence to or seriously offended him/her through means which are in violation of the Criminal Code, see section 48(2). The injured party has to petition for the disqualification of the perpetrator, though.

Has a person been disqualified to inherit, he/she can partly or fully regain the right to inherit through a will, see section 48(4) for further details.[86]

§3. The System of Descent

I. The Classes of Heirs

A. *Surviving Spouse*

160. The position of the surviving spouse, concerning inheritance, depends on whether the deceased has any other heirs. A description of a spouse's legal position cannot however, be, limited to the rules applied to the right of succession, as these

86. See Anne Louise Bormann, Finn Taksøe-Jensen & Ib Hounsgaard Trabjerg, *Arveloven af 2008 med kommentarer (The Inheritance Act of 2008)*, 265 et seq. (1st edn, Thomson 2008); Anitta Godsk Pedersen & Hans Viggo Godsk Pedersen, *Familie- og Arveret (Family and Succession Law)*, 276 et seq. (8th edn, Karnov Group 2013), and Irene Nørgaard, *Arveret (Succession Law)*, 147 et seq. (6th edn, Jurist- og Økonomforbundets forlag 2013).

must be seen in connection with rules of a more variable nature, in order to obtain a more realistic picture of the spouse's legal position. There is also, in Denmark, a special institute with the name *uskiftet bo,* which means that the spouse can delay the transfer of joint ownership with (common) beneficiaries, so that the spouse can continue to maintain undivided possession over the entire joint estate, see below in section V.

1. The Surviving Spouse's Position When the Deceased Has Living Beneficiaries[87]

161. If the deceased has living beneficiaries, the surviving spouse's legal inheritance is half of the total inheritance, see the Inheritance Act section 9(1). The spouse's inheritance is therefore not influenced by the number of living beneficiaries. This must however be seen in connection with the fact that there is, in normal situations, a joint property ownership or separate property agreements with divorce, such that the spouse has half of the joint estate as statutory share of community property. In these typical situations, the spouse will therefore get three-fourths of the joint estate, whereas the living beneficiaries will receive one-fourth as inheritance.

When the division of the estate between the spouse and the beneficiaries of the deceased takes place, the spouse has the first right during the division before any of the other beneficiaries. The surviving spouse has the right to remove in advance items that are only for personal use as long as their worth is not in discrepancy to the worth of the spouse's rightful inheritance. The same applies for items that are intended to be used by children, see the Inheritance Act section 11(1) and (2). Because the items are removed in advance they are not included in the evaluation of the estate.

According to the Inheritance Act section 11(2), the spouse has the right to supplement his/her inheritance of the estate's profit in smaller estates. The law according to section 11(2) is not to be understood as a right of the spouse to remove assets of a certain value in excess of his/her inheritance. The provision allows the spouse to supplement the inheritance in such a way that, when combined with the person in question's own separate property agreement, it is of a value up to DKK 600,000. The size of the supplement inheritance is in this way not only dependent on the size of the deceased's estate, but also of the surviving spouse's estate. The amount is also regulated with regard to the price index in such a way that it follows price index changes. (In the year 2015 the amount is DKK 720,000, which is approximately

87. See Anne Louise Bormann, Finn Taksøe-Jensen & Ib Hounsgaard Trabjerg, *Arveloven af 2008 med kommentarer* (The Inheritance Act of 2008), 205 et seq. (1st edn, Thomson 2008); Rasmus Kristian Feldthusen, Ingrid Lund-Andersen & Linda Nielsen, *Arveretten* (Succession Law), 26 (4th edn, Gjellerup/Gads Forlag, 2014); Anitta Godsk Pedersen & Hans Viggo Godsk Pedersen, *Familie- og Arveret* (Family and Succession Law), 242 et seq. (8th edn, Karnov Group 2013); Irene Nørgaard, *Arveret* (Succession Law), 55 et seq. (6th edn, Jurist- og Økonomforbundets Forlag 2013), and Ingrid Lund-Andersen & Ingrid Magnussen, *'Danish Report' in European Family Law in Action.* Volume IV: Property Relations between Spouses, 25 et seq. (ed. Katharina Boele-Woelki, Bente Braat & Ian Summer, Antwerp, Oxford, New York 2009), can be seen in www.ceflonline.net.

EUR 96,000.) The right to supplement inheritance comes before an eventual will and the rightful inheritance of living beneficiaries, including their indefeasible share. It can be applied to both the joint estate and the deceased's separate estate.

162. The intention of supplement inheritance is to ensure the spouse a certain minimum after the division of the estate. It is therefore natural, in the calculation of the DKK 600,000, to include the benefits accumulated in connection with the death of deceased, for example value of the widow's pension, annuity and life insurance sums that are given to the surviving spouse and reimbursement for the loss of a supporter, see section 11(3) of the Inheritance Act. On the other hand the value of the surviving spouses special rights as described in the Legal Effects of Marriage Act section 15(2) is only included to the extend they would be a part of the community property in case of divorce or legal separation, see section 11(3). When the spouse inherits after section 11(2), the rules concerning division that apply after the death of a surviving spouse, when a spouse is a sole beneficiary, find almost similar application, see section 16 of the Inheritance Act.

Also concerning the right to demand the division of the estate's contents after evaluation, the spouse has the first right above the other beneficiaries in the will. According to the Inheritance Act section 6, every beneficiary in the will is entitled to demand division of the contents of his/her inheritance after valuation. If more than one beneficiary demands the same division, then lots are drawn on who will have the first right to the item(s) in question. If the item(s) in question is of particular sentimental value to the family, then the beneficiary who represents that particular branch of the family should be entitled to receive it, see section 6(2). If the spouse desires the same item as one of the other beneficiaries desires, then the spouses' wishes should be respected, see the Inheritance Act section 12(2) and 13(2). However, if the beneficiary is a child of the deceased but not of the surviving spouse, the child should have the item if the item in question is of particular sentimental value to that child, unless the item is of the sort mentioned in section 11(1) – for example, items that are only for personal use as long as their worth is not in discrepancy to the worth of the spouse's rightful inheritance and items that are intended to be used by children – is a property used as matrimonial home or is of the sort mentioned in section 91(2), see sections 12(2) and 13(2). Items mentioned in section 91(2) are items included in the joint estate and serving as a part of the family home, the surviving spouse's business or the family's car.

Concerning the assets of the estate that are included under joint ownership or a divorce agreement, the spouse has not only the right to a division as desired but also to demand the property even though the value is above his/her inheritance, if he/she pays the excess amount to the other beneficiaries in cash, see the Inheritance Act section 12(2). In this way the spouse can reduce the other forced heir's right to demand money by desiring the estates property for himself/herself. The surviving spouse must though respect the deceased's will, providing it has not exceeded its competence of testation, see the Inheritance Act section 14.

If the inheritance to the deceased's under age beneficiaries cannot be completed without the exchange of property or money, that is necessary for the surviving spouse to maintain the home or business, or the surviving spouse being without other items that are required to allow this, then the division can be delayed, see section 35. The inheritance is to be completed five years after the day of the death of the deceased unless the Probate Court decides a delay for further five years, see section 36. Normally the surviving spouse does not have to pay the inheritance until the children come of age, see sections 35 and 36 for further details. If a delay is granted, safety requirements must be made (see the Inheritance Act section 37).

2. The Spouse as the Sole Beneficiary

163. If the deceased does not leave any heirs of the body, then the spouse alone is the sole beneficiary, see section 9(2) of the Inheritance Act. Even though the spouse is the sole beneficiary when there are no children involved, the family of the deceased is not entirely out of the picture. Attached to the rule in section 9(2) there is a division rule in section 15, where the family of the deceased, when the surviving spouse dies, inherits a part of the inheritance. If the surviving spouse dies, after inheriting by the rules stated in section 9(2), without becoming married again, without having inherited a cohabitating partner (without marriage) on behalf of a will for cohabitating couples (section 87), without leaving a partner who has a right to inherit on behalf of a will for cohabitating couples (section 87) and without leaving living children, the estate is divided in such a way that half is given to the family of the first deceased and half is given to the family of the longest living spouse. If there are only beneficiaries to one of the spouses, they will inherit it all, see section 15(2). If the surviving spouse has made a will concerning a part of the estate the rest of the estate is divided according to section 15(1) and (2), unless something else follows from the will, see section 15(3).

Should the longest living spouse have children, or become remarried, then the right to inherit by the family of the first deceased is extinguished. The longest living spouse has also the right to make a will concerning the estate without considering the family of the first deceased, see section 15(4).[88]

B. Descendants

164. The closest family beneficiaries to the deceased are his/her children. Children inherit in an equal manner. If one child is dead, then the inheritance to this child is divided equally among the deceased's living children. Beneficiaries who are further removed inherit in the same manner see the Inheritance Act section 1. This regulation expresses the so-called per stripes rule, where each of the deceased's children form a branch and in this way, what is inherited by a dead child is inherited by his/her children equally. This will be illustrated by an example. If a deceased leaves

88. See for further details to this section Anne Louise Bormann, Finn Taksøe-Jensen & Ib Hounsgaard Trabjerg, *Arveloven af 2008 med kommentarer (The Inheritance Act of 2008)*, 107 et seq. (1st edn, Thomson 2008), Anitta Godsk Pedersen & Hans Viggo Godsk Pedersen, *Familie- og Arveret (Family and Succession Law)*, 246 et seq. (8th edn, Karnov Group 2013), and Irene Nørgaard, *Arveret (Succession Law)*, 59 et seq. (6th edn, Jurist- og Økonomforbundets Forlag 2013).

two children these will each inherit half. If these two children are dead and have left 2 and 3 children respectively, these children will inherit the parents share of the inheritance in such a way that the family with two children will each inherit half of the half that their parent inherited, this means a quarter of the entire estate each, whereas in the family with three children they will each receive a third of the half that their parent inherited. If one of the three children is dead and has two children then they will each inherit his sixth of the estate and will therefore each receive one-twelfth of the estate.

The deceased's spouse and children are considered to define the first line of inheritance. As long as there are beneficiaries within this line, then it is not recognized by the law that more distant relatives have the right to inherit.

Until the 1 January 2008, the Inheritance Act contained a rule concerning the right of priority of the children of the deceased to inherit up to their 21st birthday. However, these rules do not exist any longer.[89]

C. Ascendants

165. If there are no relatives in the first line of inheritance, then the estate is left to those within the second line of inheritance, which is the line of the parents; the parents and their issues. Between the parents, the inheritance is divided in half. If one of the parents is dead then his/her children will inherit this share in the same way as above according to section 1(2). If there are no children after one of the spouses, then the other spouse or his/her children will inherit everything, see the Inheritance Act section 2.

If there is no one in the second line of inheritance, then the inheritance will be passed on to the third line, that is the grandparents. The inheritance is divided in such a way that half is given to the grandparents on the mother's side and half to the grandparents on the father's side. In this way each of the grandparents will inherit a quarter. If one of the grandparents is dead then his/her children, but no other more distant relatives, will inherit his/her share. If there are no children by the dead grandparent, then the other grandparent on either the mother's or father's side or their children will inherit the dead grandparents share. If there are only beneficiaries on either the mother's or father's side then they will inherit everything, see the Inheritance Act section 3.

D. Collaterals

166. As described in sections A and B, it is stated by the law that distant relatives will not come into consideration as beneficiaries if the deceased has a living

89. See for further details about these rules Ernst Andersen, *Arveret (Succession Law)* (Juristforbundets Forlag 1967), 285 et seq.; Svend Danielsen, *Arveloven*, 269 et seq. (4th edn, Juristforbundets Forlag 1997); Hans Viggo Godsk Pedersen, *Familie- og Arveret (Family and Succession Law)*, 146 et seq. (5th edn, FSR 2001); Irene Nørgaard et al., *Arveret (Succession Law)*, 22 et seq. (3rd edn, DJØF 1998), and Finn Taksøe-Jensen, *Arveret (Succession Law)*, 2nd edn (Copenhagen: DJØF, 2000), 65 et seq.

spouse or children (first line of inheritance). If there are no members of the family within the first line, then the parents will become the beneficiaries. If one of the parents is dead, then their children will inherit this parent's share. This is the deceased's siblings or their children. This group is the second line of inheritance. If there are no members within this line, the inheritance will be given to the grand-parents. If one of them is dead then their children, but not any other descendants, will inherit this share. This means that cousins do not have any right to inheritance according to the Danish law.

The Danish system is therefore built up in such a way that there are no beneficiaries from a lower line as long as there are beneficiaries in a line of inheritance that is higher. This means that if the closest relative is a niece or nephew (second in line of inheritance) and an uncle (third in line of inheritance), then the niece or nephew will inherit everything.

II. Representation

167. According to the Danish law, it is a well-known principle that the children of the deceased beneficiary will inherit the share that the deceased has inherited. As explained in section I, each of the beneficiaries' children is considered as a branch of its own. If the beneficiary has three children, then each of these will inherit a third of this share. If one of these three children are dead and has two children then these two children will inherit their parent's third, and in this way they each will inherit one-sixth.

There is though one limitation to this law such that, the relatives in the 'grand-parent line' cannot fully use this law concerning the inheritance that is meant for the grandparents, if they lived, as only the children of the grandparents, but not more distant relatives, can inherit the share inherited by the grandparents, see above in section I.D. This law does not apply as a usual rule when the deceased has written a will. If a beneficiary is dead at the time of the execution of the will, then whether or not the children of the beneficiary are entitled to inherit the deceased beneficiary's share is affected by the interpretation of the coeased has written a will. If a beneficiary is dead at the time of the execution of the will, then whether or not the children of the beneficiary are entitled to inherit the deceased beneficiary's share is affected by the interpretation of the conditions stated within the will.

III. The Anomalous Succession

168. In Denmark, there are no general rules of returned succession. However, there is a limited reversion right concerning some adoptions which took place before 1 January 1957, see §4 for more details.

IV. Adoption

169. Adopted children are considered by the law as having the same legal inheritance rights as children of birth, unless stated otherwise in the laws governing adoption, see the Inheritance Act section 4. The implications concerning inheritance for adopted children have changed while not affecting legal position of the older adoption orders. It is therefore necessary to investigate, when the adoption was made, in order to assess the effect on the inheritance. Adoptions of an older date can still be provided with additions from the newer Adoption Acts. If this is the case, then the inheritance is decided by using the rules laid out in the newer rules.

If the adoption was completed before 1 April 1923, then the adopted child will inherit, and be inherited from, in accordance with the usual rules. Concerning the adoptive parent, the right to inherit is decided in accordance with the contents of the adoption grant. If it is not specified in the adoption grant that the child has the homely right of inheritance, then the adopted child will not inherit from the adoptive parent. Even if rightful inheritance from the adoptive parent does exist, rightful inheritance from the family of the adoptive parent does not exist nor can the beneficiaries of the adopted child inherit from the adoptive parent.

Concerning adoptions which took place between 1 April 1923 and 1 January 1957, the rules for inheritance are decided by the Adoption Act from 1923, unless the grant has been endorsed to as aforementioned. According to the Act from 1923, the adopted child and his/her beneficiaries will inherit from their blood relatives. The adopted child and his/her beneficiaries have also the same inheritance rights as birth children of the adoptive parent, but not after the relatives of the adoptive parent. On the other hand, the adopting parent will not inherit from the adopted child if he/she has any blood relatives who are his/her beneficiaries. There is through a limited reversion right; this means that the surviving adoptive parent has the right to inherit an equal amount to what the adopted child himself/herself inherited from the first deceased adoptive parent.

If the grant was made after 1 January 1957, or it has been updated with endorsements from this Act, there will be a complete change of family in such a manner that the adopted child becomes a complete member of the adoptive parents family as if the adopted child was a one of their own children, and the original rights of inheritance of the child and his/her family is cancelled.[90]

V. Undivided Possession of the Estate[91]

170. For most people it is a serious economic burden if their spouse dies and in connection with this a division of the estate is required among the children of the

90. See for further details Ernst Andersen, *Arveret (Succession Law)* (Juristforbundets Forlag 1967), 20 et seq.; Anne Louise Bormann, Finn Taksøe-Jensen & Ib Hounsgaard Trabjerg, *Arveloven af 2008 med kommentarer (The Inheritance Act of 2008)*, 49 et seq. (1st edn, Thomson 2008); Anitta Godsk Pedersen & Hans Viggo Godsk Pedersen, *Familie- og Arveret (Family and Succession Law)*, 241 et seq. (8th edn, Karnov Group 2013), and Irene Nørgaard, *Arveret (Succession Law)*, 44 et seq. (6th edn, Jurist- og Økonomforbundets Forlag 2013).

91. See in general to this section Anne Louise Bormann, Finn Taksøe-Jensen & Ib Hounsgaard Trabjerg, *Arveloven af 2008 med kommentarer (The Inheritance Act of 2008)*, 121 et seq. (1st edn, Thomson 2008); Anitta Godsk Pedersen & Hans Viggo Godsk Pedersen, *Familie- og Arveret (Family and Succession Law)*, 359 et seq. (8th edn, Karnov Group 2013), and Irene Nørgaard, *Arveret (Succession Law)*, 83 et seq. (6th edn, Jurist- og Økonomforbundets Forlag 2013).

deceased. In many cases, the surviving spouse or registered partner will have the possibility to decide whether or not to remain in possession of the estate, which means that the spouse can keep the estate as a whole. As separate ownership with divorce is considered as joint ownership with death of one-half of the partnership, then there is the possibility of having possession of the estate involved with separate ownership from divorce. On the other hand it is not possible to delay the division of items that were individually owned by the deceased (absolute separate property).

Undivided estate means, that the division of a joint home can be delayed to a later point in time; often until the death of the surviving spouse. The surviving spouse receives complete responsibility of the entire estate, also including all of the deceased's debt. This applies also as far as tax matters are concerned, as the surviving spouse will in the year of the death of their spouse be responsible for the taxes of both their incomes, as well as the surviving spouse takes over the applied tax values of the deceased, see the Taxation of Estate Act section 59. The tax is calculated from the deceased's and the surviving spouse's income, by using personal deduction in each case, and the tax makes up the sum of the calculated tax amount, see Taxation of Estate Act section 62 and the following sections.

A. *Conditions Applying to the Undivided Estate*

171. In order for the surviving spouse to be in undivided possession of an estate, the spouse must be solvent, see the Inheritance Act section 19. If there are children of the deceased who are not children of the surviving spouse, then the estate must be given to them unless they give their consent that the surviving spouse can continue to have undivided possession of the estate. If the child(ren) has(have) a legal guardian, then the consent must be given by the legal guardian. The consent of the legal guardian must be approved by the executor of the estate, though. Approval is given when it is deemed to be the most responsible action to take for both parties, after taking into consideration the needs of the beneficiary and the spouse's situation, see the Inheritance Act section 18. According to the rules laid down in section 18(3), it is the responsibility of the surviving spouse to assume the responsibility of providing for the minor(s) that were previously the responsibility of the deceased, when the estate is given to the spouse as an undivided estate. The executor of the estate does not usually give approval for the spouse to receive the undivided estate unless the minor is provided for in the home of the surviving spouse. That a beneficiary is bankrupt does not prevent him/her in allowing the deceased's spouse to have undivided possession of the estate, see the Bankruptcy Act section 34(3). A beneficiary can give their consent that the estate remains undivided in advance.

While it is true that a spouse that desires that the estate remain undivided must be solvent, it is not necessary that the deceased was solvent. As the surviving spouse also becomes responsible for the debt that the deceased had accumulated, if they receive the right to maintain the estate undivided, it may not be in the spouse's best interests if the deceased was insolvent. If the debt of the deceased is not major when seen in connection with the surviving spouse's assets, it is likely that maintaining the estate as undivided will be less of a liability than a division of the estate.

The deceased cannot prevent the surviving spouse from attaining the estate as undivided in his/her will, but the size of the divisible estate can be limited in the will to the assets of the spouse plus the combined indefeasible share. This is equal to five eights of the entire estate.

B. The Effect – Control

172. A consequence of receiving the undivided estate is that the spouse also becomes personally responsible for all of the deceased's responsibilities; see the Inheritance Act section 25. This has the consequence, that not only the joint estate but also the individually owned assets of the surviving spouse are liable. If the deceased was insolvent, then the surviving spouse or creditor can request of the Probate Court that the administration of the estate be handed over to the executor. If the request is granted, then the spouse will avoid involvement of his/her own belongings, if all the goods received from the division are returned, see section 25(2). As it is difficult to assess the true situation concerning the responsibilities of the deceased within a reasonable time span, it is necessary to call in the creditors of the deceased by preclusive advertisement for creditors see section 81 of the Administration of Estates Act.

Any assets that the surviving spouse may attain at a later point of time normally are included in the undivided estate unless a valid decision is made that they should remain solely as individual assets, see the Inheritance Act section 23. Concerning the rights that cannot be passed over, or are in some other way personal, the rules involved with the division of an estate can only be applied to the extent that they are applicable with the rules that apply for these special rights, see section 23(6). The regulation is worded in the same way as the Legal Effects of Marriage Act section 15(2), that is concerned with the division of ownership between spouses while they are both living. As far as pension schemes and insurances are concerned, the Inheritance Act contains special rules. According to section 23(2) life insurances and pensions and similar amounts which the surviving spouse attains from the deceased will not be included in the undivided estate if the estate is divided during the lifetime of the surviving spouse. According to section 23(3) the surviving spouses own life insurances, pension schemes and similar rights will not be included in the undivided estate if the estate during the lifetime of the surviving spouse.

While the regulation concerning individual ownership is also important concerning a division of ownership after the death of one spouse, the regulation in the Inheritance Act section 23 concerning personal rights will only be important with division of ownership during the lifetime of the surviving spouse.

The Inheritance Act section 23(7) gives the spouse the right to keep inheritance or any other gift outside of the undivided estate by demanding the division of ownership to occur within three months after the recital of the inheritance or gift.

While the personal rights of the surviving spouse are only included in the undivided estate as far as is legally feasible according to the rules that apply to these rights, the rights of the deceased are fully included in the undivided estate, unless they ceased to exist after death. This is a natural consequence of the fact that these rights are not excluded from the rules that apply to joint fortune. It is merely decided for these rules, that the rules concerning joint fortune can only be applied to the extent that they are in agreement with the rights.

While alive the spouse has full ownership of the estate, see the Inheritance Act section 24. In connection with a third party, it is possible for the spouse to show legal proof of ownership of the assets with a letter of administration. This ownership has some limitations, though, such as the fact that the spouse is not the true owner of the entire estate. The spouse is only entitled to ownership together with the beneficiaries of the deceased. The running of the estate must therefore be in accordance with the rights of the other beneficiaries. If the spouse abuses this right of ownership of the estate, then the beneficiaries can force a division of the estate according to section 29, as there can also be talk of a claim of compensation and maybe even a reversal of the presents according to the Inheritance Act sections 30 and 31. These rules are discussed further below in sections C and D.

If a will has been drawn up, it is obvious that the surviving spouse is only able to own the part of the estate that is left to him/her, see the Inheritance Act section 24(2). There is though a slight expansion of this share by the qualitative competence of the will, as he/she can reside over the individual items within his/her qualitative competence, even if they do not belong to his/her property, unless this is against the wishes of the deceased as written in a will drawn up after the regulation the Inheritance Act section 91 concerning assets belonging to this estate.

C. The Division

173. The undivided estate is divided, if this has not occurred previously, when the surviving spouse dies. The spouse is, in theory, entitled to divide the estate whenever he/she wishes to, see the Inheritance Act section 26(1). The division does not necessarily have to happen with all of the beneficiaries of the deceased; one can divide part of the estate with one or more of the beneficiaries while maintaining undivided estate with others. Nor can there be talk of an undivided estate, if all of the immediate beneficiaries to the deceased die see the Inheritance Act section 34.

Under certain conditions, it is necessary for the spouse to divide the estate to the beneficiaries of the deceased. This is applicable if the spouse remarries or enters a registered partnership with another person, see the Inheritance Act section 26(2). This section also states, that a beneficiary cannot give up the right to division of the estate without relinquishing the inheritance.

If the spouse is in possession of an undivided estate together with the under-age children of the deceased and these children are not joint children, then he/she is required to divide their share of the estate with each of them when they reach the legal age if they demand it, see the Inheritance Act section 27(1). If one of the under-age beneficiaries should die, the spouse is required to divide this share between the other beneficiaries, unless they are in agreement that the division is not necessary, see section 27(2). If these beneficiaries are under-age then the consent is given by their legal guardians with the approval of the executor of the estate, see section 27(3).

If a beneficiary can substantiate that the spouse, by abusing his/her disposal of the estate, has reduced its worth substantially or brought it in danger then he/she can demand that the spouse divide his/her share of the estate. The same applies if the spouse has neglected his/her responsibility towards him/her, see the Inheritance Act section 29(1). The second section of the regulation shows as examples of dispositions that can be considered abuse of disposal as being investment of unnecessarily high annuity, unreasonable spending of funds, buying an unreasonable large life insurance or pension and giving presents or other favours that are not compatible with the worth of the estate.

The amount that is considered abuse must be seen in relationship to the size of the estate to a certain degree, but it cannot be considered abuse if the spouse uses the resources of the estate on expenses that can be considered normal expenses. It will normally only be considered misuse if the spouse increases the daily expenditure to such a degree that it exceeds what is considered the norm of society concerning expansion of consumption and it decreases the worth of the estate.

The purchase of an annuity is very easily interpreted as irrelevant, as an annuity is a personal right that is held separate from the division of the estate as a whole. Still, the purchase of an annuity, that is considered of a reasonable size seen in relation to the spouse's wealth, cannot be the sole reason to demand a division of the estate. The beneficiary has a certain protection though, as he/she will be able to demand compensation if the spouse requests a division of the estate within a short time of the purchase of such an annuity, see the Inheritance Act section 30.

In order to assess whether a gift or other favour is out of proportion to the size of the estate's wealth, a total assessment of the relationship between the spouse and the estate is required. If one or more of the beneficiaries has earlier received large presents, then it cannot be considered disloyal disposition if the spouse gives the other beneficiaries equally large presents. If the spouse has substantial incomes, it is possible, considering the circumstances that substantial presents can be given without it being considered disproportionate to the size of the estate's wealth. If the beneficiaries earlier have agreed to the disposition, for instance in exchange of a beneficial and irreversible will being made by the spouse, then the disposal cannot be seen as 'abused'.

174. A special clause exists concerning farm estates, where it is normal that the division of the estate to a beneficiary or their spouse can be arranged at a special 'family price'. The reasoning for the acceptance of this special price is normally that the beneficiary concerned has participated in the running and maintenance of the farm while receiving no payment or only a very small compensation for his/her work. It is considered in case law, that a spouse that resides in an undivided estate can execute such a division, without it being considered misuse and therefore be the basis for a demand that the estate be divided.

The examples given in the Inheritance Act section 29(2) are typical examples of misuse, but this list is not intended to be complete. Another situation might be that the spouse to a large degree separates the relationship between the undivided estate and his/her personal property to the extent that it damages the estate. A division can be demanded not only when there has been dispositions of such a nature that the estate's worth has been reduced, but can also be demanded when there has been dispositions of such a nature that there has been a real danger for a substantial reduction in value. The latter could be when, for example, the spouse has taken unnecessary risks without consideration for the economic welfare of the estate.

Even though one or more of the beneficiaries has demanded a division of the estate, it is not necessary to divide the estate to all the beneficiaries, but only in regard to those who have demanded the division.

D. Compensation Right: Annulment of Presents

175. If the surviving spouse has, due to misuse of his/her disposal over the undivided estate, has reduced its value in such a way that it affects the children of the deceased, they can demand compensation in form of the remaining estate, or if it is deemed necessary, for half of the lost amount from the spouse's personal property, see the Inheritance Act section 30(1). In section 30(2) it is mentioned that a beneficiary can demand compensation if the surviving spouse has purchased personal assets and rights that can be partly or completely held separately in the event of a division of the estate (assets and rights as dealt with in the Legal Effects of Marriage Act sections 15(2) and 16(a). Even though a disposition would not be misuse, understood in the sense that it could be the grounds upon which to demand a division of the estate, it must be accepted that the situation can under the circumstances be reason enough to demand compensation where the spouse just before he/she himself/herself has asked for such a division of the estate. The compensation is taken from the remaining estate, or if necessary, up to half of the missing amount can be taken from the personal assets of the spouse. If the surviving spouse has used his/her own personal property for the benefit of the undivided estate compensation can be claimed by the division of the estate by the spouse or the spouse's beneficiaries, see the Inheritance Act section 30(3).

In the Inheritance Act section 30, only dispositions are discussed that are performed while the spouse was in possession of the undivided estate. Dispositions that were performed while both spouses were alive are covered by the Legal Effects of Marriage Act section 23.

If the surviving spouse has used funds from his/her own personal property for the benefit of his/her share of the property, it is accepted that he/she can demand compensation for these funds from his/her share of the property in advance. The same right falls to the deceased's beneficiaries, if the estate is first divided when the surviving spouse dies. If the spouse that dies first has used funds to the benefit of his/her private property, then his/her beneficiaries can demand compensation for this from the remaining estate in advance, see the Legal Effects of Marriage Act section 23.

If the surviving spouse has given away the majority of the estate, it will not be possible for the beneficiaries to receive compensation for the total amount lost in the remaining estate. It is therefore made possible, in the Inheritance Act section 31(1), that the beneficiaries can demand the gift annulled, as long as the receiver knew, or should have known, that the giver was in possession of an undivided estate and that the gift was out of proportion to the size of the estate. The same applies to a life insurance sum paid out if the insurance has been bought for the funds of the undivided estate, see section 31(2). The gift or the payment can only be annulled if the estate is divided, or the beneficiary that has filed the complaint has shown that he/she desires a division of the estate, see section 32(1). A beneficiary can independently file a complaint and demand that the estate is divided in spite of objections from the other beneficiaries. In terms of annulment the phrase 'favours that are out of proportion to the size of the estate', can be considered the same as those that are applicable when desiring a division of the estate, as described in section 29 above. After the death of the longest living spouse gifts and other favours cannot be annulled if the beneficiaries of the first deceased spouse can be fully compensated for the inheritance after the last mentioned without annulment of the favour, see the Inheritance Act section 31(3).

The annulment will only rarely be rejected because of the ignorance of the receiver as such large favours are normally only given to beneficiaries or other persons that are closely connected to the person who gives the gift. Such persons that are closely connected to the giver are normally aware that the surviving spouse is in possession of an undivided estate, and have a reasonable idea of the estates worth.

While there are no time limits concerning the desire for a division of the estate or the filing of a compensation demand, it is required that the beneficiary files a case for an annulment within one year of gaining knowledge of the gift. This can be better described as the time where he/she, when it is a question about a partially mutual burden and a partial gift, first became aware of the terms involved in the exchange. A case may though be raised within five years after the final execution of the gift, see the Inheritance Act section 32(2) and (3).

E. Execution of Division of the Undivided Estate

176. Concerning execution of division of the undivided estate there is a supposition that everything that the spouse owns belongs to the undivided estate, see the Inheritance Act section 33. The surviving spouse or his/her beneficiaries are therefore responsible in producing proof of separate ownership for whatever can be considered as separately owned.

The division of the assets of the undivided estate is executed in accordance with the regular rules applying to the division between beneficiaries and their spouses. This does not only apply to the purely qualitative rules concerning the right of execution and release, but also the spouse's benefits of division in the Inheritance Act sections 12 and 13 are applied. Concerning the division of the estate, the division of the inheritance is executed in accordance to the Inheritance Act section 28. The inheritance may be executed when the estate is divided; this means that inheritance is only given to the beneficiaries of the first deceased that are alive at the time of the division. As inheritance of the estate by a beneficiary who dies in the meantime is not incorporated, if this beneficiary has a spouse, it may be necessary to demand that if the estate is to be undivided, an irreversible will with the beneficiary's spouse as a subsidiary beneficiary has to be made.

As the inheritance is first executed at the time that the estate is divided there is no need to separate the part of the inheritance which would rightfully belong to the spouse if the estate is first divided when he/she dies. The division of the estate is in this case half to the beneficiaries of the spouse who died first and half to the beneficiaries of the spouse who died last. If the spouse who died first has in his/her will limited the dividable estate to the surviving spouse's statutory share of community property plus the combined indefeasible share, then this must be respected when dividing the estate between the family groups. The relationship of division of the estate between the family groups is not normally affected if the deceased has written his/her will to the benefit of the surviving spouse, as it cannot be assumed without any special basis, that such a will, will benefit the beneficiaries of the surviving spouse.

If the estate is divided while the surviving spouse is alive, then the inheritance from the first deceased spouse to the surviving spouse is calculated in such a way that if the first deceased has not written a will, then the surviving spouse inherits half of the deceased's statutory share of community property, which means that the surviving spouse inherits three-fourths of the joint estate, while the beneficiaries of the first deceased inherit one-fourth of the joint estate. If there are no beneficiaries to the first deceased, then the surviving spouse receives free disposal of the estate, see the Inheritance Act section 34 and division when the longest living spouse dies is executed in accordance to the rules in the Inheritance Act section 16, which are discussed above in section I.A.

If the first deceased died before 1 January 2008, the estate is to be divided in accordance with the former rules. The differences are mainly that the surviving spouse will inherit one-third of the estate while the beneficiaries of the deceased will inherit two-thirds which means that the surviving spouse will claim two-thirds of the entire estate and the beneficiaries after the deceased one-third after the estate has been divided.

§4. The Rights of the State on the *Bona Vacantia*

177. If there are no legal beneficiaries to the deceased or beneficiaries of the will, the estate becomes the property of the state, see the Inheritance Act section 95(1).

If the deceased has drawn up an invalid or contestable will and there are no legal beneficiaries, the state is allowed to raise an objection to the will. In section 95(2), it is though warranted, that the Ministry of Justice can decide that objections will not be raised to the will, which must be seen as the expressed last wishes of the deceased.

The Ministry of Justice can also under special circumstances renounce the inheritance in the favour of a partner from a steady relationship, step-children of the deceased who grew up as so, persons who have grown up with the deceased as stepbrother/sister, the relatives of the deceased if the estate in whole or partly originates from a common relative or other persons or institutions that were close to the deceased, see section 95(3).

If there are no legal beneficiaries and the deceased has not drawn up a will, it depends on special circumstances if the inheritance is to be renounced. Renouncement in favour of a steady partner can only be expected to occur if the relationship has been going on for a certain length of time.[92] There can also possibly be put weight into the factor of whether or not there has been a certain degree of joint economy. Why the couple have not married is not a factor taken into consideration, unless there is reason to believe that the deceased did not enter marriage in order to prevent his/her partner from inheriting.

If the state does not renounce the inherit, this decision can be brought to the Probate Court within three months, see the Inheritance Act section 96.

92. Anne Louise Bormann, Finn Taksøe-Jensen & Ib Hounsgaard Trabjerg, *Arveloven af 2008 med kommentarer (The Inheritance Act of 2008)*, 514 et seq. (1st edn, Thomson 2008); Anitta Godsk Pedersen & Hans Viggo Godsk Pedersen, *Familie- og Arveret (Family and Succession Law)*, 248 et seq. (8th edn, Karnov Group 2013); Rasmus Kristian Feldthusen, Ingrid Lund-Andersen & Linda Nielsen, *Arveretten (Succession Law)*, 201 et seq. (4th edn, Gjellerup/Gads Forlag 2014), and Finn Taksøe-Jensen, *Arveret (Succession Law)*, 161 et seq. and 257 et seq. (2nd edn, 2000).

Chapter 2. Testamentary Succession

178. If an individual wishes his/her estate to be divided differently than it would be after the normal legal rules, he/she can do so by making a will.

The drawing up of a will is in many ways different from bilateral agreements, especially concerning the fact that the dispoition is a one-way disposition, that is first put in to action, when the individual that draws up the will dies. This is the reason that the Inheritance Act contains special rules concerning the capacity of the individual, the formal requirements of the will, the interpretation and the contents, testamentary freedom as there are also rules concerning the will's invalidity.

A will, that does not fulfil the demands made for a will to be considered valid, can be declared invalid. In section 79 of the Inheritance Act, there is a rule which states that an objection against the validity of a will can be put forward by anyone, who is in line to inherit, if the will is declared invalid. The state is also able to object to a will, if there are no legal beneficiaries.

A will can often be used as a basis for a division of an estate, even though it does not fulfil all of the demands needed to be deemed valid, as long as there is not raised an objection to it; the will is contestable. If the will is against the interests of the public or the rights of a third party, it will often be considered void and cannot be used as the basis for a division of the estate. If there are other essential things that are lacking, these can also be reason to consider the will null and void, for example, if it is only in the form of a rough copy. The contesting of a will versus the effects of nullity will be discussed further below in connection with the individual cases.

If the estate is divided on the basis of a 'will' that is a nullity, then in connection with tax and duty the inheritance will be considered as acquired by the legal beneficiaries. The inheritance will also be seen as a gift to the receiver who will have to pay income tax of the value of the inheritance, unless the person is one of the individuals that has to pay gift tax. The difference between the contesting of a will and the effects of annulment is also of importance in connection to the creditors of the beneficiaries. According to the Bankruptcy Act section 34(1), the inheritance is considered a part of the estate of a debtor, unless it is otherwise stated in the valid will (i.e., a provision of settlement) or that the bankrupt estate has excluded itself from inheritance.

If there is included an order in the will that limits the inheritance of a debtor and there is a mistake in the will which causes the will to be void, the debtor will inherit and the money will be included in his/her estate. It is a consequence of this that the debtor cannot relinquish the inheritance. If the estate is divided before the bankruptcy because of such a regulation, this must be considered as a relinquishing of the inheritance which rightfully falls upon the debtor, which leads to the relinquishing as being encompassed by the annulment rule in the Bankruptcy Act section 65.[93]

93. See Lars Lindencrone Petersen & Anders Ørgaard, *Konkursloven*, 570 et seq. (12th edn, Karnov Group 2013), and Anders Ørgaard, *Konkursret*, 57 et seq. and 105 et seq. (11th edn, Jurist- og Økonomforbundets Forlag 2014).

§1. Capacity to Make a Will

179. Any person who is over 18 years of age or has entered marriage is entitled to reside over his/her estate by means of a will, see the Inheritance Act section 62(1). Any person who is over 15 years of age is entitled to reside over assets by means of a will if the person had the right to dispose freely over these assets in accordance with section 42 of the Guardianship Act, see the Inheritance Act section 62(2). The testator may lose the ability to sensibly reside over his/her estate because of mental illness, handicap, temporary loss of sanity or a similar condition, see the Inheritance Act section 74. Even though the testator was not able to reside sensibly over his/her estate, this does not mean that the will should be disregarded in its entirety. The will can disregard dispositions that could be said to be caused by abnormal mental conditions, while other dispositions can be maintained.

If a notary has stated, in an endorsement to the will in accordance with the regulation in the Inheritance Act section 63, that the testator must be considered to be capable of sensibly drawing up a will, then this must be accepted as proven, unless there are special circumstances that raise doubt to the validity of the endorsement, see the Inheritance Act section 70. A similar assumption is not applicable even if witnesses to a will have added a similar endorsement, see section 71. A will that is made by a minor or by a testator, that was not able to sensibly reside over the estate, is normally only contestable. Then, if the will has been made by a small child who is not able to understand the meaning of the will, or by a testator who is 'out of their mind' or near unconsciousness, the will is considered null and void outright. The will is invalid if the contents of the will are made through force, fraud or other unsuitable influence or by exploiting the testator because of his/her simple-mindedness, weakness or dependence, see the Inheritance Act section 75. The importance of force is not so commonly used as the reason for the contesting of a will. The rules concerning the signature or the acknowledgment of witnesses or notary almost totally exclude the possibility that a will can be made through use of force.

On the other hand, fraud or other unacceptable influences or abuse are easier to apply if one wants someone to make a will. It is though not every influence of the testator that can be considered grounds to render the will invalid. Only the more systematic and cunning influences are considered unsuitable.[94]

The stated reasons for invalidity in the Inheritance Act section 75 correspond to the vitiating factors in the Law of Contract. While the reasons for invalidity in the Law of Contract can be divided into strong and weak reasons for invalidity, the same does not apply in the Inheritance Act. With the regulations concerning the will there does not have to be the same considerations to a contracting party as there is with mutual liability agreements. The parts of the will which suffer from a vitiating

94. See Anne Louise Bormann, Finn Taksøe-Jensen & Ib Hounsgaard Trabjerg, *Arveloven af 2008 med kommentarer (The Inheritance Act of 2008)*, 343 et seq. (1st edn, Thomson 2008), and Anitta Godsk Pedersen & Hans Viggo Godsk Pedersen, *Familie- og Arveret (Family and Succession Law)*, 256 et seq. (8th edn, Karnov Group 2013).

are therefore invalid without consideration being taken for the good faith of the favoured.

§2. DIFFERENT TYPES OF WILLS

180. In the Inheritance Act sections 63–66, there are many demands to the form of the will that must be observed. A (standard) will has to be written and signed or acknowledged by a notary – a notarial will – or by two witnesses – a witnessed will, see sections 63 and 64. If the testator is in an emergency situation, such as he/she is not able to write a will which is in accordance with the normal rules, he/she is able to write a so-called emergency will (nuncupative will). An emergency will must still fulfil certain requirements, though.

I. Normal Wills

181. A testator can freely choose whether he/she will make a notary will or a witnessed will. At first the difference between these two is only that a notary will is signed or acknowledged by a notary, whereas a witnessed will is signed or acknowledged by two witnesses. There is though a greater chance that a notary will, will actually form the basis for a division of an estate than a witnessed will. Partly because a notary will stands stronger than a witnessed will because an endorsement by the notary that the testator was capable of sensibly residing over his/her estate has to be used as the basis for a division unless it can be proved otherwise. Of more importance, though, is the fact that the will cannot be lost if it is a notary will. There will normally be a clause written in a notary will which states that the copy of the will that is filed in the notary files has to be used as the basis for the division of the estate if the original is lost. Also when a notary will is made it is registered in the Central Register of Wills. It is therefore always possible to find out when a person dies if they have made a notary will, and if so to find out, by reading the contents of the copy, what was written. Such security is obviously not available for witnessed wills.

In the Inheritance Act section 64, can be found the precise rules for witnessed wills. There has to be at least two witnesses, who have to be present at the same time as witnesses to the will as desired by the testator and they must sign their names directly after the testator has signed or acknowledged the will. A witness to the will may not be a beneficiary of the will or be a relative of someone that is a beneficiary. Nor can a person be a witness if the will contains orders that benefit people or institutions that the witness has special interest in at the time of the making of the will. Special rules concerning what the witnesses should include in their endorsement of the will can be found in section 64(5).[95]

---

95. See Anne Louise Bormann, Finn Taksøe-Jensen & Ib Hounsgaard Trabjerg, *Arveloven af 2008 med kommentarer (The Inheritance Act of 2008)*, 368 et seq. (1st edn, Thomson 2008); Anitta Godsk Pedersen & Hans Viggo Godsk Pedersen, *Familie- og Arveret (Family and Succession Law)*, 253et seq.

Despite the rules laid down in sections 63 and 64, a testator can dispose over furniture and personal chattels by a will which just is written and subsequently signed, see section 66.

II. Emergency Wills (Nuncupative Wills)

182. A person who is unable to draw up a will which complies to the standard form, because of illness or some other form of emergency situation, can draw up an emergency will, see the Inheritance Act section 65. Up to 1 January 2008 an emergency will could only be an oral witnessed declaration or a so-called holographic will. A holographic will is a will that is made by the testator's own handwriting and subsequently signed. However, from 1 January 2008 an emergency will can be any other form of authentic will, see the Inheritance Act section 65.

The drawing up of emergency wills is only permitted when the testator is unable to draw up a will by the normal rules because of illness or some other emergency situation. In case law it is recognized that an emergency will can be warranted for people with suicidal tendencies, as they will often suffer from a psychological blocking against writing a will by the normal procedures.

An emergency will is only valid for a limited time, even though it is made in an emergency situation. If more than three months have passed, in which there has been no reason why a will could not have been drawn up by normal procedures, the emergency will is rendered invalid.[96]

III. Non-compliance of the Recognized Procedures Concerning Format

183. If the will does not comply with the regulations concerning format, it is declared invalid, if the will is contested, see the Inheritance Act section 69. It is not necessary in order to disregard a will, that the will has been contested. If it is not contested, the will can still be used as a basis for the division of the estate, if it is deemed to give a realistic picture of the deceased's final wishes. If, on the other hand, the will is a rough copy it cannot be used as an estimation of the final wishes of the deceased. A rough copy is therefore considered null and void which cannot be used for the dividing of the estate.

Provided that it can be assumed that a disposition gives a realistic view of the final wishes of the testator, even dispositions that are not in the required form, can be used as the basis for the division of the estate, provided none of the beneficiaries object. This applies to, for example, deposits into bank accounts in another person's

(8th edn, Karnov Group 2013), and Irene Nørgaard, *Arveret (Succession Law)*, 168 et seq. (6th edn, Jurist- og Økonomforbundets Forlag 2013).

96. See Anne Louise Bormann, Finn Taksøe-Jensen & Ib Hounsgaard Trabjerg, *Arveloven af 2008 med kommentarer (The Inheritance Act of 2008)*, 380 et seq. (1st edn, Thomson 2008); Anitta Godsk Pedersen & Hans Viggo Godsk Pedersen, *Familie- og Arveret (Family and Succession Law)*, 254 et seq. (8th edn, Karnov Group 2013), and Irene Nørgaard, *Arveret (Succession Law)*, 178 et seq. (6th edn, Jurist- og Økonomforbundets Forlag, 2013).

name, envelopes with the name of the person written on them or items marked with the person's name.

§3. The Joint Will

184. The Danish Inheritance Act contains some special rules concerning joint wills. Usually, it is anyway the case that mutual wills will normally be set up in a single document, so that at the same time it is also a joint will. A mutual will can obviously be changed if both parties are in agreement. As a starting point a mutual will can be revoked by one of the parties concerned, but the revocation is only valid if the other party is notified, unless this is impossible because of special circumstances, see the Inheritance Act section 80. The notification is normally considered impossible if one party is so psychologically weak that he/she is not able to comprehend what the message means. In this case, it is recognized that a retrieval can be allowed if the message is given to a guardian, if any, or is implicated in an open manner, for example, by the drawing up of a new will for the notary. If one of the parties revokes a mutual will, this will is normally revoked in its entirety. However, revocation is impossible if the will is made irrevocable according to the rules in the Inheritance Act section 68.

A special rule for spouses can be found in the Inheritance Act section 81. If the mutual will between spouses contains orders concerning the division of the inheritance, it is possible for the surviving spouse to change the orders concerning his/her individual property and his/her part of the estate with the exemption of the legitimate portion to the descendants. This does not apply to the inheritance which according to the will is given to the descendants of the first deceased or to half of the inheritance which according to the will is given to their common descendants, see the Inheritance Act section 81(2). However, it is possible to state otherwise, see section 81(3). The rule in section 81 also applies to other mutual wills, see the Inheritance Act section 82.

If a mutual will between spouses contains orders concerning the division of the inheritance after the death of the longest living spouse and if the surviving spouse is committed not to change or revoke the will, then his/her right to dispose over the assets *inter vivos* is limited, see the Inheritance Act section 83. The surviving spouse is not allowed to give gifts or some of the inheritance in advance if the amount is out of proportion to the size of the estate. Neither is the surviving spouse allowed to give a favour in form of a life insurance if it bought for an amount which is out of proportion with the size of the estate. If the surviving spouse has acted to the contrary to these rules the beneficiaries can demand the gift annulled as long as the receiver knew, or should have known, the facts, see sections 83(2). The same applies to a life insurance sum paid out, see section 83(3). After the death of the longest living spouse, gifts and other favours cannot be annulled if the beneficiaries of the first deceased spouse can be fully compensated for the inheritance after the last mentioned without annulment of the favour, see the Inheritance Act section 83(4).

Cohabitating partners (without marriage) has since 1 January 2008 had the opportunity to make a will for cohabitating couples, see the Inheritance Act sections 97-89. In that will it can be decided that the couple are to inherit each other as if they were married. However, in the will it is possible to state some limits of the effects which means that it not necessary to give the partner all the benefits a spouse normally has. To do this it is necessary that it is a steady relationship. According to the Inheritance Act section 88 some conditions must be met as a condition to make such a will. The couple may not be married and most of the conditions for marrying must be met. Furthermore, according to section 88(2) the will is only valid, if they lived together at the time of the death of the first deceased partner and (1) waited, had or have had a common child, or (2) had lived together for the last two years.[97]

§4. Revocation of a Will

185. The revocation of an order in a will must be done in the form of a will, see the Inheritance Act section 47.

Until 1 January 2008 a revocation might be informal. If it can be proved that an informal revocation had taken place before that date it will still have effect. Even though a will is not revoked it can be considered invalid because the circumstances have changed. According to a rule in the Inheritance Act section 67(2), a will that is set up to benefit a spouse should be considered invalid after a separation or a divorce, unless special circumstances speak against this. The same applies with the end of a steady relationship, see section 67(3). A testator can normally freely draw up, change or revoke a will. There are though limitations for this with mutual wills, see above in §3.

It can be required that more detailed agreements concerning inheritance are made. From the viewpoint of the beneficiaries this can be a total or partial relinquishing of the right to inherit. From the spouse's viewpoint maybe also a total or partial relinquishing of statutory share of community property. In contrast to this, it can also be necessary to prevent the testator from changing the division of the estate between the beneficiaries. Therefore, it is also recognized that a testator can sometimes find it necessary to commit himself/herself not to draw up, change or revoke a will. Such agreements or promises are only binding if they are given in the form of a will, see the Inheritance Act section 68. It must also be communicated to the beneficiary involved or another person who can receive the promise on the behalf of the beneficiary.[98]

97. See Anne Louise Bormann, Finn Taksøe-Jensen & Ib Hounsgaard Trabjerg, *Arveloven af 2008 med kommentarer (The Inheritance Act of 2008)*, 451 et seq. and 466 et seq. (1st edn, Thomson 2008); Anitta Godsk Pedersen & Hans Viggo Godsk Pedersen, *Familie- og Arveret (Family and Succession Law)*, 273 et seq. and 279 et seq. (8th edn, Karnov Group 2013), and Irene Nørgaard, *Arveret (Succession Law)*, 241 et seq. (6th edn, Jurist- og Økonomforbundets Forlag 2013).

98. See Anne Louise Bormann, Finn Taksøe-Jensen & Ib Hounsgaard Trabjerg, *Arveloven af 2008 med kommentarer (The Inheritance Act of 2008)*, 451 et seq. (1st edn, Thomson 2008); Anitta Godsk Pedersen & Hans Viggo Godsk Pedersen, *Familie- og Arveret (Family and Succession Law)*, 279 et seq. (8th edn, Karnov Group 2013), and Irene Nørgaard, *Arveret (Succession Law)*, 283 et seq. (6th edn, Jurist- og Økonomforbundets Forlag 2013).

§5. Provisions in a Will

186. A will that has an illegal intention or an intention that is dishonest is seen in the eyes of the law, with support in the Danish Law section 5(1)(2), as being null and void. If a favour in the will has the condition that the beneficiary must commit an illegal action, then that part of the will must be considered null and void. The testator can request legal conditions in order to inherit, though. The reason for the condition can though be of such a nature that it must be ignored because of 'integrity' or 'distasteful considerations', if the testator is trying to influence the beneficiary's personal relationship. It is at this point of time, neither in theory nor in practice, clear where the line for the allowable conditions is placed. Such conditions are presumably rare in Denmark.[99]

A condition within a will is invalid if it demands a use or destruction of parts of the estate and this condition has no reasonable meaning, see the Inheritance Act section 78. The testator must be given a large degree of freedom to decide, for example, whether or not letters and certain personal effects should be destroyed and to support certain causes even though these may not be normally considered appropriate. The regulation is therefore only concerned with unreasonable dispositions, see also the expression in the regulation 'obviously without reasonable sense'. It could seem appropriate to consider such dispositions as null and void immediately, but it is stated in the law that invalidity only becomes applicable when an objection is raised.

A testator can normally not leave it to another person to decide who should be his/her beneficiaries. It is accepted, though, that the testator can give the power to decide on the finer parts of the will to the executor of the estate. Such matters could be the compilation of details concerning trust instruments, deciding who should inherit smaller amounts or the usual personal belongings that are not worth a great deal, as well as the division of the separate assets between the beneficiaries.

It is written in the Inheritance Act section 60(2), that property of the deceased cannot by means of a will be given to descendants of descendants not yet alive at the time of the testator's death. This regulation is similar to section 84 of the Constitution which is directed towards the establishment of family settlements that are characterized by allowing the estate to be passed down through the generations in accordance to a special set of inheritance rules within a particular family. It is characteristic for such a family settlement, that the individual 'beneficiaries' do not become the owners of the capital that is their inheritance, but only receive the right to dispose of it as they see fit. By preventing the user of the capital the ability to waste the money by 'stupid' fiscal arrangements and by preventing that the usual rules for inheritance are applied, it is possible to collect large sums of capital within the hands of few. Section 60(2) in the Inheritance Act does though set a limit to the extent of which this can occur. The order does not prevent a testator in giving a son

---

99. See Ernst Andersen, *Arveret (Succession Law)* 82 et seq. (Juristforbundets Forlag 1967); Anne Louise Bormann, Finn Taksøe-Jensen & Ib Hounsgaard Trabjerg, *Arveloven af 2008 med kommentarer (The Inheritance Act of 2008)*, 422 (1st edn, Thomson 2008); Anitta Godsk Pedersen & Hans Viggo Godsk Pedersen, *Familie- og Arveret (Family and Succession Law)*, 259 (8th edn, Karnov Group 2013), and Irene Nørgaard, *Arveret (Succession Law)*, 157 et seq. (6th edn, Jurist- og Økonomforbundets Forlag 2013).

the right to dispose over a property or the interest of a certain capital, and further giving a grandchild the same rights in the event of the son's death, and so on, as long as he only names an individual that is born at the time of his death and one unborn after this. It is first considered not to be in accordance with section 60(2) if there is named two unborn successors – successive inheritance – in a row. It is, on the other hand, considered to be in accordance with section 60(2) to make a cumulative inheritance plan, for example, by deciding that the unborn children of the residing successor should share his capital in the event of his death. It is neither against the rules laid out in section 60(2) to make an alternative line of inheritance concerning the unborn people at the time of the testators death, for example, to decide that the capital should be given to the children of the most recent successor or, if he has no children, then the second to last successor's children.

The Inheritance Act section 60(2) does not prevent the establishment of a family fund – family scholarship, foundation or fund – when it is not based upon property and when it is left to the discretion of the board to decide which relatives should benefit from the fund. It is neither wrong, when considering the rules in section 60(2), to make orders within the fund to the benefit of certain relatives. The Act of Parliament concerning funds and associations does restrict further access to favour members of certain families. The Act concerning funds and institutions, section 7, and Acts concerning corporate privately owned business funds, section 28, prevent funds, that were established after 1 January 1985, to give preferential support to members of a certain family or families other than the individuals, that lived at the time of establishment and one other in relation to the unborn generations. In section 7(2) and section 28(2) of the Acts, the restriction is expanded so it also includes orders that give members of a certain family or families the preferential right to certain jobs or in some other way, such as a work compensation, to build up economic goods from the fund or from a company in which the fund has the deciding influence. The restriction does though not encompass the job as a member of the board.

If there is an order in the will that is not in accordance with the rules in section 60(2) it is considered null and void. The executor of the estate must make sure that the invalid order in the will is disregarded.[100]

§6. Restrictions

I. The Legitim

187. The testator can by making a will, of course, only dispose of the property that he/she owns. If he/she has at his/her disposal the property of a third party, or for example, if he/she decides to settle the inheritance that he/she would inherit from the property of a spouse, orders concerning these items will be considered null and

100. See for further details Anne Louise Bormann, Finn Taksøe-Jensen & Ib Hounsgaard Trabjerg, *Arveloven af 2008 med kommentarer (The Inheritance Act of 2008)*, 335 et seq. (1st edn, Thomson 2008); Anitta Godsk Pedersen & Hans Viggo Godsk Pedersen, *Familie- og Arveret (Family and Succession Law)*, 261 et seq. (8th edn, Karnov Group 2013), and Irene Nørgaard, *Arveret (Succession Law)*, 157 et seq. (6th edn, Jurist- og Økonomforbundets Forlag 2013).

void. As far as the testator's property is concerned, there exists quantitative limitations for the testamentary freedom of the will of the testator who has children or a spouse. A testator who is married with a joint estate is also bound by qualitative restrictions in the testamentary freedom.

A. *The Quantitative Competence*

188. One-fourth of the rightful inheritance that the children and spouse of the testator receive is indefeasible share, see the Inheritance Act sections 5 and 10. That an inheritance is an indefeasible share means that it cannot be denied from the beneficiaries by means of a will. However, the testator has the opportunity to restrict the inheritance to each of his/her children to DKK 1,000,000, see the Inheritance Act section 5(2). The amount is regulated with regard to the price index in such a way that follows price index changes. (In the year 2015, the amount is DKK 1,190,000, which is about EUR 160,000.)

The testator does not normally have the right to decide over the indefeasible share in his/her will, see the Inheritance Act section 50(1). Until 1 January 2008, the indefeasible share gave the beneficiary a qualitative protection as well. The forced heir had a valid right to a share of the estate, which could not be reduced to a purely monetary demand if he/she objects to this. However, due to the Inheritance Act section 50(2) the testator can state in his/her will that a 'forced heir' shall have his/ her inheritance paid in cash.[101]

If a beneficiary is under 18 years, the testator can decide to whom the indefeasible share shall be given if the beneficiary dies before the age of 18 years without having married, see the Inheritance Act section 51. If a 'forced heir' cannot sensibly make a will and this be considered lasting, there is a possibility under the circumstances for the testator to decide to whom the indefeasible share shall be given when the beneficiary dies, see section 52 where further conditions are laid down.

If the deceased has given an advance of the inheritance to a beneficiary, such that this is to be deducted from the beneficiary's will, this is included in the calculation of the indefeasible share, see the Inheritance Act section 47(1). This can mean that the testator has the right to reside over more than three-fourths of the remaining estate. If the advance was larger than the calculated share of inheritance of the beneficiary, the amount included can only be as large as the share of inheritance, answering hereby to, see section 47(1). The testator can in this way then reside over more than three-fourths of the remaining estate as ordered by the will.

If the advancement of the inheritance is taken from the joint estate and given to a common child of a couple, and a reduction in the inheritance is to take place when the first parent dies so it is in accordance to the judicial implication in the Inheritance Act section 44, then it is necessary that the will of the first deceased is changed,

101. See Anne Louise Bormann, Finn Taksøe-Jensen & Ib Hounsgaard Trabjerg, *Arveloven af 2008 med kommentarer (The Inheritance Act of 2008)*, 56 et seq. (1st edn, Thomson 2008); Anitta Godsk Pedersen & Hans Viggo Godsk Pedersen, *Familie- og Arveret (Family and Succession Law)*, 262 et seq. (8th edn, Karnov Group 2013), and Irene Nørgaard, *Arveret (Succession Law)*, 238 et seq. (6th edn, Jurist- og Økonomforbundets Forlag 2013).

as far as necessary, in order for this reduction to be possible. If the reduction is larger than the inheritance of the beneficiary from the first deceased parent, and his/her inheritance from the surviving spouse is for the same amount, then there is only added to statutory share of community property and the indefeasible shares the value of his/her legal inheritance from both parents, see section 47(2).

In the cases where a beneficiary has relinquished his/her inheritance, and there are other forced heirs, it has been doubtful whether or not this share should be given to the testator so that he/she can reside over it by will. This is though now accepted in case law, see U 1993.799/1Ø. A requirement for this to occur is though, that the beneficiary who has relinquished his/her right to inherit, or his/her relatives are alive when the testator dies, as the other forced heirs' share is increased when another forced heir dies.[102] If the beneficiary has received compensation in connection with relinquishing his/her rightful inheritance, it must be assumed that this is the same as an advancement of inheritance and is included when calculating the share of inheritance and indefeasible share.

B. *The Qualitative Competence*

189. If the testator has any forced heirs, he/she is entitled to reside freely over the individual items, as long as they are part of the estate in excess of the legitimate portion. If the testator is married, then there are special rules that apply depending on whether the items are individually owned or included in the joint estate. He can freely reside over the items in the separate property provided that their worth does not exceed the value of the legitimate portion, see the Inheritance Act section 90.[103]

Concerning the joint estate he/she is allowed to reside over three-fourths of the value of his/her statutory share of community property, but he/she can only reside over the items that he/she has contributed to the marriage, see the Inheritance Act section 91(1). The right to reside over the assets of the estate is in the meanwhile – as is the right to reside while alive and married – limited, so he/she cannot limit the spouse's ability to maintain the household and business.

According to the Inheritance Act section 91(2), the other spouse's consent is required concerning the drawing of a will over the following assets, provided they are included in the joint estate:

(1) Property that serves as the family's home or where both of the spouses' or the other spouse's business is involved. The order must be assumed to include the

102. See Anne Louise Bormann, Finn Taksøe-Jensen & Ib Hounsgaard Trabjerg, *Arveloven af 2008 med kommentarer (The Inheritance Act of 2008)*, 242 et seq. (1st edn, Thomson 2008), Anitta Godsk Pedersen & Hans Viggo Godsk Pedersen, *Familie- og Arveret (Family and Succession Law)*, 264 (8th edn, Karnov Group 2013), and Irene Nørgaard, *Arveret (Succession Law)*, 133 et seq. (6th edn, Jurist- og Økonomforbundets Forlag 2013).

103. See Anne Louise Bormann, Finn Taksøe-Jensen & Ib Hounsgaard Trabjerg, *Arveloven af 2008 med kommentarer (The Inheritance Act of 2008)*, 481 et seq. (1st edn, Thomson 2008); Anitta Godsk Pedersen & Hans Viggo Godsk Pedersen, *Familie- og Arveret (Family and Succession Law)*, 264 et seq. (8th edn, Karnov Group 2013); Irene Nørgaard, *Arveret (Succession Law)*, 241 et seq. (6th edn, Jurist- og Økonomforbundets Forlag 2013).

same property as is mentioned in the Legal Effects of Marriage Act section 18, see above in Part 3, Chapter 1 §3.
(2) Contents of the joint home and the other spouse's necessary work tools. It may be assumed that the contents and necessary work tools in this order are the same as mentioned in the Legal Effects of Marriage Act section 19.
(3) A motor vehicle which has been used by the other spouse.

The Inheritance Act section 91 does not contain a corresponding prohibition to the one in the Legal Effects of Marriage Act section 19, concerning the disposal of items that are bought for the use of the children. The surviving spouse has the right to remove the relevant items in advance, see the Inheritance Act section 11(1). This makes it unnecessary to include these items in the will.

If the qualitative competence is exceeded according to section 91(2), the will is contestable. The spouse can of course refrain from objecting to the particular benefit. The contesting of a will does not necessarily mean that the will is worthless in a legal context, as a changed interpretation of the will can lead to the payment of the individual in question for an amount equal to the value of the contested asset. It can therefore be a good idea to omit to contest the will under certain conditions.

The surviving spouse must, in principle, accept the will of the decedent spouse. In small estates the spouse can, with the first right in the division of the estate as explained in the rule in the Inheritance Act section 11(2) concerning the right to supplement the inheritance with up to DKK 600,000, make a large reduction in the will.

As a starting point, the testator cannot reside over the indefeasible share in his/her will. There do exist different exceptions to this rule, though.

The testator can, in his/her will, decide that the inheritance that is given to a beneficiary has to become part of that individual's separate property, see the Legal Effects of Marriage Act section 28(a).

The testator can also, by way of his/her will, make decisions concerning the inheritance that restrict the inheritance in such a way that the beneficiary cannot reside over the inheritance, but only the profit from it.

The testator can also give a beneficiary the first right to claim his/her inheritance in the form of certain particular assets, see the Inheritance Act section 50(2). Finally it must be mentioned that there, until 1 January 2008, were special rules which gave the owner of an agricultural property a certain extension of the testamentary freedom. These special rules do not exist any longer.

II. Maintenance Provisions

190. The rules concerning the indefeasible share in the Inheritance Act sections 5 and 10, and the spouse's right to a supplement inheritance from the Inheritance Act section 11(2), can be considered as rules, that are made to ensure the surviving family a certain minimum inheritance. The rule in the Inheritance Act sections 35–39, concerning the option of the surviving spouse to receive respite in the form of payment of the inheritance left to the under-age children of the deceased under special conditions, is a rule that is also concerned with ensuring the surviving spouse a certain minimum. Apart from these rules, there are no specific rules concerning inheritance in the Danish legal system which are made to ensure the surviving family of a deceased.

§7. Interpretation of a Will

191. When interpreting an order in a will, one is not bound by the Danish legal system to follow the will word for word. In principle, one can freely interpret the contents and one is also able to disregard certain orders in the will, if the testator is considered to have been lead astray. This is stated in the Inheritance Act section 77. If, for example, an order in the will is clearly motivated as a payment to an employee for honesty and good service and it turns out that the person in question has been involved in fraudulent conduct towards the deceased, it is then within the law to disregard the inheritance.

If a will has, because of a typing error or some other mistake, an order that is not as intended, then it should be given out according to the true intentions of the testator, if these can be deciphered, see the Inheritance Act section 76. It is obvious from the above, that the most important is what the testator had intended with his/her will, and not necessarily how it has been written. On the other hand, it is natural that the courts will be very careful with adjusting orders in a will unless there is a very good basis on which to do so. As an example of this one can look at the judgment from the Supreme Court in U 1982.319 H, where the Supreme Court could not find evidence, that it was not the intention of the deceased to only give the 'favourite nephew' a grandfather clock, even though the value was less than what the other beneficiaries received.[104]

If an order has been formulated in such a way, that it is impossible to ascertain what the testator wished, then it must be disregarded as it is completely without reason, see the Inheritance Act section 76.

104. See for further details Anne Louise Bormann, Finn Taksøe-Jensen & Ib Hounsgaard Trabjerg, *Arveloven af 2008 med kommentarer (The Inheritance Act of 2008)*, 407 et seq. (1st edn, Thomson 2008); Anitta Godsk Pedersen & Hans Viggo Godsk Pedersen, *Familie- og Arveret (Family and Succession Law)*, 265 et seq. (8th edn, Karnov Group 2013), and Irene Nørgaard, *Arveret (Succession Law)*, 191 et seq. (6th edn, Jurist- og Økonomforbundets Forlag 2013).

Chapter 3. Acts *Inter Vivos* Related to the Estate

§1. Estate Planning

192. As a part of the planning of the transfer of the estate from the testator to the beneficiaries, the testator has several different possibilities to enter agreements with the beneficiaries. On the other hand, the beneficiaries cannot, while the testator lives, make agreements between themselves concerning the division of the estate after the testator's death without the testator being involved in the process as well. It is in accordance with the Inheritance Act. Section 41, which states that a beneficiary cannot sell, mortgage or in any other way reside over an inheritance, that he/she is expecting, in the same way an inheritance is excluded enforcement proceedings. An agreement concerning the transfer or the relinquishing of an expected inheritance, that is given to another beneficiary, is null and void. On the other hand a beneficiary can relinquish an expected inheritance to the testator himself/herself, see the Inheritance Act section 42. The relinquishment can be given with or without compensation. The relinquishment of an inheritance also commits the children of the beneficiary in question, unless their right to inherit has been a condition. Such a relinquishment of an inheritance while still giving the children the right to inherit can be motivated by the wish to allow the children to inherit and save the Inheritance Tax between the first and the second generation. A relinquishment can also be motivated by the wish to keep the inheritance away from an insolvent beneficiary's creditors. It is also possible to give the beneficiary the right to the interest from the capital. In this way the beneficiary is considered, while the capital does not fall into the hands of creditors.[105]

A testator also has the possibility to arrange a deal with some of the beneficiaries, that they partly or totally relinquish their right to inherit, if the testator favours one or more of the beneficiaries by way of his/her will. Such an arrangement can formally be seen through by way of relinquishment – if necessary, subject to the making of the will – as well as an irrevocable will. According to the Danish legal system, a testator can agree to relinquish the right to make or reverse or change his/her will. It is stated in the Inheritance Act section 68(2), that such an action is valid if the testator makes the commitment in the form of a will. As it is promise to the beneficiaries, it is obvious, that this promise must be given to the beneficiaries.[106]

---

105. See Anne Louise Bormann, Finn Taksøe-Jensen & Ib Hounsgaard Trabjerg, *Arveloven af 2008 med kommentarer (The Inheritance Act of 2008)*, 231 et seq. (1st edn, Thomson 2008); Rasmus Kristian Feldthusen, Ingrid Lund-Andersen & Linda Nielsen, *Arveretten (Succession Law)*, 195 et seq. (4th edn, Gjellerup/Gads Forlag 2014); Anitta Godsk Pedersen & Hans Viggo Godsk Pedersen, *Familie- og Arveret (Family and Succession Law),* 282 et seq. (8th edn, Karnov Group 2013), and Irene Nørgaard, *Arveret (Succession Law),* 123 et seq. (6th edn, Jurist- og Økonomforbundets Forlag 2013).

106. See Anne Louise Bormann, Finn Taksøe-Jensen & Ib Hounsgaard Trabjerg, *Arveloven af 2008 med kommentarer (The Inheritance Act of 2008)*, 385 et seq. (1st edn, Thomson 2008); Rasmus Kristian Feldthusen, Ingrid Lund-Andersen & Linda Nielsen, *Arveretten (Succession Law)*, 107 et seq. (4th edn, Gjellerup/Gads Forlag 2014); Anitta Godsk Pedersen & Hans Viggo Godsk Pedersen, *Familie- og Arveret (Family and Succession Law),* 281 (8th edn, Karnov Group 2013), and Irene Nørgaard, *Arveret (Succession Law)*, 248 et seq. (6th edn, Jurist- og Økonomforbundets Forlag 2013).

§2. DONATIONS

193. As long as the person is alive, he/she can normally reside freely over the contents of his/her estate, also in the way of giving the possessions away. This has though the limitations according to the Legal Effects of Marriage Act if the person is married, as there are also limitations in connection with the creditors if the person involved is insolvent. The beneficiaries though, cannot hinder that the testator gives his/her fortune away to others.

If the testator wishes to benefit certain individuals or causes, while wanting to keep his/her estate intact until his death, then he/she must make out a will. This principle is maintained by section 93 of the Inheritance Act. According to the law, the rules for wills also apply for promises of presents, that cannot be carried out until the time of his death, and presents that are given from his/her deathbed.

As can be seen, the Inheritance Act section 93 encompasses two types of dispositions; deathbed donations and donations that do not take effect until the time of the death of the giver, the real *donatio mortis causa.* As a special group, that is not mentioned in the regulation, it is sometimes applied to death-risk donations.

I. Death Bed Donations

194. When a person considers his/her death to be approaching, it is not such a loss for the giver when donations are given, as it is for the beneficiaries. Expressed in another way, it is not such a binding disposition for the individual involved, as it is in reality only binding for the beneficiaries. It is therefore natural that the rules laid out in the section 93 of the Inheritance Act, have to be followed. Even though the rules which apply to wills have not been followed, the disposition will be followed as a formless disposition of the will, if no beneficiaries contest.

It is not a deciding factor, according to section 93, when the gift is given. The disposition is normally seen in light of the conditions which applied at the time, when the giver of the gift is bound by the laws according to the promise of the gift; in other words the time when the receiver of the promise became aware of its existence.

According to the formulation, 'donations that were given shortly before the donator's death at a time where the death must be seen as near and the donator was aware of that', there is considered to be a very short time span between the giving of the gift and the death of the giver. On the other hand, it is not enough that there is such a short time interval. In order for a gift to be considered a deathbed gift, the giver must have predicted his/her death to be near and been motivated to give the gift because of this factor.[107]

107. See Anne Louise Bormann, Finn Taksøc-Jensen & Ib Hounsgaard Trabjerg, *Arveloven af 2008 med kommentarer (The Inheritance Act of 2008)*, 499 et seq. (1st edn, Thomson 2008); Anitta Godsk Pedersen & Hans Viggo Godsk Pedersen, *Familie- og Arveret (Family and Succession Law)*, 291 et seq. (8th edn, Karnov Group 2013).

II. Death-Risk Donations

195. Death-risk presents are often classed under the Inheritance Act section 93. A death-risk gift is a donation where the giver is considered to be in a dangerous situation. Under such conditions, for example, just before a dangerous operation, it will often be provided that the gift will be returned if the giver survives. So these donations may as well be seen as pro forma dispositions since the donator often will have the opportunity to get that sort of gifts back if he/she survives the calculated risk.

III. Death Donations[108]

196. The real death donations are really promises of donations, which cannot come into effect as long as the giver is alive, see the Inheritance Act section 93. It is exactly the requirement, that the gift cannot be realized until after the death of the giver, that means that this arrangement has no bearing on the giver but has importance to the beneficiaries. It is on the other hand not of importance, that the gift has not been given at the death of the giver, if it was the intention of the giver that the gift should have been given while he/she still lived, without consideration of death. It is important if the terms of agreement where such that the gift would most probably be given first after the death of the giver.

In an insolvent estate, where the ranking of the creditors has been set, it is not of great importance whether a promise of a gift is a death gift, as the demands according to promises of donations are enclitic to the demands of Bankruptcy Act section 98. If precautions are taken towards the realization of a promise of a gift, without it being adequate to bring the disposition away from the term death gift, this will have relevance as the part given must be returned, unless it can be separated as a special disposition, that is valid. If a deceased had, for example, promised a large sum to an individual at his/her death, but had managed to transfer a part of the amount before dying, this part must be considered a valid gift. It is an entirely different matter whether the estate was insolvent, as the gift under the circumstances could be annulled according to Bankruptcy Act section 64.

Sometimes the giver wishes to give a gift, but also wishes to be able to partly or completely enjoy the benefits of the gift, as long as he/she lives. It can be done to a certain extent without the gift being considered a death gift, see below in section A concerning the boundaries between donations given in life and death donations. Mutually burdening agreements sometimes also contain regulations concerning how matters should be tackled in the event of the death of one party. It is therefore also possible that a problem can arise when trying to distinguish between the

108. See in general to this section Ernst Andersen, *Arveret (Succession Law)*, 217 et seq. (Juristforbundets Forlag 1967); Anne Louise Bormann, Finn Taksøe-Jensen & Ib Hounsgaard Trabjerg, *Arveloven af 2008 med kommentarer (The Inheritance Act of 2008)*, 490 et seq. (1st edn, Thomson 2008); Anitta Godsk Pedersen & Hans Viggo Godsk Pedersen, *Familie- og Arveret (Family and Succession Law)*, 294 et seq. (8th edn, Karnov Group 2013), and Irene Nørgaard, *Arveret (Succession Law)*, 353 et seq. (6th edn, Jurist- og Økonomforbundets Forlag 2013).

regulations natural to a mutually binding agreement and death donations, see below in section B.

A. *Presents Given During Life versus Death Donations*

197. In order for a gift to be considered a lifetime gift, the giver of the gift must have put a substantial restriction on himself/herself. This can be a problem if the giver has retained the right to use or receive interest benefits from the gift. If it is agreed that the giver can get the gift back, if he/she needs it, it is obvious that there is no substantial restriction placed on the giver, and the gift is considered a death gift.

With the giving of property with lifelong right of enjoyment to the giver, it is limited how much of a burden the promise of the gift falls upon the giver. It is though recognized, that such a disposition can be considered a lifetime gift, if the receiver is given a registered deed over the property. In this way, the giver is not able to reside over the property by selling or mortgaging it. If, on the other hand, no steps are taken towards the registering of a deed, the disposition will normally be considered a death gift.

If it is personal property that is in question, then it is normally required that the items in question have been handed over to the receiver. As far as securities registered in the Securities Agency are concerned, the arrangement is considered a lifetime gift despite the lifelong benefit to the giver in the form of interest, if the actual delivery has been registered. An actual delivery is normally required when the gift is a lump of negotiable documents, while with ordinary claims it is probably required that the debtor is notified. The giver is probably also able to maintain his/her voting right to the shares, as long as he/she is still prevented from selling or mortgaging them. Concerning the transfer of money from a bank or savings account, the giver must in the same way have made arrangements, which make the actual transfer a reality. The giver is actually not entitled to reside over the gift after promising it to another, but something is normally required to prove the reality of the promise.

The issuing of a document of indebtedness, that is free of interest and payments as long as the giver is alive, places no burden on the donator and is therefore a death gift. If the giver has realized the mortgage right for the amount, some restriction is put on the giver, which is presumably enough to make the assumption that the gift is a lifetime gift. If the document of indebtedness is with interest, and can therefore fall due with a breach of contract, it must be considered a lifetime gift.

A death gift must after normal principles be seen as liable to the Inheritance Tax within the estate, as it is considered a part of the estate left behind by the deceased. As long as the gift is considered a lifetime gift and the receiver is within the mentioned group of people, the actual delivery is put under the restrictions laid down in the rules of the Inheritance Tax Act chapter. If this is not the case, the gift is taxed as income tax.

B. Death Donations versus Mutually Burdening Agreements

198. In mutually burdening agreements it sometimes occurs that one part will reap certain benefits at the death of the other party. This is often the case in partnership agreements and in joint ownership agreements. There can also be problems concerning death presents when it comes to nursing agreements.

In partnership contracts it is often agreed, that the other partners, with the death of one partner, have the right to liberate beneficiaries according to the given guidelines. This can, for example, be an agreement that the value of the shares is to be measured according to certain principles, and that the payment of the shares can occur in portions over a certain time interval. It is normally accepted, that such regulations are valid as mutually burdening agreements, even though the other partners have an economic benefit, when the regulation is reasonably well grounded when considering the continuation of the business.

With shareholder agreements there can be admitted the option or right to purchase by the other shareholders, if a shareholder wishes to get rid of his/her stock. Such agreements may also bind beneficiaries. If the other shareholders by a mutual agreement have the right of purchase when a partner dies, this can be interpreted as a mutually binding agreement, if the regulation is otherwise a natural part of the agreement.

In joint ownership agreements concerning individual assets, normally real estate, there can also be a need to make allowances as to the situation if one of the partners dies, for example, concerning the option to buy by the surviving member(s). As this option will by itself normally be of small (relative) worth, and otherwise well within reason, there can really be no doubt as to whether this agreement is valid or not. In the same manner should a right to buy according to an impartial evaluation and on normal terms be deemed valid.

A mutual option to buy at a predetermined price can be a natural part of a mutually binding agreement, which must be respected by beneficiaries.

If a regulation of the conditions is one sided in such a way that an equal burden is not placed on both partners (though of a different character), it is considered a gift. If it is a prerequisite that the gift can first be realized at the time of death, it is considered a death gift.

An agreement that grants the surviving partner certain benefits with the death of the other partner contains in principle a certain element of risk as it is not known who will benefit from the agreement. This is especially seen with nursing agreements or other working agreements. If the person who is the nurse receives a decided compensation to nurse an individual until the time of his/her death, it will be – seen in a purely economical sense – a good business for the nurse if the work burden is short lived and a bad business if it is long term.

A prerequisite for allowing such dispositions as mutually binding agreements is, however, that the 'payments' at the time the contract was made must be seen as compatible.

§3. TRUSTS

199. In Denmark it is not possible to establish a trust in the same way as it is known in, for example, the English legal system. Some of the benefits, that could be desired of such a trust, can be acquired by other means, for example, by making a fund, by tying up assets or by granting profit in the form of a right to the interest attained.

§4. INSURANCE CONTRACTS

200. In Denmark it is possible to draw up different types of insurances that insure the bereaved. Some of these contracts are made in such a way that the person who draws up the agreement can also get capital or other equivalent benefits paid out, if the individual lives, if this is necessary, whereas the bereaved receive a benefit, if the individual is dead.

A life insurance can be drawn up as a purely risk insurance, understood in such a way that there has to be paid a certain sum of money, if the person whose life is insured, dies. An insurance of this type will normally have a limited time span for coverage, such that it will only be paid out if the insured dies before a certain age. Capital savings are often connected to this, so that on top of the risk coverage a certain sum of money has to be paid to the insured if he/she lives beyond a certain age, see the Insurance Contracts Act section 107.

If the insured has not named a beneficiary to this insurance money, and if the sum has to be paid out at the time of the death of the insured, then this money is to be paid out to the 'closest relatives', see the Insurance Contract Acts section 105b(l). If there are no 'closest relatives' the money is included in the estate of the deceased, see the Insurance Contracts Act section 105b(l). The same applies if the insured has decided that no one is to have the sum paid out, see section 105b(2). A beneficiary will normally be stated, which can be done by notifying the insurance company in writing, or by including this information in the policy of the insured, or by an endorsement to the insurance policy, see the Act's section 103. When a beneficiary is stated, the money is paid directly to this person and kept separate from the estate, see the Act's section 102(1). This means, among other things, that the beneficiary receives the insurance money irrespective of whether the estate is solvent or not.

The appointing of a beneficiary can be done by naming a specific person, but is normally done through standard procedures. In the Insurance Contracts Act section 105, rules are drawn up concerning the meaning of some of the more commonly used regulations. In section 105a the meaning of the expression 'closest relatives' is laid down. If the expression 'closest relative' is used, it is accepted that the spouse is the beneficiary; if there is no spouse the partner in a steady relationship is the beneficiary; if there is both a spouse or a partner from a steady relationship and children, the spouse or partner will have the right to the entire amount. If there is no spouse or partner it is accepted that the children are the beneficiaries in accordance with the legal laws governing inheritance. If there are no living descendants, it is accepted that the other beneficiaries are taken in the same order as for the normal inheritance, where they are granted intestate inheritance or testamentary gift. In section 105a(2), it is stated that a partner in a steady relationship only can be a beneficiary in accordance with this section if the partners were living together at the time of the death of the deceased, and have lived together for the last two years as they were spouses, expecting, having or have had a common child.

If the appointing of a beneficiary has been done before 1 January 2008, it is still according to the rules as they were before that date. The main difference is that a partner in a steady relationship is not mentioned in those rules. In these cases it is possible that a partner in a steady relationship is to be regarded as the closest relative, however if there are children it is not common.

A favour can under certain circumstances be considered extinguished, even if it has not been withdrawn. In the Insurance Contracts Act section 106 it is explicitly stated that a favour to a certain individual will be withdrawn if he/she does not live longer than the person whose life is insured; therefore the heir's beneficiaries do not take his place in regard to the deceased, unless this is specifically stated. It must also be accepted, that a spouse that is named as a beneficiary will lose this right if he/she is separated or divorced, according to the principles stated in the Inheritance Act section 67, unless there are grounds for the opposite. The same applies with the breaking of an engagement and the termination of a steady relationship, see section 67(3). If the beneficiary is accused by the law to have caused the death of the insured, it can be decided according to the Inheritance Act section 48, and the Insurance Contracts Act section 18, that the accused cannot receive the insurance money and that his/her statutory share of the community property may not be increased because of this.

201. The insurance money is paid to the beneficiary, as already stated, independent of the estate, see the Insurance Contracts Act section 102(1). In the Insurance Contracts Act section 104(2), there is a rule though that gives, within certain limits, the spouse and descendants the right to contest the validity of the benefit. If a beneficiary is named to the life insurance and this must be regarded as unfair to the spouse and other rightful beneficiaries a court can settle that the insurance sum is to be paid out partly or in whole to the spouse or a rightful beneficiary. However, the amount cannot exceed the amount they would have had, if the life insurance money was considered part of the estate and given to the beneficiary by will in accordance to the indefeasible share and the statutory share of community property. This right can be made valid as separate to the estate, which has the implication, that it can also be used even if the estate is insolvent.

Similar rules apply as far as pension savings in banks concern, see the Act concerning some Legal Aspects of Pension Savings in Banks sections 2–5b.

Savings that were intended as pension can be made so that an amount within certain limits, which is saved in a special account, is exempt from normal income tax. In return a duty is paid from the saved amount when it is paid out. The sum is paid out when the insured reaches a certain age. If the insured dies before he/she reaches this age the sum is paid to the beneficiary, if there is such a person.

Pension savings, which are paid out in instalments, often have an agreement included which gives the spouse the right to receive the pension, for a certain length of time or for the entire lifetime of the spouse, if the other spouse dies. There will often also be added a right to the pension for the children until a certain age, for example, 21 or 24 years in such an agreement.

A substantial number of these agreements concerning pensions are connected to the place of employment. It is though also normal that the additional agreements are drawn up as a supplement to these agreements connected to the place of employment.[109]

§5. OTHERS

202. It is sometimes desired by an individual, that his/her estate is given to charity of some type or the individual wishes to ensure the continuation of his/her business. Apart from a payment to the decided purpose while alive or by way of a will, it is possible to support a certain charity by way of a fund. In a similar fashion, the continuation of a company can be secured by establishing a fund.

A fund is a self-governing institution, that is, the wealth of the fund must be irrevocably separated from the estate of the creator of the fund. The fund is managed by a board of at least three members. The individual that establishes the fund, has the fund, his/ her spouse, or people that are connected to the named individuals as relatives or in-laws from the same or other generations which are as close as siblings, cannot constitute a majority of the board, without the consent of the authority which is connected to funds in the Danish Commerce and Companies Agency. Thereby it is attempted to prevent the situation whereby the founder has the right to exclusively reside over the fund's assets.

As there is no individual that owns the capital of the fund, except for the fund itself, there is no election to decide the board of directors. The election of new members only occurs according to the rules laid down by the regulations of the fund. It is very common that the board supplements itself. Under special conditions, it is possible for the authorities concerning funds to remove members of the board, if they do not fulfil the requirements needed in order to be on the board.

Funds that are not businesses are included in the Act concerning funds and certain societies. Such a fund must have a fund capital of at least DKK 250,000 (approx. EUR 34,000). The capital normally has to be maintained, whereas the profit can be administered by the members of the board in accordance with the regulations (typically to charity).

If it is desired that a business is maintained by way of a fund, the fund will normally have a certain number of shares in the company sufficient to ensure a deciding influence. The fund is in this way covered by the Act concerning business funds. When the deciding influence is held by a fund a continuance will be ensured, where it is not dependent on the division of the inheritance, with a subsequent risk of a

109. See for further details Rasmus Kristian Feldthusen, Ingrid Lund-Andersen & Linda Nielsen, *Arveretten (Succession Law)*, 215 et seq. (4th edn, Gjellerup/Gads Forlag 2014); Anitta Godsk Pedersen & Hans Viggo Godsk Pedersen, *Familie- og Arveret (Family and Succession Law)*, 337 et seq. (8th edn, Karnov Group 2013), and Irene Nørgaard, *Arveret (Succession Law)*, (6th edn, Jurist- og Økonomforbundets Forlag 2013), Ch. 19.

lack of control of the shares and where expenses can make it necessary to sell the shares. At the same time, the company is to some extent secured against contested takeovers.[110]

110. The Acts regulating funds are annotated by Lennart Lynge Andersen, *Fondslovene*, (5th edn, Gjellerup 2003).

Chapter 4. Acquisition and Administration of the Estate

§1. The System of Acquisition

203. The authority which receives the information first, that someone has died, be it the funeral authorities or any other authority in Denmark, must as soon as possible notify the Probate Court, that will call a meeting to decide how the estate should be treated, see the Administration of Estates Act sections 4 and 7. Until it is decided how the estate is to be treated, it is the responsibility of all individuals, who are in possession of assets which belonged to the deceased, to keep these in a safe way. If the storage cannot be done without difficulty or great cost, the Probate Court will exempt the individual of the responsibility. Where circumstances make it necessary, it can be decided by the Probate Court that the assets of the estate are to be partially or completely registered or taken into protection. The Probate Court can appoint a temporary manager who can make the necessary decisions, see the Administration of Estates Act section 8.

When a decision is made as to how the estate is to be treated, the assets are given to the individual(s), who will administer the estate. A so-called letter of administration is issued by the Probate Court which, in relation to a third party, gives the appointed individual(s) authority to reside over the assets, see the Administration of Estates Act section 9.

§2. The Administration of the Estate

204. In Denmark, an estate can be divided by an authorized manager of the estate or by private distribution of the estate, all depending on the circumstances. The estate can also be finished without a final administration of the estate. This applies especially to certain small estates and, depending on the circumstances, is given to the spouse.

I. The Distribution of the Estate

205. The administration of the estate, without division of the estate, can be done according to the Administration of Estates Act, section 18, when the value of the assets after paying expenses for the funeral, the handling of the estate as well as the specially insured debt, does not exceed DKK 25,000, which is also regulated by the price index according to the Act's section 21, (DKK 41,000 – a little over EUR 5,500 in the year 2015). The administration can be given to an individual or individuals, who are, according to the Probate Court, the closest relatives, or maybe to an institution that the deceased had a certain connection with, to the person who has paid or has promised as paid or has promised to pay for the funeral, to the community or to the state's treasury.[111]

111. See Anitta Godsk Pedersen & Hans Viggo Godsk Pedersen, *Familie- og Arveret (Family and Succession Law)*, 321 et seq. (Karnov Group 2013), and Kjærgaard Møller et al., *Dødsboskifteloven (The Annotated Administration of Estates Act)*, 127 et seq. (DJØF 1998).

II. The Distribution to the Surviving Spouse

206. The administration to the surviving spouse can occur when the value of the total estate does not exceed DKK 600,000, see the Administration of Estates Act section 22 and the Inheritance Act section 11(2). The last mentioned contains a rule that the spouse always has the right to extract as much of the total inheritance that the value hereby combined with the surviving spouse's statutory share of community property as well as the ordinary share of inheritance, as well as individual property makes up to DKK 600,000 (DKK 720,000 in the year 2015).

Even though the administration according to the regulation requires that the spouse take over the responsibility of the debts of the first deceased, there are modifications to this. According to the Administration of Estates Act section 23, the responsibility can be limited to the received, if the estate of the deceased was insolvent and it is taken under administration by an authorized administrator of the estate at a later point of time.

III. Private Distribution of the Estate

207. Private distribution of the estate can be done in two ways, a normal way or a simplified way.

It is a condition before a private distribution of the estate can be executed, that the assets of the estate as well as a possible security is accepted to be enough to cover the debts of the estate, as well as serious consideration, including the beneficiaries inability to pay, does not allow private distribution of the estate. That a beneficiary is in the process of a bankruptcy, is legally incapable or absent, does not necessarily rule out a private distribution of the estate, when at least one of the beneficiaries can accommodate the distribution, without being a guardian or guardian appointed by the Probate Court, and is capable of fulfilling his/her responsibilities as they occur, see the Administration of Estates Act section 25. On the other hand, the person will be the only one responsible for the claims that can be directed towards all of the beneficiaries.

When handing over the estate for private distribution, the beneficiaries must issue an advertisement for creditors, if this has not already been done, see the Act's section 25(4). Any of the beneficiaries can demand that the estate is not to be divided before the debts of the estate are paid or properly insured, see the Act's section 26(4). If the estate is partially or totally divided before this is done, then the beneficiaries are jointly and severally liable for the debt, see the Act's section 27(1). This does not apply though to beneficiaries that were bankrupt, or represented by a guardian or a guardian appointed by the Probate Court, as they are only responsible for what they received and only pro rata to the extent that they were entitled to by their shares of the inheritance and the statutory share of community property, see the Administration of Estates Act section 27(2). This limitation is valid even though one or more beneficiaries is not liable for his/her share. The missing amount is therefore the joint responsibility of the beneficiaries who are not bankrupt.

If it is later proven that the estate is insolvent, the beneficiaries can limit the liability by demanding the estate to be handled by an authorized executor and give away the assets received from the estate, whereas those that are not encompassed under the above-mentioned limitations in section 27, subsection 2, are responsible for the entire demands that can be directed towards the beneficiaries; this means everything that is given to the beneficiaries, see the Act's sections 29 and 30. Under special circumstances, the Probate Court can make a decision to give the estate over to an executor if the creditors or legatees wish this and there is a real risk, that a continuation of the private distribution of the estate will expose the involved with a loss, see section 30 of the Act.

Also, the latest day of completion is one year from the time of death, and the distribution of the estate is sent to the Probate Court in two copies within three months of the last day, as the beneficiaries have though at least nine months from the time of death, see the Administration of Estates Act sections 30–32. The Probate Court will send one of the copies to the tax authorities.

In smaller estates, where it is not necessary to pay inheritance tax or accessory inheritance tax, where the deceased did not have a private business, where the estate was not taxable, where there are no tax-deductible shares, where there were no legatees and where there were no beneficiaries, who are represented by a guardian or a guardian appointed by the Probate Court, the private distribution of the estate can be performed by means of the simplified process. The important essence of the simplification is that it is only necessary to make a statement over assets and liabilities – with the day of death as the latest day of completion – at the administration of the estate. The same can happen if the spouse was the only beneficiary and he/she has taken over the taxable position of the deceased, see the Administration of Estates Act sections 33–35.[112]

IV. Distribution of the Estate by an Authorized Manager

208. If the estate is not divided by one of the above-described methods, then it is divided by an authorized manager. In the Administration of Estates Act it is described in more detail, that an estate is to be handled by an authorized manager if (1) a beneficiary desires this; (2) the estate is considered to be insolvent; (3) all the beneficiaries either are represented by a guardian or a guardian appointed by the Probate Court, or they are bankrupt or unable to fulfil their responsibilities as they occur; (4) the deceased has decided this in his/her will; (5) there are no beneficiaries to the estate, or it is uncertain who the beneficiaries are; (6) it is decided that the estate has to be administered in such a way because of the Act's section 23 (transfer to the spouse), section 30 (transfer after a private distribution is started), section 76(3) (transfer because the surviving spouse has neglected his/her duties when dividing the estate), or the Inheritance Acts section 25(2) (transfer after delivering to the undivided estate); or (7) it isn't decided within a reasonable time limit, that the estate should be handled in a different way.

112. See Anitta Godsk Pedersen & Hans Viggo Godsk Pedersen, *Familie- og Arveret (Family and Succession Law)*, 323 et seq. (8th edn, Karnov Group 2013), Kjærgaard Møller et al. *Dødsboskifteloven (The Annotated Administration of Estates Act)*, 171 et seq. (DJØF 1998).

For every legal area, the Ministry of Justice appoints a certain number of lawyers to handle estates, see the Administration of Estates Act section 11(1). Others can be appointed as managers, if the deceased has decided this by way of his/her will, but such a regulation can be overlooked, see sections 11(2) and 38 of the Act. The appointment of an executor is considered to be a regulation that the person appointed is to be the manager of the estate, see section 118. If the beneficiaries wish to get a certain manager, this is normally accommodated by the Probate Court, see section 37(2), but otherwise it is the Probate Court that decides who the manager is to be.

The manager of the estate must issue advertisement for creditors if this has not happened before the estate was transferred, see the Administration of Estates Act section 46. If the information shows that the estate may be insolvent, the manager will immediately request the Probate Court to determine this, see section 43. The manager of the estate will also draw up, before the date of completion of the advertisement for creditors, an opening status that contains description over all the assets and liabilities in the estate with details on values at the time of death, the estate's expected profits and expenses as well as the administrator's evaluation of whether the estate is insolvent or not, see section 52 of the Act. If the estate is accepted as being insolvent, then the administrator will immediately ask the Probate Court to make arrangements for insolvency proceedings. If it is discovered at a later point in time that the estate is insolvent, then the manager of the estate will act in a similar fashion and ensure that a decision is made as to the course of action concerning insolvency proceedings. When an estate is declared insolvent, the essential consequence is that the laws applying for bankruptcy are applied, see the Administration of Estates Act section 70.

The estate manager makes the decisions concerning the affairs of the estate. Essential questions must though be placed before the heirs. If there is disagreement among the beneficiaries, an estate meeting has to be called so they can vote. The votes are weighted according to the beneficiaries' shares of the inheritance and statutory share of community property. The manager of the estate can, under certain circumstances, disregard the result of the vote, but the beneficiaries can, if this is the case, demand that the Probate Court decides on the matter. Otherwise estate meetings are called as the need arises. It should normally occur if a beneficiary demands it, and it has to occur if the Probate Court demands it, see the Act's sections 53, 55 and 96.

The final day for an administration of the estate is two years after the day of death. It has to be put forward for acceptance at the last estate meeting no later than two months after the final day, as there is always a limit of nine months from the day of death until the handing in of the statement, see the Administration of Estates Act sections 66–68.[113]

113. See Anitta Godsk Pedersen & Hans Viggo Godsk Pedersen, *Familie- og Arveret (Family and Succession Law)*, (8th edn, Karnov Group 2013), 313 et seq. and Kjærgaard Møller et al., *Dødsboskifteloven (The Annotated Administration of Estates Act)* 227 et seq. (DJØF 1998).

V. Advertisement for Creditors

209. Advertisement for creditors can be issued after the decision is made as to how the estate is to be administered or, with the permission of the Probate Court, before this time, see the Administration of Estates Act section 81. Advertisement for creditors must be issued in the case of a private distribution of the estate and when an executor of the estate is appointed, see section 81(2). The advertisement for creditors must be printed once in the *Official Gazette,* but the Probate Court can decide that the advertisement for creditors should also be printed in local papers. Apart from the personal information, the advertisement for creditors must contain information concerning a possible decision of insolvency.

The time limit for notification is eight weeks after the notice. The notification must be done in writing and list the demands of creditors as well as possible demands for interest and expenses. If the advertisement for creditors contains information concerning possible insolvency proceedings, then possible demands from creditors for a position of preference should also be mentioned. If the decision for the handling of insolvency is first made at a later point of time, then the manager of the estate will brief the notified creditors that they have eight weeks in which to report an unreported demand for a position of preference, see the Administration of Estates Act section 82.

The advertisement for creditors in decedent estates is barring other claims, see the Administration of Estates Act section 83(1). There are exceptions, though, by section 83(2), to this rule which states otherwise, that whatever is not reported before the time limit, is not valid. This applies to (1) demands, that are put forward in writing after the time of death and are in the hands of the estate before the end of the time limit; (2) demands, that rest upon proprietary rights, when the item was in the possession of the estate and marked in such a way that it was clear who owned it, or the estate was aware of who owned it, or there were circumstances which should raise suspicion as to who could be the rightful owner; (3) demands, that are secured by a mortgage, or in a similar way, demands secured by a pledge in a owner's mortgage is taken out only if the estate is, or should be, aware of the creditor's identity; and (4) demands of taxes and duties to the extent that is decided in other laws.[114]

114. See Anitta Godsk Pedersen & Hans Viggo Godsk Pedersen, *Familie- og Arveret (Family and Succession Law)*, 328 et seq. (8th edn, Karnov Group 2013), and Kjærgaard Møller et al., *Dødsboskifteloven (The Annotated Administration of Estates Act)*, 387 et seq. (DJØF 1998).

Selected Bibliography

Boele-Woelki, Katharina, Bente Braat & Ian Summer (eds). *European Family Law in Action. Volume I: Grounds for Divorce; Volume II: Maintenance between Former Spouses.* Antwerp, Oxford, New York: Intersentia, 2003.

Boele-Woelki, Katharina & Angelika Fuchs (eds). *Legal Recognition of Same-Sex Couples in Europe.* Antwerp, Oxford, New York: Intersentia, 2003.

Boele-Woelki, Katharina, Bente Braat & Ian Summer (eds). *European Family Law in Action. Volume IV: Property Relations between Spouses.* Antwerp, Oxford, New York: Intersentra, 2009.

Bormann, Anne Louise, Finn Taksøe-Jensen & Ib Hounsgaard Trabjerg. *Arveloven af 2008 med kommentarer (The Inheritance Act of 2008).* Copenhagen: DJØF, 2008.

Christensen, Stine Krone. *Forældreansvarsloven med kommentarer (Act on Parental Responsibility).* 2nd edn. Copenhagen, Thomson Reuters, 2014.

Danielsen, Svend. *Arveloven med kommentarer (The Inheritance Act).* Copenhagen: DJØF, 2005.

Danielsen, Svend. *Værgemåsloven med kommentarer (The Guardianship Act).* Copenhagen: DJØF, 2006.

Danielsen, Svend. *Ægteskabsloven – kapitel 4 and 5. Retsplejeloven kapitel 42 (The Annotated Marriage and Matrimonial Causes Act).* Copenhagen: DJØF, 1993.

Danielsen, Svend & Mogens Hornslet. *Lov om ægteskabets retsvirkninger (The Annotated Legal Effects of Marriages Act).* 2nd edn. Copenhagen: DJØF, 1986.

Dübeck, Inger. *Personers Rettigheder (The Rights of Persons).* 1st edn. Copenhagen: DJØF, 1997.

Estrup, Henrik & Nikolaj Aarø-Hansen. *Navneloven med kommentarer (The Act on Names).* Copenhagen: DJØF, 2006.

Eyben, Bo von & Helle Isager. *Lærebog i erstatningsret (Liability for Torts Act).* 8th edn. Copenhagen: DJØF, 2015.

Feldthusen, Rasmus Kristian, Ingrid Lund-Andersen & Linda Nielsen. *Arveretten (Succession Law).* 4th edn. Copenhagen: Gjellerup, 2014.

Kleis, Birgit and Niels Beckman. *Indfødsretsloven med kommentarer (The Act on Danish Nationality).* Copenhagen: DJØF, 2004.

Lund-Andersen, Ingrid, Noe Munck and Irene Nørgaard. *Familieret (Family Law),* 5th edn. Copenhagen: DJØF, 2003.

Lund-Andersen, Ingrid and Irene Nørgaard. *Familieret (Family Law),* 2nd edn. Copenhagen: DJØF, 2012.

Lund-Andersen, Ingrid, Familieøkonomien (*Financial Relations in the Family*), Copenhagen: DJØF, 2011.

Møller, Mogens Kjærgaard, et al. *Dødsboskifteloven (The Annotated Administration of Estates Act).* Copenhagen: DJØF, 1998.

Selected Bibliography

Nielsen, Linda. *Familieretten (Family Law)*. 6th edn. Copenhagen: Gjellerup, 2012.
Nørgard, Irene. *Arveret (Succession Law)*. 6th edn. Copenhagen: DJØF, 2013.
Ørgaard, Anders. *Konkursret (Bankruptcy Law)*. 9th edn. Copenhagen: DJØF, 2006.
Pedersen, Anitta Godsk & Hans Viggo Godsk Pedersen. *Familie- og arveret (Family and Succession Law)*. 8th edn. Copenhagen: Thomson Reuters, 2013.
Petersen, Lars Lindencrone & Anders Ørgaard. *Konkursloven (The Annotated Bankruptcy Act)*. 11th edn. Copenhagen: Thomson Reuters, 2014.
Pritchard, John. *The New Penguin Guide to the Law.* 3rd edn. Penguin, 1993.
Redmond, P.W.D. & Peter Shears. *General Principles of English Law.* 7th edn. M&E Law, 1993.
Taksøe-Jensen, Finn. *Skifte af dødsboer (Administration of Estates)*. Copenhagen: Thomson Reuters, 1998.

Index

The numbers here refer to paragraphs numbers.

Abortion, 46, 47, 71
Absentees, *see* missing persons
Absolute separate property, *see* separate property
Abuse of control, 174, 175
Address protection, 41, 43
Administration of estate, *see* estate
Adoption, 9, 60, 61, 66, 101–107, 169
Advertisement for creditors, 209
Alcoholics, 18, 56
Annulment
  of marriages, 79–80, 83, 148
  of transfers, spouses, 129-130
  of gifts, spouses, 129-130
  of gifts from undivided estate, 175
Anomalous succession, 168
Artificial insemination, 9, 100
Ascendants, 165
Assets
  division of matrimonial property, 146
Authorized manager, 204, 208

Baptism, 59
Brain death, 49

Capacity, 11
  legal capacity, 8
  liability for torts, 27
  personal work, 25, 111
  to dispose of property, 12
  to enter into contracts, 25
  to make a will, 172, 179
  to succeed, 157
Chastisement of children, 54
Cheque Act, 69
Child pornography, 55
Children, 9, 53-55
  children born in wedlock, 61, 93
  children born out of wedlock, 61, 93
  paternity, 93–100
Children's work, 25, 111
Citizenship, 65
  acquisition, 66
  loss, 67
Civil status, 38
Claims against separate property, 154
  compensation by division of matrimonial property, 149
  compensation by division of undivided estate, 175
Classes of heirs, 160
Cohabitation without marriage, 91–92
Collaterals, 166
Commorientes, 158
Community property, 118, 122, 135, 140, 152
Compensation, 34
  division of matrimonial property, 149
  undivided possession of estate, 175
Compensation and legal incapacity, 25–29
Compulsory medical treatment, 48, 72
Compulsory military service, 65
Consent to deal
  furniture, 123
  household effects, 123, 135
  matrimonial home, 84, 89, 1122, 135
  tenancy, 87, 124
Constitution, 3, 51, 66
Contact, 110
Contract modification, 153
Control of property, 140, 143

Damage, 29
Death, 33, 49, 155
Deathbed donations, 194
Death donations, 196
Death-risk donations, 195
Descendants, 164
Disappearance
  heirs, 37

missing persons, 31–32, 156
Distribution of estate, *see* estate
Division of estate
after evaluation, 162
Division of Family Assets Act, 143
Division of matrimonial property, 143, 173
assets, 146
compensation, 149
grounds for, 144
liabilities, 146
qualitative, 151
tax return, 146
unequal, 148
Division of missing persons' property
assets, 35, 36
heirs, 37
the State, 36
Divorce, 83
bigamy, 79, 85
effects, 90
grounds and conditions, 83, 85
homosexuals and lesbians, 85
violence, 85
DNA-tests, 97
Domicile, 64, 81
of missing persons, 33
Drug addicts, 53
Damage, 29
Death, 33, 49, 155
Deathbed donations, 194
Death donations, 196
Death-risk donations, 195
Descendants, 164
Disappearance
heirs, 37
missing persons, 31–32, 156
Distribution of estate, *see* estate
Division of estate
after evaluation, 162
Division of Family Assets Act, 143
Division of matrimonial property, 143, 173
assets, 146
compensation, 149
grounds for, 144
liabilities, 146
qualitative, 151
tax return, 146
unequal, 148
Division of missing persons' property
assets, 35, 36
heirs, 37
the State, 36
Divorce, 83
bigamy, 79, 85
effects, 90
grounds and conditions, 83, 85
homosexuals and lesbians, 85
violence, 85
DNA-tests, 97
Domicile, 64, 81
of missing persons, 33
Drug addicts, 53

Elections
Danish local authorities, 65
Danish Parliament, 65
European Parliament, 65
Embryo, 47
foetus, 47
Emergency will, 182
Emigration, 40
Epidemics Act, 57
Estate
administration of, 204
authorized manager, 204, 208
deceased persons, 156
distribution to surviving spouse, 206
meeting, 208
planning, 192
private distribution, 204, 207
temporary manager, 203
Euthanasia, 48
Expected inheritage, 192

Filiation, 93–100
Forced heirs, 188
Franchise, 65
Funds, 202

Gifts, 127
annulment, 129
tax, 127, 178
undivided possession of estate, 173
Goodwill, 136
Guardianship, 8, 9, 11, 12, 16, 53, 66, 71, 113
consent of guardian, 25
duties of the guardian, 17
joint permanent guardianship, 21
limited permanent guardianship, 20
permanent guardianship, 17–19
scope of guardianship, 17, 23
temporary guardianship, 17, 22

Health condition, 17–19
Heart death, 49
Household expenses, 119
  loans, 119
Household effects, 123, 135, 152

Indefeasible inheritance, 188
Indication
  ethical, 47
  eugenic, 47
  medical, 47
  social, 47
Inheritance
  expected, 192
  indefeasible, 188
  rightful, 188
Insemination, 100
  donor, 100
  husband, 100
Insurance contracts, 28, 29, 200-201
  life insurance, 34, 137, 200
Integrity, 8, 9, 44
  physical, 46
  psychological, 51
  social, 52
Invalid contracts, 26
In vitro-fertilization, 47, 100
Irrevocable will, 192

Joint custody, 108
Joint liability, 119, 141
  tax, 134
Joint parental authority, 108
Juror, 65

Kinship, 117

Lay judge, 65
Legal capacity, 8, 12, 15, 69
legal incapacity, 12, 13, 24–26
Legal duties, 8
Legal Effect of Marriages Act, 78, 118
Legal matrimonial regime, 135
Legal rights, 8, 53-58
Legal status, 8, 9
Liabilities
  division of matrimonial property, 147
Liability, 27–29
  compensation, 28
  limited liability, 28
  torts, 27–29
Liberty, 8, 9, 44
Life insurances, 34, 137, 200
Life-testament, 48

Maintenance, 88, 108, 112, 190
Manic-depressive persons, 24
Marriage, 15, 73
  capacity to marry, 74
  nature of, 73
  void, 79, 80
  voidable, 79, 80
Marriage settlement, 127, 131, 139
Matrimonial Causes Act, 74, 79, 83, 88
Matrimonial home, 89, 121, 152
  consent to deal, 121
  consent to make a will, 187
Matrimonial property
  control of, 122, 140
  division of, 145
Mental condition, 70, 80
Mental illness, 17, 18
  commitment, 72
  constraint, 72
  detention, 72
  fixation, 72
  the use of force, 72
  treatment, 72
Minister of justice, 36
Minor, 12, 15, 28
Missing persons, 30–37, 156
Mutual will, 184

Names, 59-64
  change, 64
  composition, 59
  first name, 62
  last name, acquisition, 61
  middle name, 63
National Hospital's Donor Register, 49
Nationality, 65–68
Negligence, 28
Notary will, 181

Ordinary contracts between spouses, 126
Organ donation, 46, 49
Organ transplants, 46, 49

Parental authority, 15, 53, 108
  joint parental authority, 108
  sole parental authority, 108
  transfer of, 108
Parents, 53, 74, 105
  divorced, 53

unmarried, 93
Partnership, *see* registered partnership
Paternity, 93–100
Pension schemes, 34, 137
Personal registration, 38–43
Central Person's Register (CPR), 38
Local Authority Register, 38
personal identity number, 38, 41
Personal rights, 136
Personality rights, 44–53
Persons
elderly demented persons, 15, 71
natural persons, 9
legal persons, 10
mentally handicapped, 9, 70-72
Political rights, 65
Pregnancy, 47
Presumption of death, 32–34, 156
Priority of the children, 164
Privacy, 8, 9, 44
Private registers, 51
Probate Court, 35, 203
Provisions in a will, 186
Psychiatry Act, 48, 70, 72
Public Records Book, 38, 42

Registered partnership, 73, 81–82
Rescission
of contracts, 26
of guardianship decisions, 23
Residence, 69
Nordic countries, 68
Retention
compulsory, 72
Revocation of a will, 185
Rightful inheritance, 188

Schizophrenic persons, 24
Separate property, 132, 135, 139
contracts, 132
by marriage settlement, 132
by third party, 133
Separation, 84
grounds and conditions, 85
license, 85, 86
Separation of property, 132, 135, 154
absolute, 132
Spouses relationship with creditors, 141
State Church, 39
Sterilization, 71
Suicide, 48
Supplement inheritance, 161
Surplus rule, 128
Surrogacy, 100
Surviving spouse, 150, 205

Testamentary succession, 178 et seq.
Torts, 12, 27 et seq.
Treaties, 5

Undivided possession of estate, 135, 170
Unfaithfulness of spouses, 78, 85, 86
Unsound mind, 29
Unworthiness to succeed, 159

Vagabonds, 56

Ward, 11, 12, 17, 22, 24–27, 74
Wedlock, 61, 93
Will, 178
capacity, 179
contesting of, 178
emergency, 182
form, 181
irrevocable, 192
mutual, 184
nullity, 178
objection against, 178
provisions, 186
revocation of, 185
Witnessed will, 181

www.ingramcontent.com/pod-product-compliance
Lightning Source LLC
Chambersburg PA
CBHW071447230926
51846CB00001B/368
* 9 7 8 9 0 4 1 1 8 2 5 9 3 *